Blissfully Blended

ISBN 978-1-60260-521-3

Published by Barbour Publishing, Inc., P.O. Box 719, Uhrichsville, Ohio 44683 www.barbourbooks.com

Our mission is to publish and distribute inspirational products offering exceptional value and biblical encouragement to the masses.

Printed in the United States.

365 Devotional Readings for Stepmoms

Introduction

When one hears the term *stepmom*, a whole lot of images come to mind—and a lot of them aren't nice. Friends and family with the best of intentions may make comments or give not-so-helpful advice on how to connect with your stepchildren that could leave you confused, hurt, or struggling to figure out what's best for your blended family.

Inside *Blissfully Blended* you'll find reminders of God's love for you as you take on the important role of mother to someone else's children, as well as encouragement to face the challenges each day brings.

With a devotional reading for each day of the year, you will be able to focus your thoughts on God's wisdom and promises throughout the Bible to help you turn your struggles into successes. You'll be encouraged by the real-life triumphs of stepmoms and gently challenged at times to make beneficial changes to your own attitudes and actions.

Being a stepmom is a huge responsibility. But with your heavenly Father by your side, you have access to all the wisdom, resources, and strength you need to accomplish everything He has called you to do—to be the best stepmom you can be. We hope *Blissfully Blended* is an encouragement along the way!

The Publishers

Let the Walls Fall Down

Day 1

For he himself is our peace, who has made the two one and has destroyed the barrier, the dividing wall of hostility.

EPHESIANS 2:14 NIV

A recently married woman struggled to keep the peace between her new husband's two daughters and her own teenage daughter. They argued over everything—parents' affections, space in their shared bedroom, and even what to watch on television or what to eat. The bickering continued, despite the woman's best attempts. She wondered at times if the wall between the two families would ever come down, if they'd all be able to live in peace. At times it seemed impossible.

Perhaps you can relate to this woman's story. Maybe you're struggling to hold two seemingly separate families together. There's good news today! God is the author of peace, not confusion. And when He offered His Son as a sacrifice on the cross, the barrier that separated man from God—and man from man—was destroyed. If you know the Prince of Peace, it is possible to live in peace.

Today acknowledge your need for peace to the Lord. If you've built up any walls in your heart, confess them and ask the Lord to tear them down. He's the only one capable of truly destroying the barriers keeping us apart.

Father, I confess I've let walls rise up between me and those I love. Tear them down, Lord! Show me how to have Your kind of peace—the kind that destroys barriers. Amen.

Day 2

Getting Plutoed

Lift your eyes and look to the heavens: Who created all these?
He who brings out the starry host one by one, and calls them each by name.
Because of his great power and mighty strength, not one of them is missing.
Isaiah 40:26 niv

For all of you who worked in elementary school to memorize a solar system with nine planets, brace yourselves. There are now only eight planets. According to a 2006 ruling of the International Astronomical Union, Pluto has been demoted. It is now considered a "dwarf planet."

God must struggle to suppress a grin after hearing that earthly news bulletin. What must He think of man's vagaries? He was the one who had the idea for Pluto to begin with—along with Mars, Earth, Jupiter, the Milky Way, Andromeda Galaxy's spiral of starlight, and M-15's globular cluster. He not only created the solar system, but He knows the name of each object in that velvety black sky.

And not one of them is missing, said Isaiah. Not a single one.

If God can keep track of every star in the heavens, He can handle the unique problems of your family. Looking at objects that are 2.5 million light-years distant puts our troubles and tribulations into a more proper perspective. Even when our problems seem to be of cosmic proportions, God has them covered.

Heavenly Father, the heavens are a constant display to
remind us of Your great power and mighty strength. Amen.

Shut Off the Outside Noise

If we're confident that he's listening,
we know that what we've asked for is as good as ours.

1 John 5:15 msg

The sound of waves crashing against the boulders along the coastal shore can overwhelm you. The waters thunder, drowning out every sound for miles. Any other noise falls silent, not even making a whisper in your ear. It's as though the majesty of the waters demands your full attention.

Imagine now that you could silence your busy life with the gentle roar of God's voice. Different versions of the Bible describe the voice of Almighty God as "rushing waters" or "the sound of many waters" (Ezekiel 43:2 NIV, NKJV). When you take time with God, you can shut off the outside noise and listen intently to His voice on the inside of you.

Picture the tenderness of God's love for you crashing powerfully against the breakers of your soul. Turn your ear to the inside and listen to the Spirit of God speak to the deep places of your heart.

You have the ability to tune out everything and tune in the voice of God. He alone can flood you with His supernatural peace in the midst of any storm. His strength will uphold you at all times. Allow His words to flood you today.

Dear God, I've been so busy. Forgive me when I'm too busy to listen.
Help me to take a breath and experience Your presence
and hear what You have to say. Amen.

Day 4

Every Other Weekend

"So is my word that goes out from my mouth:
It will not return to me empty, but will accomplish what
I desire and achieve the purpose for which I sent it."
Isaiah 55:11 NIV

Drake hadn't been a Christian when Lucy met him, but he started coming to church with her and came to know the Lord a year before they married. Drake's ex-wife and son, Ryan, were still not Christians. Lucy and Drake encouraged Ryan to come to church with them during his weekends with his dad. He seemed drawn in by the youth group activities but remained aloof to the gospel message.

Lucy knew Ryan's mother told him there was no such thing as God when he was home, and that he struggled over what to believe. Lucy often found herself angry with his mother but knew she had no right; Ryan's mother could teach her son whatever she liked. Lucy was only a stepmother.

But wait, she thought. God had put her in Ryan's life for a reason, and she could show Ryan God's love by example. She could pray for wisdom on how to present the truth of God's Word when he was in their home. She knew that she needed to trust God for Ryan's salvation, even if he was only exposed to the truth every other weekend. Perhaps someday even Ryan's mother would come to know God.

Dear God, it says in the Bible that Your Word doesn't come back void.
Please help me to keep praying for and witnessing to
those who don't know You. Amen.

Day 5

A Sure Thing

Know therefore that the LORD your God is God;
he is the faithful God.
DEUTERONOMY 7:9 NIV

Reliable, loyal, dependable, trustworthy, dedicated, committed. If the news is any indication, people do not exhibit an abundance of these character qualities today. Sure, we want reliable cars and loyal dogs and dependable computers and cell phones. But are we trustworthy friends and committed spouses? Are we teaching our children dedication by displaying that quality in the lives we live before them? Are we faithful?

While the human race may be experiencing a drought of faithfulness, our God definitely is not. As today's verse states, "he is the faithful God." He doesn't just have the character quality of faithfulness. Rather, He *is* faithful. You never have to wonder if this time He will act faithfully or whether next time He will decide not to be faithful. As surely as you can depend on water to freeze at thirty-two degrees Fahrenheit and the sun not to turn into the moon and your children to ask you three hundred questions today, you can know that God is faithful. He is continuously committed, eternally trustworthy, enduringly dependable. He is reliable, loyal, dedicated, devoted, unchanging, unfaltering, unwavering. He is infinitely, interminably, incessantly, inevitably *faithful*. You can depend on it.

Dear Lord, thank You that Your promises are sure and
Your commitment to me is eternal. I know I can depend
on You to be constantly and forever faithful. Amen.

Hot Lips

Put away perversity from your mouth; keep corrupt talk far from your lips.
PROVERBS 4:24 NIV

Our speech is a hot topic throughout God's Word. James wrote that no man can tame his tongue (James 3:7–8); and Paul said not to let any unwholesome talk come out of our mouths, but only what is helpful for building others up (Ephesians 4:29). In spite of cultural changes that have taken place since biblical times, one thing hasn't changed: We cannot keep our mouths shut!

Our speech is probably the biggest factor in whether we live peaceful, happy lives. In Matthew 15:18, Jesus said that out of the heart, the mouth speaks. Our tongues are just muscles in our bodies. Our speech, however, pours out of our spirits. Speech control is actually self-control. If we can control our speech, we can better control our lives. That sometimes seems like an impossible task.

But there's hope! If we ask God to help us control our speech, He will. And practice makes perfect. If we refrain from gossip today, it will be easier tomorrow. If we bite our tongues and don't spew angry words this time, we'll eventually see our angry tirades cease. If we choose to shower the people around us with loving, encouraging words, then lovely speech will soon become a lovely habit. Over time we'll find that our speech is not the only thing that has improved. Our hearts will be better, too!

Dear Father, thank You for helping me control my speech. Let my words be a source of healing and encouragement to others. Amen.

Day 7

What Did You Say?

What you say can mean life or death. Those who speak with care will be rewarded.
PROVERBS 18:21 NCV

It wasn't supposed to come out like that; that's not what was meant. What do we do now?

An unkind word can cut to the quick—once it's said, it can never be unspoken. So says scripture: Our words can mean life or death. Who hasn't reeled from a verbal lashing from a teacher or a parent or a friend? Arguments often lead to things best unsaid in the heat of the moment. We have the choice of unleashing a tidal wave of blessing or curses upon those in our realm of influence.

As stepmoms, we might be in the crosshairs of someone else's potshots. But reacting in the moment with an angry retort might do more harm than good. Words can either establish new levels of understanding, trust, friendship, and intimacy or unravel all we've tried to establish.

The nature of our words does have a highly effective quality on another person's life. We need to be quick to stay our tongues and fast to ask God for wisdom. Hard to do? You bet it is. Only through His power will we be able to choose our words with care.

Dear heavenly Father, guard my tongue that I might be the giver of life and joy. Amen.

Day 8

Continuing the Work

He who plants and he who waters are equal (one in aim, of the same importance and esteem), yet each shall receive his own reward (wages), according to his own labor.
1 Corinthians 3:8 AMP

Parenting can be a difficult job at the best of times, and being a stepmom has its own set of challenges. It's like taking over a garden from the one who created it and caring for it while the first gardener is watching. In other words, it may be uncomfortable at times, and ideas may clash.

Paul uses this analogy and points out that the one who plants and the one who waters are equal. No allowance is made for feelings of inferiority. If we are willing to embrace our stepchildren as our own and water them with love, discipline, and boundaries, life will be much easier for all those concerned.

Just like tending a garden, raising children involves much labor and effort. Weeds need to be pulled and edges trimmed. Tempers need to be tamed and bad habits dealt with. At the end of the day, the final result is what really matters, not defining who planted and who watered. What greater reward could there be than seeing children grow into responsible, caring adults who love and respect God?

Dear loving Father, help me to be content in my role as I tend the lives You've placed in my care. Let my ultimate aim be to communicate Your love to them. Amen.

Beware of the Enemy

Be self-controlled and alert. Your enemy the devil prowls around like a roaring lion looking for someone to devour.

1 Peter 5:8 NIV

As we do the work God has set out for us, our enemy prowls around waiting for a weak moment—disappointment, rejection, frustration, detours, or hardship—when he can attack full force.

Satan knows exactly what we are doing and why and how. He looks for ways to deter us from being the mother our children need. When he casts doubts in our minds, our defense needs to be the full armor of God, especially the sword of the Spirit and prayer. With those two in place, Satan will be defeated.

Our enemy will try to instill jealousy and envy in our hearts and in the hearts of our children as they seek love and attention from us. He will cast doubts about what we are doing for our families and seek to destroy our spirit. Armed with the Word of God and clothed in a mantle of prayer, we will defeat him and let God retain control of our lives.

Parent with confidence in the One who began a good work in you. He will guide you. Let not your heart be troubled or afraid, the God of salvation is with you even when you make mistakes. He will guide your efforts as you strive to be the best stepmom to the children He brought into your life.

Heavenly Father, help my family today to fight off the attacks of our enemies. Protect us with Your Word and bring our enemy to defeat. Amen.

Day 10

Encouraging Words

Do not let any unwholesome talk come out of your mouths, but only what is helpful for building others up according to their needs, that it may benefit those who listen.
EPHESIANS 4:29 NIV

In a quaint neighborhood, two light green houses sat next to each other for fifty years. The houses each had one boy, one girl, and a set of parents living inside. They looked like identical families.

One brother and sister grew up in an encouraging environment. They always heard how well they were doing in school and how much they'd improved their grades. Their parents encouraged them to do their best, even when they lost their fourth basketball game in a row. No matter what they did, they always knew that they were loved.

The other house had a different atmosphere. The kids didn't know their parents loved them. They didn't think they were smart and never liked themselves because they never knew they could do better. When they failed at something, no one encouraged them to try again. When they frustrated their parents, they heard the anger in their parents' voices, but they never heard that they were loved.

Which house is yours? What atmosphere are your kids growing up in? Make it your purpose to keep encouraging words in your mouth. The stability of your children depends on it.

Lord, let only encouraging words come from my mouth so my kids know how much they are loved. In Jesus' name, Amen.

Day 11

Stabilizers

The LORD is exalted, for he dwells on high. . .and he will be the stability of your times, abundance of salvation, wisdom, and knowledge; the fear of the LORD is Zion's treasure.
ISAIAH 33:5–6 ESV

Automobiles have stabilizers. So do aircraft and ships. We have stabilizers (of a sort) in our clothing. Support hose and underwires fall into that category. (Girdles used to, but who in their right mind wears one of those anymore?)

Some days we wish we had some stabilizers in our home—some gyroscope, some chemical, or yes, even a girdle—to bring stability to the wobbly relationships in our blended family. Where does a stepmom turn?

God tells us that it's not from an object or even a circumstance that we gain stability. It's from Him. He dwells on high, Isaiah tells us; and that gives Him the big picture. But not only is He a God who is far off, but He is near, too (Jeremiah 23:23). He brings stability in our times—times of indecision, times of frustration, times of stress. And from Him we can get an abundance of salvation and daily wisdom.

No matter how destabilized we may feel, God remains in control. He will steady us in the rough waters we may find ourselves in today.

My great God, even when I'm discombobulated, You offer stability. Thank You that You can restore my perspective and balance. In the strong name of Jesus I pray. Amen.

Day 12

Gentle Words

A gentle answer turns away wrath, but a harsh word stirs up anger.
PROVERBS 15:1 NIV

"You can't tell me what to do! You're not my real mom!" shouted Cathy's stepson as he stormed out of the room. The emotional climate at the Millers' had been extremely volatile and unpredictable since the wedding one year ago. The blending of two families was not as simple as Cathy had hoped. Flare-ups had become routine. Harsh words were commonplace. An undercurrent of resentment and anger permeated the air. This was not what she had bargained for. How could this vicious cycle be broken?

Regardless of the circumstances that bring two families together, children must sort out many unfamiliar emotions. Suddenly, their family dynamics have been permanently altered. Their security has been rocked, their foundation shaken. Broken hearts can be healed and trust reestablished. Stepmoms can play a vital role in the process of restoration by displaying patience and understanding.

Ask the Lord to help you lovingly respond to your stepchildren. Gentle words convey understanding. Harsh words fuel anger. Do not expect your stepchildren to have the ability to respond appropriately. Be the one who makes the effort, that takes the first step. Reach out to them with kindness and empathy. Then love instead of resentment will permeate the air!

Dear Lord, teach me how to respond to my stepchildren with gentle words. May love permeate our home. Amen.

Day 13

A Sneeze in the Face

Out of the same mouth come praise and cursing.
My brothers, this should not be.
James 3:10 NIV

The little boy was only three and couldn't yet tie his own shoes, so his stepmom knelt down on the floor and tied them for him, smiling up into his little face. Suddenly, his face contorted, he drew in a sharp breath, then he let loose a thundering sneeze. She didn't have time to turn away, so she received the full force of the wet, sticky blast right in the face. And sure enough, the next day, she came down with the very same cold from which the little boy was just recovering.

Even hospital-worthy hygiene won't protect us from all our children's germs. They exude snot, tears, and saliva as easily as breathing! We can teach them to cover their mouths and blow their noses to protect the health of those around them. But it is also important to teach them that far more damaging things can come out of their mouths than coughs and sneezes: words. Unconsidered and cruel words can stay with us longer and hurt far worse than the flu or a fever.

The best way for them to learn to speak with love is for them to be spoken to with love!

Dear Lord, help me guard my tongue and speak with love. Help me teach my children the power of the tongue. And forgive me when I fail. Amen.

Holy Ground

"Do not come any closer," God said. "Take off your sandals, for the place where you are standing is holy ground."
EXODUS 3:5 NIV

Moses was tending his sheep when his world changed. While watching the flames in a burning bush that wasn't consumed, Moses heard God speak and make a request, give instructions, and promise His presence. He often speaks to us and changes our world, too.

A stepmom's "holy ground" may look like a back porch or a football field, a laundry room or a courtroom, but it doesn't matter. God is there nonetheless, ready to speak and make a request, give instruction and promise His presence when the journey before us will be long and hard.

Our holy ground waits on us to be still and seek Him, to remove our defenses and listen to His voice. Every stepmom moment is in God's hands and ours to live the best we can, with God leading the way. If we can look at the "burning bushes" in that light, perhaps we'll more readily trust God's control of what we can't even begin to understand. The travel ahead may look fearful, but the foundation on which we stand is more faithful than a sunrise. Holy ground means secure steps.

Father, thank You for Your presence when I barely have the strength to stand and for providing the stability of Your infinite grace and power. On Your holy ground, I rest. Amen.

Day 15

Jonah's Grudges

Jonah was really upset and angry. So he prayed: Our Lord I knew from the very beginning that you wouldn't destroy Nineveh. That's why I left my own country and headed for Spain. You are a kind and merciful God, and you are very patient. You always show love, and you don't like to punish anyone, not even foreigners."

JONAH 4:1–2 CEV

Jonah wanted God to conform to his rules, and he kept God in a small, Jonah-sized box. When he finally obeyed God and preached to the city of Nineveh and the entire city repented, it made him mad! He had no real desire to see those people saved, even if it meant they would change their ways and seek to honor the Lord. After all, they were wicked people! Really, really bad.

But God desires for everyone to be in right relationship with him. Every single person, even the wicked ones.

Most of us have a Nineveh-type person in our life, someone we need to forgive over and over. That frustrating individual might even be our own child! When we hold on to grudges, even righteous grudges, we become Jonahs. Jonah's story is meant to teach us that no one is beyond God's reach.

If we can look at others—even those in our family—with God's perspective, we will understand them better. We will have more patience, mercy, and kindness. It's not natural or easy, though. We need to seek God's corrective vision. And when we ask, He will give.

Lord, help me to see others from Your perspective so that I can truly reflect Your mercy, patience, and kindness. Amen.

Day 16

Being Specific

I pray for them: I pray not for the world, but for which thou hast given me; for they are thine.
John 17:9 KJV

Praying a blanket prayer for those who influence our children is very easy. We can pray for our children's teachers, classmates, and friends without knowing much about the people we're praying for. We can leave everything up to God to take care of while we sit back and relax. While there is nothing wrong with praying for those we don't know well, we must also realize the responsibility we have to be acquainted with those in direct contact with our stepchildren. We should be able to be more precise when lifting them up to God.

Jesus set a wonderful example when He was with his disciples. He knew their likes, dislikes, petty grievances, and joys. He knew exactly what to pray for them. Jesus did this by spending time with His disciples and their families.

Even when it isn't comfortable, we need to make an effort to learn more about our stepchildren and those who are around them without being judgmental. What teachers do they like? Dislike? What are their favorite activities? Music groups? Movies? Books? There are many ways to learn about them as long as we reach out in love. Then we are able to pray for those God has given us in a much more specific way.

Jesus, thank You for the example of love You've given. Help me to love my stepchildren and their friends. Amen.

Day 17

Hope for the Future

"For I know the plans I have for you," declares the LORD, "plans to prosper you and not to harm you, plans to give you a hope and a future."
JEREMIAH 29:11 NIV

Stepmothering is a tough job! One stepmom, Karen, and her husband, Mike, believed God meant for them to put their families together. Their future was to be one family. They clung to this belief during the tough times while they reared six kids. Karen advised new stepmoms, "Don't get discouraged. In time things usually work out. We're too caught up in the now. Be patient and hang in there."

How did they find hope? By believing that their children and stepchildren felt at home and that they had made a difference in their kids' lives. Mike and Karen believed that God really did have a good future in store for them.

Sometimes our kids' sour attitudes rub off on us. But we need to have God's attitude rub off on us. When you're feeling wounded and unappreciated, remember that God believes in you. He gave you this stepparenting gig and knows you'll succeed. God has a future and hope for us. If God has hope for your future, you can, too!

Dear Lord, please help me to believe I'm doing a good job with these children. Encourage me today, and help me encourage myself. In Jesus' name, amen.

Day 18

Time and Space

Don't sin by letting anger control you. Think about it overnight and remain silent.
Psalm 4:4 NLT

Maybe you're the type who has to stop and count to ten to keep from erupting when tensions mount. Or maybe you're the sort to keep it all bottled up inside, only letting it spew out on others when you've reached the boiling point. Regardless, anger can have terrible consequences for you and those around you. It needs to be dealt with at its core. You can't let it control you, or it will become your master.

Do you struggle with anger? If so, what causes it to rear its ugly head, and what can you do to squelch it? Perhaps your issues are rooted in childhood incidents or things that happened to you beyond your control. Maybe you just don't feel comfortable letting it out in spurts, so you bottle it up. Well, praise the Lord! He has the capability of handling it all: your anger and any issues that activate it.

If you allow God to do a complete work in you in this area, then you won't pass on your anger to your children or stepchildren. They will learn to deal with their challenges without erupting. And you can help them learn how to do that.

Lord, I confess my anger to You. I ask You to drive it from me—from the very root. Guard my heart and guide every word that comes from my mouth. Amen.

Work for the Lord

Day 19

Whatever you do, work at it with all your heart,
as working for the Lord, not for men.
COLOSSIANS 3:23 NIV

Katherine's father often said, "Do it right or don't do it at all." Uncertain of what "right" entailed, Katherine made it her business to observe the authorities in her life then put her shoulder to the wheel following their example. Diligence and hard work earned accolades—the dean's list at school, promotions at work, and compliments from coworkers and friends—but somehow the praise seemed hollow. Satisfaction was short-lived. There was always another job to do, another person to please. *Is this really the way God wants me to live?* she wondered.

When Jesus walked on the earth, He modeled a different work ethic. His work was God-ordained, God-led, and God-empowered. In fact, Jesus proclaimed to the world that He did *nothing* on His own—even the words He spoke were taught to Him by God.

We will never reach the perfect moment-by-moment unity Jesus shared with God, but we can tune out others' demands and seek God's promptings as we attend to daily tasks. Asking, "What would You like me to do now?" brings God into the equation. He'll respond. As He directs our activities and gives us His power to complete them, all the glory will go where it belongs—to God. This is true working for the Lord, not for men.

Father, may I cease striving to do everything "right" as defined by humans. You are my Lord and Master. Show me what to do each day, and fill me with Your strength. Amen.

Day 20

Tastefully Blending

And when his brethren saw that their father loved him more than all his brethren, they hated him, and could not speak peaceably unto him.
Genesis 37:4 KJV

Have you ever added too much of your favorite ingredient to a casserole only to discover that the flavor overwhelmed everything rather than enhancing the overall taste? Too much of a good thing can actually be detrimental, and the flavors just don't blend well.

Apparently that's the kind of thing that happened in Jacob's family. He had twelve precious sons and one daughter by four different wives. It wasn't easy for him to avoid playing favorites, and he obviously overdid it, causing a distasteful rift in the family that wasn't resolved until decades later.

It isn't easy to avoid having a favorite child, and it can be even more challenging in a mixed family, but it is important to be careful how you handle such situations. Be cautious. Do not compare your children, even in moments of frustration, or you'll set them at odds against each other. Each member of your family is a unique individual and needs to be handled with care. It is true that successfully blending a family will present many challenges; but when that mix is seasoned with love, patience, and much prayer, the results can be delightful.

Lord, thank You for never playing favorites with Your children. With Your strength I will avoid this, too. Amen.

Treasure Hunts

Day 21

Glory ye in his holy name: let the heart of them rejoice that seek the Lord. *Seek the* Lord *and his strength, seek his face continually.*

1 Chronicles 16:10–11 kjv

Treasure seekers all over the world surf the Internet to satisfy their appetites for excitement, intrigue, and wealth. One American West Web site tells of century-old legends of hidden mines, such as the Lost Dutchman Mine, supposedly concealed in Arizona's Superstition Mountains. Stories of fevered treasure seekers who risked—and lost—their lives to satisfy their craving for gold are told on every page. Fortune hunters hungry for the thrill of finding gold coins, jewels, and ship artifacts also seek online advertisements for companies that take them exploring eighteenth-century shipwrecks off the shores of Florida. Still others frequent chat rooms that help them follow the current geocache craze, spending time, energy, and money simply for the fun of pursuit and discovery. Nothing seems as important as finding the next clue!

Sometimes we Christians forget we have access to the ultimate treasure of the universe: friendship with God Himself. Moreover, He wants to be found and has left all kinds of clues in His map, the Bible. Wouldn't it be wonderful if we sought Him with the give-it-all-I've-got passion of these seekers of earthly treasure?

Lord God, how often I forget Your infinite value! Yet You do everything in Your power to draw me to You. Thanks for the treasure of Your love and faithfulness. Amen.

Day 22

I Do

"These are the children God has graciously given to me."
Genesis 33:5 NLT

Dearly beloved, do you take your husband's children as your own—to live in harmony as a functional, happy family? Will you love, comfort, and keep them, in sickness and in health, for richer, for poorer, for better, for worse, in sadness and in joy, to cherish and continually sacrifice your own desires, whether or not they deserve it, for as long as you all shall live?

Will you promise to love them unconditionally, support their dreams and goals, put up with their messes, deal patiently with their negative attitudes, and drive them wherever they may need to go no matter how much it inconveniences you? Will you solemnly vow not to criticize their birth mother in their presence regardless of her efforts to undermine your authority, realizing that you can never win by doing so? Do you pledge to bite your tongue against the harsh words that you will, at some point, be dying to say?

Finally and most importantly, will you commit to raising these children up in the fear and admonition of the Lord, teaching them to revere and obey God and to worship Him in spirit and in truth? Will you lead them, by example, in paths of righteousness, demonstrating what it means to be a Christian?

If so, signify by saying, "I do."

Congratulations! You are now a certified, genuine, honest-to-goodness stepmom, and these are the children God has graciously given to you.

Lord, remind me of my commitment to my stepchildren,
and give me the grace to fulfill it. Amen.

Being Held

He is before all things, and in him all things hold together.
Colossians 1:17 NIV

Isn't it amazing to think that this world—and your family—is being held together by God Himself? Nothing you try to do can ultimately control what happens to your family. As much as you would like to be sometimes, the truth is that you are not in control. All that you can, and should, do is trust that your heavenly Father does have control. You can rest in knowing that God loves you desperately and that each member of your family is precious to Him. Sometimes it is really hard to give up control as a mother. You think that by being overly protective you can somehow stop a major catastrophe from befalling your family. Of course, you still need to use the common sense that God gave you to help keep your family safe from harm. However, there can be a fine line between doing what you can to help protect your family and trying to take control away from God. Ask the Lord to give you the wisdom to know the difference. Give back the control that belongs to Him alone. Ask Him to give you peace in knowing that He is holding each member of your family in His hands.

Dear Father, help me to give up control and rest in knowing that You are holding all things together. Amen.

Day 24

Respectfully Yours

"You must respect your mother and father. . . . I am the LORD your God."
LEVITICUS 19:3 NCV

In a world of "me first," it's difficult to raise children to understand the concept of respect. On television shows, being disrespectful to spouses, teachers, or parents gets a laugh. In real life, the behavior is often similar. It's especially disappointing when it happens within the safety of the home. A mouthy youngster isn't disciplined, or a rebellious teen just "can't be dealt with." How then can we expect to be respected?

If you feel as if you lack the respect you deserve in your household, begin by speaking with your husband about it. He may not be aware that it is happening, he may not know that it bothers you, or perhaps he sees it as "cute." However, if you openly share your feelings, he can then work with you to come up with a game plan.

Training kids to respect authority, material possessions, and money can be a difficult task. But teaching your children to respect you and your husband will instill in them the model for respecting and obeying Christ. You will also be exhibiting a healthy Christian marriage as you work as a team toward your goal.

Dear Father, help me to respect You and others as I should so that I can be a good example to my kids. Amen.

Day 25

An Invitation

"Come, all you who are thirsty, come to the waters; and you who have no money, come, buy and eat! . . . Listen, listen to me, and eat what is good, and your soul will delight in the richest of fare. Give ear and come to me; hear me, that your soul may live."

Isaiah 55:1–3 NIV

Through Isaiah, God gives us an awesome invitation. Regardless of whether we have money, we are to come to Him and drink and eat.

All God requires is three things. First, we must *come*. In every moment of every facet of our day, the invitation stands: "Come." When vacuuming the living room, come. When showering, come. When driving down the street, come. He's waiting.

Second, we are to *be thirsty and hungry*, wanting to be in His presence. For only He can relieve our minds, and He is ready and able to carry us through thick and thin.

And finally, we are to *listen*. God emphasizes this by repeating the command over and over again: "Listen, listen to me. . . . Give ear. . .hear me, that your soul may live."

God invites us to answer His call, to thirst for His presence, to listen to His voice and feed upon Him. In doing so, we will find ourselves supping on and with the best of friends—the living water and bread, Jesus Christ. He is the richest of fare, and in Him our soul will delight.

Lord, I come to You, thirsty for Your presence. Speak to me. Love me as I delight in You, the richest nourishment for my hungry soul. Amen.

Against the Grain

Ruth. . .said to Naomi, "Let me go out into the harvest fields."
Ruth 2:2 NLT

"Your kids *are* coming this weekend?" *Just when I anticipated some downtime!* The pressure of getting heartier meals on the table for early adolescents is back on your shoulders. So what's the next move to make? Ruth's response to that question no doubt goes against the grain of popular opinion.

Ruth, the newcomer to Naomi's family, made an unlikely move. She, of all people, shouldn't be expected to get supper as she accompanied Naomi back to Bethlehem. You'd think somebody in Naomi's hometown would have furnished a steaming pot of barley soup!

But Ruth's next move was to go out to the barley field and gather the grain before she could even think of getting supper on the table. No doubt this extra load on her shoulders was lightened by the refuge she had come to find under the wings of the Almighty God. Aha! No better place than this to give you *oomph* for the next move.

Before going to your "field" to provide for your family, take time to replenish yourself under the wings of the Almighty. Surely your refreshed spirit will benefit those around your table as much as the food you prepare.

Dear God, please help me to willingly go against the grain of opinion and move in obedience to You. Amen.

Remember This

Day 27

I thank my God every time I remember you.
PHILIPPIANS 1:3 NCV

What a great example Paul set for his dear readers! He was in prison. Things couldn't get much worse. There was not much Paul could give thanks for in his current circumstance, so he looked inside and pulled out good memories! He remembered people he loved, and he thanked God.

How many times do we get so caught up in our current bad situations that we forget how good God has been? Our heavenly Father has shown His love to us in countless ways and has given us the ability to remember all the wonderful things He has done for us. He has given us food and shelter. He has surrounded us with people to love. And, no matter how bad things get, most of us can pull up at least one good, positive, praiseworthy memory.

When we find ourselves in circumstances beyond our control, circumstances that make us angry or break our hearts, we should follow Paul's example. We should think of something that makes us smile, something for which we are thankful. And we should give thanks to God for His eternal goodness.

Dear Father, thank You for all the wonderful people and things in my life. When life gets hard, help me to be thankful for those things. Amen.

Day 28

Prepared for Battle

So take everything the Master has set out for you, well-made weapons of the best materials. And put them to use so you will be able to stand up to everything the Devil throws your way. This is no afternoon athletic contest that we'll walk away from and forget about in a couple of hours. This is for keeps, a life-or-death fight to the finish against the Devil and all his angels.

Ephesians 6:11–12 msg

An athlete wouldn't dream of walking into the arena of his sport without the right equipment. Neither would a soldier enter into battle without his weapons and battle dress. So why do we attempt to face our spiritual enemy without having put on the armor our Captain has set out for us? Is it because we underestimate our enemy?

In our homes, we fight against Satan and *all* his angels for the souls of our children and stepchildren. This isn't a mere skirmish; it is a "life-or-death fight to the finish." Even if our children make professions of faith in Christ alone for their salvation, the enemy doesn't give up. He's going to do all he can to keep them from being effective servants of Christ.

God has provided the spiritual armor we need to fight the battle: the belt of truth, the breastplate of righteousness, the shoes of peace, the shield of faith, the helmet of salvation, the sword of the Spirit. It's not enough to put the armor on; learn to use it effectively. Become a warrior princess, ready to do battle on behalf of your children. You'll never regret it.

Father, thank You for equipping me for spiritual battles that will come my way. Amen.

Day 29

Simon Says

Follow my example, as I follow the example of Christ.
1 Corinthians 11:1 NCV

Sandy watched her children and her neighbor's children playing Simon Says. As she watched, Sandy suddenly realized that the game was the exact opposite of what God intended her to be as a parent. Simon Says teaches, "Do as I say and not as I do," but a godly parent is God's representative and teaches her children, "Follow me as I follow Christ."

It is an awesome responsibility to raise children. They watch what we do and call us on it if we say one thing and do another. How can we give our children clear directions—how can we tell them, "This is the way; walk ye in it," if we are not walking in that way ourselves? How can we teach our children about faith if they see us worry all the time? How can we teach them to be kind to others when they hear us gossip and backbite? How can we teach them the importance of being part of the family of God if we send them to church instead of taking them? Our children imitate us. They learn by what we do and how we behave. In order to get them to listen to our words, we must make certain that our words match our actions.

Dear Father, please help me to be a good example not only to my own children but also to every child who comes into the sphere of my influence. Amen.

Day 30

Dear Abba. . .

God is our refuge and strength, a very present help in trouble.
PSALM 46:1 NASB

Emily, Lisa's ninth-grade stepdaughter, wanted to go to a senior class party on a school night. Lisa said no. Now Emily was standing in the middle of their lawn, shouting at the top of her lungs, "I hate you! I hate you!"

Lisa stood poised, waiting to hear the unspoken words—You're not my mother!—that hung in the air between them. But they never came. Instead, her enraged stepdaughter clamped her lips shut and stomped into the house.

With a heavy heart, Lisa stumbled into the kitchen and sank into a chair, just in time to hear Emily's bedroom door slam shut.

Who knew that being a stepmother would be so hard?

Now in tears herself, Lisa wondered how to handle this latest situation with Emily. Whom could she call for advice? Her husband was working late, her mother had passed away years ago, and her close friends and neighbors were raising toddlers, not teens.

"Maybe I should sit down and write to Dear Abby," Lisa said aloud as she lowered her head onto the kitchen table. Moments later, she sprang up, sniffling. "No, not Dear Abby. I'll go to the ultimate source, the ever-present Master of wisdom."

Lowering herself to her knees, Lisa began to pray. "Dear Abba. . ."

Dear Abba, You know what's happening in my life. You see all, understand all, know all. Give me wisdom in every situation. Give me the strength to do what's right in Your eyes. Amen.

Day 31

Just a Moment. . .

Moses answered them, "Wait until I find out what the Lord commands concerning you."
Numbers 9:8 niv

When some Israelites had questions about celebrating the Passover on the way to the Promised Land, they went to Moses. And he went to God, confident of an answer. We can have the same confidence, because the same God stands ready to answer our questions, too.

Whether we're being asked for advice or desperately needing guidance of our own, we can follow Moses' example—we can wait. We can inquire. We can earnestly seek God's will before we act. And steplife promises no shortage of situations needing divine intervention and direction.

The stepmom sought that guidance with great urgency one day, sitting on the stairs grasping her knees to her chest, a decision on her shaking shoulders of what to do next. Fear, anger, and exasperation pounded in every heartbeat echoing between her ears, but she resisted the meltdown she could feel coming and asked for God to send instruction instead. She waited. She prayed. She breathed steady breaths. And in the pause, He quieted her stampeding heartbeat so she could act. May we follow her and Moses' example every time.

Father, please help me to remember that waiting to find out what You want me to do is always the best choice. Please calm my fears and guide my heart so that I may touch my family as You would have me do. Amen.

Day 32

Resisting Temptation

"By smooth words he will turn to godlessness those who act wickedly toward the covenant, but the people who know their God will display strength and take action."

DANIEL 11:32 NASB

In the passage above, Daniel is writing about a vision he received from God. The vision addresses bleak events that will occur in Israel's future. Kings who renounce God will rule over the people of Israel, wars will be fought, and the Israelites will experience much pain and suffering. As Daniel receives this vision, the angel of the Lord assures him that though the king of the north will try to turn the people of Israel from their God, he will not be successful. God will strengthen them and give them the courage to resist.

The words above are important for us today. Daniel's vision makes it clear that those who don't know the words of God and who ignore God's commands will be led astray by the smooth-talking king of the north. Only those who truly know God and are committed to the covenant will have the strength to resist the new king. We have to face great temptation each day. So much of today's society is at odds with the message of Christ. However, believers who have a strong relationship with Jesus can rely on God to give them strength to resist the smooth words of temptation they encounter each day.

Dear Lord, I commit myself anew to knowing You better. Imprint Your words on my heart so that I might resist temptation when it comes. Amen.

Perfect Conditions

Those who wait for perfect weather, will never plant seeds.
ECCLESIASTES 11:4 NCV

Perfect conditions. What are they, exactly? It's human nature to dream of what we could accomplish if only so-and-so would cooperate, or if only the weather were perfect, or if only every circumstance would neatly fall into place. But in reality that rarely, if ever, happens.

So if we waited on everything and everyone being in place at the same time, nothing would ever get done. God has much He wants to accomplish on earth through His children. And, thank God, much does get done every day—in spite of difficulties, in spite of pain, in spite of children or stepchildren or husbands who don't seem to want what we want when it comes to spiritual goals.

We can have the best plans in the world, with everything considered, planned for, contingency plans in place, and so forth. But the enemy of our soul delights in circumventing all our best-laid plans in an attempt to get us to curse God (see Job 1–2) and bring dishonor to His name. The next time you're faced with imperfect conditions, remember Proverbs 16:3 (NLT): "Commit your actions to the LORD, and your plans will succeed."

The outcome may not look as you envisioned it, but the essence of your plans and dreams will be realized as you place your complete dependence on Him.

Father, thank You for helping me to get things accomplished—in spite of less-than-perfect conditions. Amen.

Day 34

Customs

Daniel. . .in his upper room. . .knelt down. . .and prayed and gave thanks before his God, as was his custom since early days.

Daniel 6:10 NKJV

We have all sorts of customs: something we do over and over as a family until that action or event becomes familiar or comfortable. We have certain foods we eat for different holidays, special vacations spots we return to, or family reunions that occur at timely intervals. Some of us have a family night each week when we play games or do something special just for our household.

Traditions are a wonderful way to instill godly values in our children. They can be a great way to bond. The best way to have our children develop a custom is to have it become a part of our lives as well. We have to consider what is important to impart to our children. Do we pray with them? Do we teach by example to read and study our Bibles daily? Do we make God the focus of our lives, not an afterthought, and show our child how to do the same?

God wants us to talk with our children about His importance in our lives. He wants us to share a love for Him and His saving grace so that our children will pass on this important decision to their children. This is a custom worth handing down from generation to generation.

Father, thank You that I can come before You in prayer. Help me to teach this important truth to my children. Amen.

Can I Quit?

Day 35

Let us not become weary in doing good, for at the proper time we will reap a harvest if we do not give up.

Galatians 6:9 niv

Melody went from being a childless single to a married stepmom with full-time custody of three girls. Added to that mix came a challenging (exasperating!) relationship with the girls' mother. Melody knew it wasn't going to be easy to step into a ready-made family, but she never dreamed it would be as difficult as it turned out to be. *It was probably just as well not to know*, she thought. She would have run for the hills. Many times, she confessed, she daydreamed about quitting, packing her bags, and heading back to her less complicated single life. But she would never quit. She was raised to follow the principle "Do what's right, even when it's hard." Every day, some days more than once, Melody asked God for the grace to endure this difficult season and be the best mother she could possibly be.

Years later, Melody is reaping the joys and blessings of enduring the race. At a recent baby shower for her new granddaughter, she heard her stepdaughter tell a friend that she wanted to be a mother just like Melody.

By Your grace, Lord, help me to endure the struggles that seem inherent to being a stepmother. Keep my eyes on the prize: to reap the joys and blessings of an obedient life. Amen.

Day 36

Hard to Swallow

They sang: Saul has killed a thousand enemies; David has killed ten thousand enemies! This song made Saul very angry.

1 Samuel 18:7–8 cev

You've come to expect attention from others. Your latest story keeps your family or friends on the edge of their seats. Your new cooking creation keeps them talking. Then, out of nowhere, it's your coming-into-her-own stepdaughter's wit or wasabi that grabs them. So what are you to do with that pit in your stomach when heads turn in a different direction?

Well, King Saul chose to help himself to gluttonous helpings of envy because David had greater success against the Philistine enemies and got the applause. Saul had liked this young chap as a helper around the palace, but his attitude changed drastically when David turned hero.

When your "helper" turns "hero," the best cure for a pit in the stomach is a generous portion of God's graciousness, the capacity to enjoy someone else's accomplishment! It may still not be easy to get down, but God promises you a much better aftertaste!

Please forgive me, Lord, for envying a younger upstart.
Help me to step back when it's her turn to step up. Amen.

What Thanks Do I Get?

Day 37

And thy Father which seeth in secret himself shall reward thee openly.
Matthew 6:4 KJV

You're the glue that keeps everything together. The pantry stocker, cookie baker, and toilet paper roll replacer. Without you, the beds would go unmade and the homework would never leave the backpack. You put your heart and soul into solving problems and soothing hurts. And when your family is tucked in safely for the night, you trudge off to bed, at times wondering, *Does anyone ever notice?*

Does anyone appreciate the neatly folded underwear? The new toothpaste? The spaceship birthday cake that took six hours to make? Does your stepchild understand how hard you're trying to make him feel loved? Is going the extra mile really worth it?

Bending over backward is a lot more satisfying when you receive a standing ovation. And while you may not hear any applause coming from your loved ones, you can rest assured that God is cheering. He notices your hard work and is rewarding you in ways that you may not even realize. The answers to prayer that come just in the nick of time, the extra blessings that arrive when you least expect them—all of those things are God's way of telling you to keep up the good work.

Dear heavenly Father, You know that there are times when I need a pat on the back. Remind me that You not only see my efforts, but are pleased with them, as well. Amen.

Day 38

Anger Released

In your anger do not sin. Do not let the sun go down while you are still angry, and do not give the devil a foothold.
Ephesians 4:26–27 NIV

Janet sat cross-legged on her closet floor, scribbling furiously on a legal pad. How could the stepfamily she'd chosen to love find so much reason to hate her? It wasn't fair! Angry words exploded from her pen, filling page after page, until she reached exhaustion.

Leaning against the wall, breathing slowly, Janet finally settled down. "Help me, Father, to see what You see," she prayed. As she read the words she'd penned, the truth shocked her. She realized she'd become a bitter woman. Tears drenched her cheeks. "I promised to love my stepfamily, Lord, but I haven't. Please help me!"

When we allow anger to fester, Satan gains a foothold within us. The bitter root spoken of in Hebrews 12:15 grows, causing hostility. But we don't have to cooperate with Satan's plan to destroy our relationships and our peace. We *can* let our anger go!

Are you angry? If so, remember, God cares deeply about your hurts. He already knows everything you're hiding inside—so tell Him about it. As you throw yourself upon His mercy and grace, God will show you His point of view. Bitterness will flee. You will finally be free to extend true love and forgiveness to others.

Father, help me empty myself before You of all the hurts I've self-righteously stored in my heart and mind. May Your grace cover me and my family and set us all free. Amen.

God's Household

Day 39

Consequently, you are no longer foreigners and aliens, but fellow citizens with God's people and members of God's household.

Ephesians 2:19 NIV

The task of merging families isn't always easy, is it? Sometimes you can feel like an outsider. A foreigner. And try as you may, you can't always force people to bond. Oh, you can put them together in the same house, but you can't assume they'll all get along and act as a family should act.

Thank goodness it's not that way in God's family. In His house, we're no longer foreigners and aliens. We're members of His family. Fellow citizens! And His home is big enough to hold millions! (Talk about a lot of siblings!) He is the ultimate parent and knows just how to keep His kids in line.

So what does this mean for you? Perhaps you've already experienced the joy of joining two families into one peaceful one. Maybe your husband's children from a prior marriage have settled into a comfortable relationship with you. If things have gone smoothly, congratulations! If you're still struggling in this area, remember to keep the Lord in His rightful place as head of your household. With God as your Father, you really can become one big happy family!

Dear Lord, today I acknowledge once again that You are Lord. . .not just of my life, but of my household. Thank You that I am no longer a foreigner or an alien. I'm Yours! Take Your rightful place, Father. May this home truly be Yours. Amen.

Day 40

Smart Love

When wisdom entereth into thine heart, and knowledge is pleasant unto thy soul; discretion shall preserve thee, understanding shall keep thee.

Proverbs 2:10–11 KJV

I love you, Anna. I told you that at our wedding. I'll never change my mind."

Last night Will's honest brown eyes had looked deep into hers, reminding Anna of the wonderful day six months before when they pledged their love before God.

Anna had needed his reassurance. She'd struggled after his son's mother, Katie, called with her latest ploy. Seven-year-old Aiden had read twenty library books. He wanted both his mom and dad to celebrate with him at McDonald's. Her car had broken down; could Will pick them up around six then fix it afterward? Anna's husband kindly but firmly told Katie she could join him, Anna, and Aiden Saturday to celebrate. He gave her the number of an economical garage. As Anna listened on the other end, her stomach unknotted. And when Will held her, she enjoyed his warmth and love.

Friday, when Katie brought Aiden for the weekend, Anna wanted to give the woman a triumphant smile or two. But she resisted the temptation and let Will discuss parenting details with her without hovering near. Over time, Anna realized Katie lived a lonely, self-centered existence without God. Her own understanding not only made their relationship bearable, but blessed Aiden and her grateful husband, strengthening their marriage and adding to her own happiness.

Lord, how often Your commands benefit not only others, but me as well! Help me act with Your compassionate wisdom. Amen.

Day 41

A Cause for Rejoicing

For men are not cast off by the Lord forever. Though he brings grief, he will show compassion, so great is his unfailing love.

LAMENTATIONS 3:31–32 NIV

The prophet Jeremiah is the author of Lamentations, a book in which he pours out his sorrows. Known as "the weeping prophet," Jeremiah is heartbroken over the disobedience of the Israelites and their rejection of God. He mourns because the destruction of Jerusalem is imminent, and he knows that the people of Israel will endure God's wrath and punishment as a result of their rebelliousness.

Jeremiah's heart breaks for his people; but in the midst of this darkness, he finds a ray of hope. God will not be angry forever. He is the God of compassion and love, and while the people of Israel will experience grief for a time, God will relent from His anger. Even as Jeremiah weeps, he is able to praise God's compassion and unfailing love.

We have an even greater reason to praise God than Jeremiah did. Through God's compassion and infinite love, He sent His Son, Jesus Christ, to die on a cross for our sins. We do not have to wait for God to relent from His anger and to draw us back to Himself again. Rather, we simply must repent from our sins, asking for forgiveness and rejoicing in God's great compassion and love.

Dear Lord, I'm sorry for my disobedience to You. Thank You for Your awesome compassion and love, and thank You for sending Jesus to take away my sins. Amen.

Day 42

Love, Knowledge, and Understanding

I pray that your love will overflow more and more, and that you will keep on growing in knowledge and understanding. For I want you to understand what really matters, so that you may live pure and blameless lives until the day of Christ's return.

PHILIPPIANS 1:9–10 NLT

Do you ever feel overwhelmed as a mom? Not sure how to solve the next problem or finish your endless list of tasks? God wants us to succeed as mothers. That doesn't mean we have to be perfect. We will still make mistakes. But God wants us to come to Him and find the answers to what really matters. This verse gives us some keys to success.

First, we have to wrap everything we do as a mom in love. If our solutions and tasks aren't wrapped in love, then they are meaningless. Second, we have to continue to seek the Lord daily for knowledge and understanding. Get into God's Word and ask the Holy Spirit to help you understand the Word and apply it to your daily life. We also need to be understanding of our family members. Ask God to help you understand the needs of each individual in your family.

Your family is precious to God! Playing a game or having a good conversation with one of your children who needs a little extra attention can sometimes have more eternal impact than crossing another task off your list.

Dear Father, give me the desire to seek You each day. Help me to understand what really matters in life. Amen.

Embracing God's Plan

Day 43

There is no differnce in men in this new life. . . . Christ is everything. He is in all of us.
COLOSSIANS 3:11 NLV

As a five-year-old American living in Japan, Sarah knew she was different. Her blond hair, in stark contrast to the jet black hair of her classmates, was a dead giveaway. People stared. They patted her head. In her heart she knew she didn't fit in. Those same emotions came flooding back thirty years later when she became a stepmother. All of her friends had biological children, and she felt like an outsider.

Motherhood may come through birth, adoption, or marriage. Regardless of how the title is bestowed, the Lord has given us a unique privilege. We impart love. We give encouragement. We offer guidance. Stepmothers, like any mother, influence and shape the lives of those entrusted to our care.

Embrace God's plan for your life. Acknowledge that He is sovereign. He has given you an opportunity to shape children's lives. Do not focus on ways you might be different from your friends. With Christ, differences do not matter. Seek to be used by the Lord. Cultivate relationships with your stepchildren. Look for ways to sow God's truth into their hearts. God has you right where you are for a reason. You most certainly fit in!

Dear Lord, thank You for giving me the opportunity to parent my stepchildren. May I look to You for guidance. Amen.

Day 44

What's Mine Is. . . Yours?

"If you have two shirts, share with the person who does not have one. If you have food, share that also."
Luke 3:11 NCV

Deb pulled the white sweater out of her closet that her fifteen-year-old stepdaughter, Lisa, had borrowed the weekend before. She was not a bit happy to see the stain on the front of the sweater.

"Oh, I'm sorry," said Lisa when Deb confronted her. "I spilled salad dressing on it, but I figured you could get it out." Deb realized right then that they needed to set up some boundaries.

"Lisa, I don't mind if you borrow my things. God has given them to me, and I want to share them. In fact, God is the owner of everything. He, in His goodness, has loaned everything to us to take care of during our time on this earth.

"But when we borrow something from someone, we need to ask for permission first. Then, when you have been granted the privilege of borrowing the item, treat it carefully and return it in the same condition. If it's beyond repair, it is your responsibility to replace it. But I don't think that's the case with this sweater. Let's go see if we can work on getting this stain out."

Jesus, thank You for all You have blessed me with. Help me to teach my children how to be good stewards with what they borrow. Amen.

Day 45

Rotten Egg

Hatred stirs up dissension, but love covers over all wrongs.
PROVERBS 10:12 NIV

Hatred. What an ugly word. It describes an invisible yet almost tangible emotion that bubbles up inside one's soul and spills over to everyone who comes near. Hate cannot be contained and, contrary to popular belief, cannot be focused on just one person.

Hatred doesn't do nearly as much damage to its target as it does to its vessel. Just as a rotten egg will contaminate a dozen good eggs in a bowl, hate will contaminate any love in one's soul. A person who hates is miserable and wants everyone else to be miserable. So that person stirs up dissension and anger and grief and gossip and slander. And it's never enough.

Love can't be contained, either. It's like a beautiful artesian well that bubbles up and springs forth life and health and nourishment to everyone in its reach. When love—*real love, God's love*—is stored in a person, then forgiveness and patience and kindness abound. While hate brings hurt feelings and bitter words and violence and destruction, love brings joy and smiles and sweet laughter and healing. Hate tears down. Love builds up.

Dear Father, thank You for Your love. Please help me to get rid of any anger, bitterness, and hatred in my heart, and fill me with Your perfect love. Amen.

Guard the Tongue

Reckless words pierce like a sword, but the tongue of the wise brings healing.
PROVERBS 12:18 NIV

As a teenager, Susan went to live with her father and stepmother. At first Susan hated having to leave her mother, and her attitude toward her stepmother was one of intense dislike and mistrust. But it seemed that no matter how hurtful she tried to be when speaking with her stepmother, the response was always one of love and encouragement. Finally, Susan realized that her words were received with a spirit of love that only God could provide. Her animosity turned to respect for a woman who spoke wisely.

Being a stepmother sometimes means biting the tongue and not saying the words that come to the mind. When stepchildren hurt with their words, we must not let our own words come back with the same hurt toward the child. Words spoken in love and with wisdom can eventually heal the rift that comes between child and stepparent.

Being able to swallow those words of harmful retort or reprimand is difficult. But God is faithful; and when we call upon Him to help us guide our stepchildren into acceptable behavior, He is there with us to give support and encouragement.

Heavenly Father, guide us today so that our words do not pierce and wound but bring hope and healing to others. Amen.

God Hears You

I love the LORD, because He hears my voice and my supplications. Because He has inclined His ear to me, therefore I shall call upon Him as long as I live.

PSALM 116:1–2 NASB

The president of the United States is considered the most powerful man in the world. His time is scheduled to the minute, supporters seek his autograph, and frenzied reporters pummel him with numerous questions. He tries to answer all of them, but he is able to answer only one question at a time—and rarely can he answer every question.

Thankfully, God doesn't hold press conferences where we have to compete for His attention. Since He is the ultimate master of multitasking, He can handle millions of people all over the world all at the same time who are begging, pleading, even demanding that He do something about their situations. Does He say, "Just a minute, this gentleman was first," or "Could you repeat that? I missed the first part"? Of course not! He hears every word of every prayer uttered by every person every second. He inclines His ear to everyone who calls upon Him. In fact, the verse suggests that the God of the universe *bends down* to hear you. So if you feel your household is falling apart around you, know that God hears your prayers. Any time, any day, no matter how many others are praying, He inclines His ear to *you*. Now that's powerful!

Father, I am so grateful for the privilege of coming to You in prayer. Thank You for hearing every prayer and being faithful to listen and answer. Amen.

Day 48

The Water Brooks

In the morning, O Lord, you hear my voice; in the morning I lay my requests before you and wait in expectation.

Psalm 5:3 NIV

When a deer is chased by a predator, it looks for a place of safety, a place that is difficult for the enemy to find. The water brook offers protection and refreshing. Water from the water brook provides a second wind that the deer needs to escape the one pursuing him.

As a stepmom, you may feel that no matter what you do, it's never enough. Someone is always pushing your buttons; and no matter how thoughtful and giving you try to be, drama still happens in the end.

When you are tired, you become vulnerable. You probably push yourself to do more and be more for your family. To be the best you can be for yourself and for them, you need to eat well, get enough sleep, and take care of yourself by visiting the "water brooks" God has given you.

In the midst of disappointment, discouragement, and transition, run to your place of refreshing. Slip into your quiet place and allow His presence to fill your heart with living water. Draw hope from the life-giving God. He is with you always, so take a few minutes to get alone with Him.

Heavenly Father, I need You. I need Your strength and Your hope. Help me to depend on You and to run to You instead of trying to do things for myself. Amen.

Day 49

A Rocky Road

I will rejoice in the Lord, I will joy in the God of my salvation. The Lord God is my strength; He will make my feet like deer's feet, and He will make me walk on my high hills.

Habakkuk 3:18–19 NKJV

Sometimes life seems like an uphill battle. We strive, we fret, we panic. It's just too difficult to stay the course—to keep on keeping on. We're tempted to throw up our hands in frustration and quit. That's when we must realize we're in the perfect position: hands raised in surrender.

God's promises are true. When we relax in His care, He will bring us safely through all our difficulties. He didn't promise a life with no problems. He did promise to carry us through. In Proverbs 3:5 (AMP), the word "trust" is extrapolated: "lean on, trust in, and be confident in the Lord." Are we leaning on the Lord? Do we trust Him with our future and the future of those in our care? Have we become confident in His Word?

Surrender and trust—two words that lead to life and joy. Choose to surrender and trust this day. He'll then bring you safely over the mountains.

Dear Lord, surrendering and trusting don't come naturally. Gently guide me so I might learn of You and become confident in Your care. Amen.

Day 50

Rest Awhile

And He said to them, "Come away by yourselves to a secluded place and rest a while." (For there were many people coming and going, and they did not even have time to eat.)
Mark 6:31 NASB

Mothering is a full-time job, and stepmothering may bring added pressures as families are blended and relationships built. In the midst of all this busyness, there comes a time when we need to head to a secluded place and rest awhile. This place doesn't have to be a desert island or a cabin in the mountains, but can be a bedroom with a Do Not Disturb sign on the door or a quiet spot at the bottom of the garden.

Wherever it is, it needs to be a place of seclusion and rest from the daily demands of life—a place where we can relax and do nothing or listen to some worship songs and read a book. It can also be a chance to do something creative and fulfilling like writing in a journal or working on a scrapbook. Even a half hour of rest can make an amazing difference to energy levels and attitude control.

If we don't take the time to rest, we will keep rushing from one appointment to another, from one duty to another, and will eventually end up exhausted. In this condition, we're no use to anyone.

Dear Lord, You are the God of peace and rest. Help me to take time to relax and recover my energies. Amen.

Day 51

Fear Not

"Be strong and of good courage; do not be afraid, nor be dismayed, for the LORD your God is with you wherever you go."

JOSHUA 1:9 NKJV

Parenting is an adventure. It can be exciting, trying, frightening, and full of twists and turns. Parenting is rarely boring. The one thing we need to remember is that we are in a God-designed adventure. He is the One who planned our story and who guides our footsteps. He has the map showing dangers. Sometimes He guides us around them; sometimes He helps us through them. Always, He is there with us.

Even though we know God is there, we can become fearful because we don't feel Him or see Him. His presence eludes us in dark times, and we have doubts. Those are the times when our faith must be put to action. What we've learned in the light, or good, times we have to trust in the dark, or difficult, times. God is there. We can have that assurance.

There is no adventure without a share of potholes in the road, delays, and wrong turns. Some of those are by our own choosing when we fail to seek God's counsel. Some are designed by the enemy or are even things God allows to happen. No matter what, God will be there to set us on the right path again. There is no need to fear. Trust Him with every step.

Lord, take my fear and distrust and replace them with total faith in Your ability to guide me. Amen.

Day 52

Easy Does It

And his servants came near and said to him, My father, if the prophet had bid you to do some great thing, would you not have done it? How much rather, then, when he says to you, Wash and be clean?

2 Kings 5:13 AMP

Naaman was a revered and successful soldier, and he had leprosy. Elisha told him to wash seven times in the Jordan River and be healed, but that sounded too easy, too low-key, to be effective; so Naaman protested, wanting to do something more complicated to achieve his goal. His servants urged him on, though, and he complied and was cured.

We want to be good stepmoms (great ones, really, maybe even go down in history, or at least in our family scrapbooks as "The Greatest *Ever*"). We want to wow the children we inherit (and their parents) with our skills, our abilities, our wisdom, and our compassion. We want to, and we may think getting there means grand gestures and superwoman powers.

But no, our sincerity and efforts shine brightly in the simplest of acts—in a kind word, a helping hand, a giving heart, a nonjudgmental stand. Our everyday understanding, willingness, and generosity in the way we live our lives will help us achieve our goals, even if no statues are involved.

Let us never discount the low-key work, because the result may be just what we wanted.

Father, please show me what You would have me do and open my eyes to all the opportunities, large and small, that You place before me. Help me see the little efforts that mean so much. Amen.

Share and Share Alike

Day 53

Don't forget to do good and to share with those in need.
Hebrews 13:16 NLT

All of us were taught early on to share. Sharing meant you made friends. Stinginess left us alone with our "stuff."

As stepmoms we may have trouble learning to share. We marry the man of our dreams. We have someone to laugh with. Someone to lavish us with attention. After a bad day at work, we have a sympathetic ear. Someone to "take our side." Life is great.

Then the stepkids come over. They love their dad's attention—in fact, they demand it. He laughs at their silly jokes. They have someone they can tell about the bullies at school. Someone who can do something about it! And there we sit—on the outside listening in. Sharing the best we've got with someone else.

In the verse above, the writer of Hebrews wasn't talking about sharing a loved one. Yet the principle stands. Just as the sharing of goods cost the early believers, sharing her husband with his children costs the new bride. The rest of that verse holds the secret to doing what's right in both circumstances. Why should the new bride generously share her husband with her stepchildren? "These are the sacrifices that please God" (Hebrews 13:16 NLT).

Father, You shared Your beloved Son with me for my good. Help me do the same with my husband for the children's good, knowing it pleases You. Amen.

Day 54

Refilling the Cup

Not forsaking the assembling of ourselves together, as is the manner of some, but exhorting one another, and so much the more as you see the Day approaching.
HEBREWS 10:25 NKJV

One of the most important parts of stepmothering is having a supportive church family. One stepmom, Karen, said that without her relationship with God and her church family, her marriage would not have survived. She and her husband drew their strength from Sunday services. They refilled their cups. And they loved God and their church family.

Their family went to church and Sunday school every week, even when they had to fight with the kids to get them dressed in church clothes instead of jeans and T-shirts. But the church family was a huge support. Karen looked up to a Christian friend and decided she wanted the same kind of peace and happiness in her life. She figured the only way she was going to get that was through regularly attending church and through a relationship with Jesus. So she worked toward that, sometimes praying alone at her church during the week.

She and her husband kept taking their kids to church week after week, stomachs churning over prechurch battles. But they got through it.

And so will we. Like this stepmom, we need to pray often and surround ourselves with a strong, supportive church family. We're not supposed to go it alone. God wants us to draw strength from others who love Jesus as much as we do.

Dear Lord, thank You for my church family. Thank You for the gift of prayer. Please bless my church family today. Amen.

Day 55

Hunt for the Treasures of Life

Whoever goes hunting for what is right and kind finds life itself—glorious life!
PROVERBS 21:21 MSG

Life's responsibilities often crowd out the beautiful moments hidden in each day. A mom can get so caught up in her daily routine that she misses the enthusiastic glimmer in her stepson's eye when he finally gets the guitar he's wanted. Or the guilty look on her husband's face when she finds him sneaking candy to their four-year-old.

Your laundry will never cease, dishes will continue to get dirty, and the bathroom shower will always need cleaning. But you won't always have a five-year-old child running around your house wearing pink shorts, a blue shirt, and fuzzy bear slippers.

Take time to notice the smile your stepdaughter gives you when you bake her favorite cookies. Enjoy the *pitter-patter* in your heart when you first hear your stepchildren say, "I think you're pretty cool." Treasure the love you see in your husband's eyes when he comes home from work and finds you cooking his favorite meal.

Hunt for the good in each day. When you do, you'll find a glimmer of glorious life in every situation you face.

Lord, I want to search for the treasures You give me each day. Help me stay alert to beautiful moments with my family and friends. In Jesus' name, amen.

Day 56

The Ultimate Space Satellite

"For the eyes of the LORD move to and fro throughout the earth that He may strongly support those whose heart is completely His."

2 CHRONICLES 16:9 NASB

Amid heated arguments, curfew debates, and enforcement of discipline, we may feel all alone. The challenges of being a stepparent sometimes seem overwhelming. In times of trouble, we may feel as if we are standing on a mountaintop with the wind whistling all around us. There seems to be no help in sight. Because all family situations and problems are as unique as the individuals involved in them, we sometimes don't know where to turn.

Yet we are never truly alone. There is One whose eyes move "to and fro throughout the earth." He's like the ultimate space satellite, seeing all, knowing all. But He is not distant. He is standing on the mountaintop with us. As we face difficulties, He is there to block the wind. And just when we think we are about to fall over the edge into an endless abyss, He grasps for our hand, holds tight, and pulls us back onto level ground. He may not erase all our problems, but He will be with us as we go through them.

All we need do is trust in Him. Look for Him. Allow Him to catch us. He'll never let go. We can give Him our whole heart. It's safe in His hands.

My Lord and Savior, I willingly give You my heart. I put total trust and faith in You, knowing You see all and know all. Hold me tight. Never let me go.

The Scream of Self

Day 57

"But you are a forgiving God, gracious and compassionate, slow to anger and abounding in love."
NEHEMIAH 9:17 NIV

Babies have no patience. They scream when they are hungry, even if Mother, with a warm bottle, is right outside the nursery door. They scream for a toy just out of reach. As they grow older, they scream to get their own way. They scream when they *don't* get their own way. They scream when we ask them to do something they just don't want to do. They scream because their needs and desires are more important to them than anything else in the world.

Adults don't usually scream to get their way, at least not out loud. But often God asks us to do something we don't want to do—or to stop doing something we really want to do—and we find ourselves screaming inside. We don't want to obey; we wonder why we should. Just like a tiny baby, we kick against the wisdom of our loving Father, who knows what we need far better than we do.

We want the children in our care to obey quickly and cheerfully because we know it is the right thing for them to do; it makes us happy, and it will make them happier also. This is what God expects from us, too. But thankfully, just like a parent, He patiently and lovingly forgives us when our obedience is less than perfect.

Dear heavenly Father, help me to listen for Your voice and to obey You quickly and cheerfully, even when I don't understand why. Amen.

Day 58

Wise Up!

If you need wisdom, ask our generous God, and he will give it to you. He will not rebuke you for asking.

James 1:5 NLT

We ask God for so many things—finances, stronger relationships, blessings, material things, and much more. But isn't it funny how we rarely think to add wisdom to the list? Sure, we ask, "Lord, help me make this decision or that decision." In the moment, we just want to get through whatever problem we're facing. But if we pray for wisdom in advance of those things, then we'll have the wherewithal to make those decisions as we face them.

Are you struggling with a decision today? Maybe something family related? Do you need wisdom, not just in a particular area, but in general? Ask the Lord. He is the all-wise God, filled with knowledge above anything we can begin to comprehend. Isn't it nice that the scripture above points out that God doesn't mind when you ask? He won't slap your hand! He won't even question your motivations. He will simply give—freely!

So ask! You have not because you ask not. Acknowledge your need before the One who knows better than anyone else how to meet it; then watch in awe as He generously pours out His wisdom. What a loving and giving God we serve!

Lord, I need Your wisdom. It's not head knowledge I'm seeking, but true wisdom from on high. Would You please shower down Your wisdom on me today, Father? Amen.

Hand-Picked by God

How shall we order the child, and how shall we do unto him?
Judges 13:12 KJV

When is the last time you stopped to consider that nothing takes God by surprise? He knew that one day there would be precious children who would need a special mother in their lives, and He chose you for the job. It might seem like an overwhelming task at times, and you might wonder how you ended up in such a position, but there is a reason.

Are you at a loss about how to fulfill your role? Turn it over to God. Like Manoah and his wife, ask the Lord how to train and treat your stepchildren. God expects you to be faithful in fulfilling this role into which He has brought you, but He never intended for you to do it alone.

You truly do have a unique opportunity. Embrace it. Learn from it. Realize that perhaps you need your stepchildren as much as they need you. Enjoy being part of their lives.

Of course, much of how you act toward your stepchildren will depend on their age; but no matter what that is, you will have a certain amount of influence on their lives. Seek God's direction so that influence will be positive.

Thank You, Father, for this position into which You've placed me. I want to have a good impact on the lives of my stepchildren. Amen.

Day 60

Yikes! Way Up There?

He makes me as surefooted as a deer, enabling me to stand on mountain heights.
2 Samuel 22:34 NLT

You may accept the challenge of a tough climb as a recreational sport, but what a different story when your journey as a stepmom demands it. Perhaps you hadn't anticipated the tricky maneuvers you'd need to make and the heights to which you would climb. Consider the following scenario:

Just as you are adjusting to the steeper incline of a blended family, your husband is notified that he has won the custody battle after all. You're excited, sort of; yet you can't fathom a steeper incline with even more responsibility on your back. At your wit's end, you cry out to God, "I can't keep going, Lord!"

That's when a firm hand helps you to keep climbing. Amazingly, you keep your balance in the iffy and scary places. Even your breathing is more relaxed. Believe it or not, your Helper says your stride is increasingly graceful.

You may not like going uphill at such an angle, but you're catching on to the truth that God will enable you to take the next step and plant your foot on a new height.

Lord, this journey's impossible without You, but I have to say that You're terrific in the scary places. Thank You. Amen.

The Power

Day 61

I also pray that you will understand the incredible greatness of God's power for us who believe him. This is the same mighty power that raised Christ from the dead.

Ephesians 1:19–20 NLT

How many times have you tried to do something that you really set your mind to, only to end up disappointed with yourself? Maybe a New Year's resolution to lose weight or to make family devotions a priority? You make a list and a plan. Maybe even purchase a lot of expensive equipment or study materials. But a few weeks or months down the road, you are right back where you started. This often happens because we think we can do things in our own power just by setting our minds to it. The Bible tells us otherwise. True life change can happen only when we are trusting in God's amazing power to help us accomplish the goal. We can do nothing on our own. When we try to do things on our own, we might see some success at first, but in the end we fail miserably. Don't set yourself up to fail! Commit your plans to the Lord. You still might have an occasional setback, but with God's power at work in you, He will give you the strength to move past the obstacle and keep on going.

Dear Father, take control over my life and my plans. Help me to do everything through Your power instead of relying on myself. Amen.

Day 62

Comfort in Rejection

And the LORD told him, "Listen to all that the people are saying to you; it is not you they have rejected, but they have rejected me as their king."
1 SAMUEL 8:7 NIV

"You're not my mother! I won't listen to you!" Perhaps you've been stung by these words despite diligent efforts to embrace your stepchildren. Rejection hurts, especially when you're serving God with pure motives.

Samuel knew all about rejection. Chosen by God to rule over Israel, he governed as God's personal representative to the nation. He did his job well. However, when Samuel transferred some responsibility to his unfaithful sons, Israel rebelled. They failed to present their concerns to the Lord, seeking earthly answers instead. The surrounding nations, ruled by kings, seemed superior; so Israel took their stand—they demanded a king for themselves.

Samuel felt the sting of Israel's rejection and ran to God in prayer. God exposed the truth. Israel hadn't rejected Samuel or the choices he made—what they rejected was God as their king. The Lord comforted Samuel and told him exactly how to respond.

Stepfamilies face tremendous pressures. Children, feeling powerless, often turn their anger on a stepparent. If you're facing rejection, despite diligently serving God in your position, run to God as Samuel did. Only the Lord can probe the depths of the problem and guide you to safety. Go. Pray. Receive comfort and wisdom—and hold on.

Father, I know You'll fulfill Your plans for my family. May my comfort come from You. I entrust my family into Your omnipotent hands. Amen.

Day 63

Overlooked

Take a good look, friends, at who you were when you got called into this life. I don't see many of "the brightest and the best" among you, not many influential, not many from high-society families. Isn't it obvious that God deliberately chose men and women that the culture overlooks and exploits and abuses?

1 Corinthians 1:26–27 msg

Raising a family is a challenge in the best of circumstances. But when you add stepchildren, who may or may not live with you full-time, and the other parent/stepparent, who may not have the same values and goals you have, the task becomes almost impossible. We feel inadequate for the job, incapable of making wise decisions, and overwhelmed by the sheer impossibility of ever having an influence for the good. How do we balance it all?

Thankfully, we are not left alone to accomplish the impossible. Paul tells us that "God deliberately chose men and women that the culture overlooks and exploits and abuses" to be His representatives here on earth. We're flawed. We have nothing that puts us above the average in any area of life, let alone parenting. Because of our faith in God, we're made fun of, maybe even opposed, by the "other" parent. They attempt to undermine our teaching and influence.

But God said that He will use our inadequacies to bring shame to those who reject Him. He takes our seeming failures and makes them successes when we trust Him to work through us. He deliberately chose you for the task of parenting the children in your home. Rejoice in that and relax.

Father, thank You for choosing and trusting me to parent the children in my home. Amen.

Day 64

On the Shores of the Nile

He became her son. And she called his name Moses.
Exodus 2:10 KJV

As Pharaoh's daughter slipped her feet into the cool waters of the Nile, she had the impression that something was amiss. Scanning the lush green landscape, she noticed a dark object nestled among the nearby reeds.

"What is that?" she mused aloud. It appeared to be a basket woven from bulrushes and daubed with pitch. Her maid hastily fetched it for her, and when the princess lifted the lid of the little ark, she gasped. A tiny baby lay swaddled inside!

"This is one of the Hebrews' children," she cried. The babe startled from his slumber and began to wail, his infant voice beseeching her for comfort. And as she cradled him against her breast, her heart filled with compassion. Had not an edict been issued concerning Hebrew sons? Surely this child was doomed for destruction. She gazed at his delicate features and stroked his silken hair.

"Fetch a nurse for the babe," she commanded. As she stood on the brink of the Nile and studied its flowing waters, a plan unfolded in her mind. She would save this Hebrew boy from the river, and someday he would become a great man.

"Don't cry, little one," she told him. "You will be my son; and I shall call you Moses, for I drew you out of the water."

Lord, remind me of the critical role I play in my stepchild's life. Moses could not have been instrumental in leading God's people out of slavery in Egypt if his stepmother had not drawn him from the Nile. Amen.

Helping the Needy

Day 65

If you feed those who are hungry and take care of the needs of those who are troubled, then your light will shine in the darkness, and you will be bright like sunshine at noon.

Isaiah 58:10 NCV

Lena felt she could not bear one week, let alone an entire summer, with her husband Garth's two teenagers. When June arrived, Cassie and Colin descended on their house like hungry bears, devouring everything in their path. Their appetites grew every year, straining Lena's food budget to the max. Worse, the skinny fourteen- and fifteen-year-olds never put on weight. Lena, who couldn't eye an ice cream carton without gaining ten pounds, watched them wolf down gallons.

As if that weren't enough, every summer she and Garth struggled to wean the kids away from their usual diet of violent video games, destructive movies, and problem friends. Because of Garth's job, Lena found herself enforcing unpopular rules. Even though she tried to balance discipline with fun times, Lena felt like an evil—and nearly bankrupt—stepmother. During a desperate devotional time, she read the above verse in Isaiah 58, which reassured her that regardless of how Garth's children viewed her now, God saw her as His light in their world. She took fresh courage and went to the grocery store once again.

Loving Father, when I'm ready to do the easy thing and quit, You invite me to share Your nature by ministering to these hungry, hurting kids. You are enough. Please help me. Amen.

Day 66

United, Protected

But we prayed to our God and guarded the city day and night to protect ourselves.
NEHEMIAH 4:9 NLT

Neighboring peoples threatened to attack the Israelites as they rebuilt the walls of Jerusalem. With enemies close about, Nehemiah couldn't fold. He couldn't call for reinforcements. He couldn't hide or abandon his work. So he made a plan. He preempted any attack with prayer and stability from within.

When the walls of our marriages, newly built or otherwise, are threatened from outside forces, we can't give up or expect someone else to save us. We need a plan, too. A stepmom's marriage is often vulnerable, and the work to save it must continue in disagreeable circumstances sometimes. Maybe former spouses cause trouble, or hurting kids lash out at what they see as the problem in their lives, or the pressures of a life complicated with too much to do and no time or money to do it all get heavier—all these things add up to a dangerous attack in the making.

A stepmom and her husband need a plan like Nehemiah's. They need a constant prayer to God for His favor and grace and their own best efforts to protect their union from anything that might threaten it. A united front sustained by love, respect, commitment, and trust is our best defense. Under God's watchful eye, we can continue to build in safety.

Father, many outside forces threaten us, and we need Your help. Please strengthen us and protect us from within so that nothing without can tear us apart. Amen.

I've Been There

So when your faith remains strong through many trials, it will bring you much praise and glory and honor on the day when Jesus Christ is revealed to the whole world.

1 Peter 1:7 NLT

Remember when you were young, thinking that adults just didn't understand kids and the problems they face? Don't look now, but you might be one of the adults that a young person thinks just "doesn't get it." In fact, he or she may be living in your house!

If the topic comes up in conversation (which you may need to initiate!), share with the child that you once had to confront the fears, problems, and concerns that he or she could be facing. Even if it isn't a two-way talk, at least the child will understand that you are a bit like he or she is—and you made it through adolescence and into adulthood just fine.

Jesus is the perfect example for all of us—young and old alike. He had to endure rejection, pain, denial, and temptation. Yet He experienced each trial and overcame it in God's strength.

The specific temptations and rejection situations may vary a bit from your younger days, but the feelings and struggles are the same. Encourage your kids to come to you and your husband for help, but especially for prayer support. You may never know what trial your child will overcome because you prayed.

Dear God, please help our children as they face the many problems of the world today. Give them Your strength to overcome the trials. Amen.

Day 68

A Father's Promise

"Don't panic. I'm with you. There's no need to fear for I'm your God. I'll give you strength. I'll help you. I'll hold you steady, keep a firm grip on you."

Isaiah 41:10 msg

One afternoon Ethan decided he no longer needed his bicycle's training wheels. After some persuasion, Ethan finally convinced his father to remove them. He felt so grown-up and independent—until he tried to ride. Suddenly, Ethan wasn't as confident, and he realized he needed his dad's help. "Don't let go!" Ethan warned his father. "Don't worry, Ethan. I've got you. I'm not going to let go." As Ethan took that first shaky ride down the sidewalk on two wheels, he was comforted in knowing that his dad was right beside him, offering support, guidance, and love.

While Ethan will eventually be able to ride his bike without his father's support, we always need God's firm grip in our lives to keep us steady. The great news is that God promises to take care of us no matter what! Throughout the Bible, we read of God's promises never to forsake us. Instead, He walks beside us, giving us strength and taking away our fear. When we are afraid, God reassures us with His comfort and love. Like Ethan's father, He promises not to let us go. What a comfort it is to know that God is always with us, keeping us steady and giving us strength!

Dear Lord, so often I panic and try to get through life on my own. Instead, help me to trust in You for strength, support, and guidance. Amen.

First Love

Beloved, if God so loved us, we ought also to love one another.
1 John 4:11 KJV

As mothers or stepmothers, we want our children to love us. Of course, we have certain standards in place to tell us if we are loved. Our children will be obedient, courteous, agreeable, and the like. When they don't subscribe to those standards, we sometimes forget our role in loving them.

As mothers, we are to set the example of loving long before our children learn to love us. We bathe them, feed them, and dress them when they are young. We provide comfort when they are sick. Each time we give of ourselves without expecting anything in return, we are saying to that child, "I love you." Regardless of whether they love us back, we must love them.

Before we knew who God is, He loved us. He cared for us, called to us, watched over us, and gave more than we can begin to imagine because He loved us. God is the author of love and sets an example for us. Have we always been obedient, courteous, or agreeable to God? No, none of us has. Yet He loves us with an everlasting love. Is it so much to ask, then, that we set aside our standards and simply love the child given to us?

Jesus, please fill me with Your love for my children. Help me see them through Your eyes and lay aside my own selfish wants. Amen.

Day 70

On My Knees

My response is to get down on my knees before the Father, this magnificent Father who parcels out all heaven and earth.
EPHESIANS 3:14 MSG

As a parent, it's not always easy to guard our responses. We're used to being in charge, and when things don't go the way we hope, we sometimes knee jerk. Blow up. React poorly. Then we wish we could take it back—or figure out a different way to respond next time.

So how do you react when things aren't going your way? Do you get down on your knees before the Father? Or do you throw your hands in the air, ready to admit defeat? God is interested not just in our actions, but in our reactions. When we blow it, we're really sharing what's been inside our hearts all along. So dealing with our poor responses means dealing with our hearts.

How do we do that? Bend your knees and spend time in God's presence. Pause to deal with things—really deal with them. It might take time, but it will be worth it. And when we pour our energies into making things better, it's a win-win situation. We draw closer to the Lord, and He pours out His mercy and blessing on us. What a magnificent God we serve!

Dear Lord, today I come to You on bended knee, asking You to guard both my actions and my reactions. Deal with any issues in my heart that cause me to react the way I do. I give those things to You. Amen.

The Water Walker

Day 71

He alone has spread out the heavens and marches on the waves of the sea.
Job 9:8 NLT

It was almost dawn, the fourth, or last, watch of the night. On this windy, stormy night, the disciples were in a boat on the Sea of Galilee. Suddenly, Jesus was passing by them, walking on the water. The disciples thought they were seeing a ghost. What else would walk on the water in the middle of a storm?

But when Jesus assured the disciples that it was Him, Peter made an odd request. "Lord, if it's you, tell me to come to you on the water," he shouted above the howling wind (Matthew 14:28 NIV). Peter stepped out on the water, without doubts, needing no proof other than Jesus' command to come to Him.

It was a short walk.

Reality started to sink in as Peter "saw" the wind then floundered. Mercifully, Jesus grabbed him and rescued him.

Saying yes to a marriage that includes another woman's children can be a little like Jesus' invitation to walk on water. It will take a miracle to keep us from sinking! More often than not, the seas are pretty choppy. The wind keeps trying to knock us over.

But it wasn't faith in *faith* that got Peter out of that boat; it was faith in a great God. And Jesus was never going to let Peter sink. He's not going to let us sink, either.

Lord Jesus, when You ask me to do more than I am able to do, help me to remember that You are the one who will keep me afloat. Amen.

Day 72

A Silver Tongue

The tongue of the righteous is choice silver; the heart of the wicked is of little worth.
PROVERBS 10:20 ESV

Have you ever been around a person who speaks only kindness, wisdom, truth, and love? These people are rare. Jesus said in Matthew 15 that our words come from our hearts. If the tongue of the righteous is choice silver, then the heart of a righteous person holds great value! The rest of us flock to this person, for just being around her or him seems to make our lives a little better.

We've all been around people who spew venom at every opportunity. Their words are like acid, causing pain and destruction to those who listen. If our words come from our hearts, then the hearts of these people are of little value to the rest of us. We don't like to be around them. They tear us down, when we all want to be built up.

We can add value to our hearts by filling our minds with good things, things that will nourish our souls. Then our speech will be an outpouring of the lovely things in our hearts, and people will be drawn to us as they are drawn to anything of value.

Dear Father, help me to fill my life with things that will please You. Let my words always offer healing and encouragement to those around me. Amen.

The Fast-Track to Mommyhood

Jesus replied, "You may go. Your son will live." The man took Jesus at his word and departed. While he was still on the way, his servants met him with the news that his boy was living.

John 4:50–51 NIV

She had been single for many years; then, simply by falling in love with a widower with four small children, she had become a mommy. It all happened so fast: their courtship, the wedding, the honeymoon. Suddenly, she was up to her eyeballs in sippy cups, dirty diapers, stuffed bunnies, and dust bunnies. The gentle learning curve most young mothers experience as they add one child at a time over the course of a few years was for her nothing short of a learning precipice. Suddenly, she, who could barely remember changing diapers as a teenage babysitter, was confronted with an eighteen-month-old, a toddler, and two elementary school children. All hers now.

But all through those early, chaotic months, she reminded herself, "Children are a blessing from the Lord." Over and over she said it, until one day she woke up and realized that it was finally true for her, too. Those children had become a blessing from the Lord. Just like the royal official who sought Jesus' healing touch for his deathly sick son, she took Jesus at his word and was not disappointed.

Dear Father, thank You for Your precious Word and the truth it teaches me that I am often too blind to see. Help me to trust Your every promise. Amen.

Thy kingdom come. Thy will be done in earth, as it is in heaven.
Matthew 6:10 kjv

The Lord's Prayer. We know it by heart. We recite it by rote. Yet do we mean it? Flippantly we utter, "Thy will be done." Do we realize the implication of those four words? In essence, we are submitting to God's will, whatever that may be. We are professing that because God is sovereign, His ways are best. We are asking God to be in charge, to have His way, to be in control. Admittedly we don't have all the answers. We defer to His better judgment. We will accept His final answer. We will trust His ways.

In heaven God's perfect will is carried out without interference. He triumphantly reigns in majesty. His glory is revealed. What if we could get a glimpse of heaven in our lives on earth? It is possible when we allow the Lord preeminence. His glory will be revealed to the extent that we truly desire that His will be done in our lives.

Someday, every knee will bow and acknowledge that Jesus Christ is Lord. Why wait? Ask Him to be Lord of your life today. Then when you pray, "Thy will be done," you will truly mean it from your heart.

Dear Lord, please take Your rightful place as Lord of my life. May I submit to Your perfect will. Amen.

Starting on the Right Path

Train up a child in the way he should go: and when he is old, he will not depart from it.
Proverbs 22:6 KJV

Although stepmothers may have stepchildren who are already grown and out on their own, others may find themselves the parent of young children. This is a golden opportunity for a Christian stepmom to instill the love of God in the hearts of little ones.

Training a child in the way he should go includes reading them Bible stories, going to church together, learning to pray together, and sharing what God has done in their lives. Stepmoms can also guide and train by their own example of what it means to be a Christian in any and all circumstances.

When children see their parents living out their testimony with honesty, integrity, and love for others, it gives the child a rich picture of what is expected as he or she grows to adulthood. Discipline is guidance toward acceptable behavior, and what better way to guide than by example? Jesus set the example for all Christians; and although we will never reach the perfect life He lived, our actions speak loudly to young hearts and minds.

The goal of a stepparent, as with any other parent, is to teach children to become caring Christian adults with a love of Jesus in their hearts, so that if they stray, they will return to His love.

Lord God, help us today to be the example You set before us as we guide our stepchildren to their future. Amen.

Day 76

In Pursuit

*But God demonstrates His own love toward us,
in that while we were still sinners, Christ died for us.*
ROMANS 5:8 NKJV

"I just don't think I'm equipped to do this stepmom thing." Sherry sighed into her coffee cup.

"No *you're* not," her sister said, "but *Someone* else is." She pointed to the Bible sitting on the table. Sherry tried to smile, but she felt too worn out. After having two sons, she had been excited to have a stepdaughter, but Lana was a difficult girl. At fourteen she was sullen and stubborn. Much to Sherry's dismay, she spent her visitation weekends shut away in her room, listening to music and talking to her friends. Sherry had hoped they would bond over cookie baking and shopping trips, but Lana seemed to resent her intrusion in her father's life and house.

"What am I supposed to do? She acts like she hates me."

"She'll come around," her sister said, flipping open the Bible. "Remember how gracious God is with us. He wants to claim us as His children, and look how we resist. But He just keeps reaching out to us."

Sherry sighed. "You're right, I forget about that sometimes. I guess if God can keep pursuing me, I can keep pursuing Lana."

"And, we'll keep praying," her sister said, taking her hand.

Dear God, You are always in pursuit of my heart—please help me to be willing to reach out to others and show them Your love, even when it is hard. Amen.

Is Anybody Listening?

Day 77

Give ear to my words, O Lord, consider my sighing.
Psalm 5:1 NIV

How often do young ears hear you call, "Dirty wash to the laundry room, please"? Whether it's *my*, *his*, or *our* children, your words may fall on selective-hearing ears. Even a call to the dinner table may go unanswered. So, is anyone out there listening?

Quickly David answers, "God hears you!" Not only did David know God heard him, but he was convinced that God was a great listener. Perhaps David had a picture in his mind that God cups His ear and leans in so He doesn't miss a word. Better still, David had the nerve to ask God to hear his sigh. In other words, the psalmist believed that God gave him His full attention without even uttering a word. Wow, that's listening!

Have you brought your words or sighs to God, telling Him how much it bugs you when your kids or stepkids fail to heed your words? You don't have to raise your voice or clamor for God's attention or verbalize your thoughts. No matter what else is going on, God is hearing everything you say with words or with sighs.

Since God is such a good listener, would it surprise you if you actually get an answer back? Listen! Do you hear those feet going to the laundry room?

O Lord, thank You for tuning in to my words. You have so many things to do, but You always give me Your undivided attention. Amen.

Day 78

A Place to Run

From the end of the earth I call to You when my heart is faint; lead me to the rock that is higher than I. For You have been a refuge for me, a tower of strength against the enemy.

Psalm 61:2–3 nasb

As unreasonable as it seemed, Lynette couldn't help it. She felt like running away.

When she had accepted Bill's proposal of marriage, Lynette knew his daughter had been part of the package. But now that the vows had been uttered, the promises made, she realized instant motherhood was taking its toll. Whenever she laid down the law with her stepdaughter, Tanya, Bill would come home and give his daughter a reprieve, making Lynette look like the bad guy or "evil stepmother." How much easier it would be just to be single again!

When we are weighed down with the burden of family problems, running away seems like a good idea. After all, it seemed to work, at least temporarily, for Lot. But it didn't work so well for Lot's wife. Because she kept looking back at what she'd had, she couldn't go forward. Instead, she turned into an immovable pillar of salt.

In times of strife and stress, when we feel faint, we need not look back but up, to the shelter and refuge of God, our tower. When we run to Him, we will find the strength and wisdom to move forward, knowing He will guard and guide our way.

Lord, my heart is faint. As I run to You, fill me with Your strength, love, compassion, and wisdom. Help me to move forward instead of looking back. Lift me high above the fray and set me down in a broad place, able to face the world again. Amen.

What Is Your Message?

So proclaim the Message with intensity; keep on your watch. Challenge, warn, and urge your people. Don't ever quit. Just keep it simple.
2 Timothy 4:2 msg

The town square had a platform where people could set up their soap boxes. Each day, crowds gathered to hear speakers who were passionate about their causes. Some were fanatical about saving the whales. Others campaigned against guns and begged for help in banning alcohol and preserving rain forests. People were interested and listened, but for all their passion, these speakers were largely ineffectual.

As Christians, we also have a message, and the heart of that message is love. We are commanded to proclaim this with intensity which means with depth, clarity, and concentrated passion. Instead of preaching and pointing fingers, we should share this message in other ways. For example, our lifestyle and behavior can be a challenge to our family, urging them to follow in our footsteps.

We may not see results overnight, but if we persevere and keep things simple, the results will follow. Don't be tempted to shout from your soap box but keep extending love and showing the message that God has placed in each of our hearts. As we do this, we will be effective in obeying God's command to us, and our loved ones will respond.

Dear heavenly Father, help me to live my life in a way that proclaims Your message of love. Help me also never to give up. Amen.

Day 80

The Growing Cycle Grows Us

Use all your skill to put me together; I wait to see your finished product.
Psalm 25:21 msg

Sometimes it feels like we give God little to work with or grow into something better. With a constant focus on our problems and our last glimmer of hope fading like a dying flashlight, we wonder, *What else can go wrong?*

We don't know, but we trust God is still at work in us and around us. *His* skill superseded our lack, so perhaps He is putting us together—if we'll allow it—to be more like Him in every way, every day, and He is working to make something perfect out of the mess we see. Surely we can help.

We can surrender to the growing cycle, understanding that what appears to us to be a fallow, unproductive time may be God's pause in our outside world to work on our inside lack. Beneath the surface, He can amend the soil of our hearts to produce beats that more resemble His. That's the finished product we desire: an *us* that looks like *Him* and loves like *Him*, that shares grace, forgiveness, compassion, wisdom, and peace like *Him*.

And the only way there is under His guiding hand and steering plow. Regardless of the weather or the pests, we can focus on the possibilities instead of on our problems and watch Him grow something better, starting with us.

Father, thank You that You're not done with me yet!
Please help me submit myself to Your tending, and
train me up in the way You'd have me grow. Amen.

God's Protection

Day 81

You have been a refuge for the poor, a refuge for the needy in his distress, a shelter from the storm and a shade from the heat.

Isaiah 25:4 NIV

When we hear words like *refuge*, *shelter*, and *shade*, we might envision images of weather events—hurricanes, blazing heat, blizzards, tornadoes, dust storms—all which cause us to seek shelter. On the other hand, our minds might turn to homeless shelters or safe houses for abused children. Perhaps we think of animal shelters or a secluded vacation spot. Regardless of the images that come to mind, protection is key. Protection from the elements, protection from harm, protection from stress—we all need protection of some kind.

In addition to all of the other amazing attributes of God, He is also our protector, and He knows all of our needs. In the midst of a storm, we take any kind of shelter we can get, even though it may not be ideal. However, God offers us perfect protection. He knows what we need before we do, and He provides for us a place of peace and protection when we come before Him. In the midst of your pain, your stress, and your fears, let God comfort you today. He offers you a refuge, a shelter, a shade—absolute in its protection, perfectly suited for you.

Dear Lord, You are my protector, and I praise You. You keep me from harm, and You comfort me in my distress. Thank You, almighty God! Amen.

Day 82

A Life of Joy

Satisfy us each morning with your unfailing love,
so we may sing for joy to the end of our lives.
Psalm 90:14 NLT

Webster's definition of *joy* is "the emotion evoked by well-being, success, or good fortune." When was the last time you experienced true joy?

Many thoughts could be swirling through your mind: your wedding day, the birth of your child, landing your dream job, finally getting that car. . . . But joy can come in what could be considered as "little" moments with your children throughout the day: listening to how their day at school went, baking cookies, playing a game. . . .

At times, as a mom, joy can seem a distant emotion. When you are tired and have just gotten the last child in bed, how can you have joy?

In 1 Thessalonians 5:16 (NLT) we are told to "always be joyful." That is not a perpetual state of giddiness; rather, it's a spirit of peace, resting in Jesus.

A joyful spirit is contagious. Find delight in the "ordinary" moments, and others will catch the joy.

Dear Father, please be my source of joy today, especially when I'm tired or things don't go as I planned. Let me rest in the fact that You are in control. Amen.

A Stepmomma's Heart

As the Father hath loved me, so have I loved you.
John 15:9 KJV

Hailey's favorite teddy bear was tucked in safely beside her. She rubbed the worn spot on his ear as she pictured the scene from her bedtime story. Poor Snow White was running through the dark forest as she tried to escape from her wicked stepmother. Gnarled roots and branches grabbed at her cape, glowing eyes peered from the tangled underbrush, and owls hooted eerily in the night. Hailey shivered under her covers.

What was it like to be alone and afraid? She hadn't liked Daddy's new wife at first. She thought she'd be mean like Cinderella's stepmother or try to get rid of her like Hansel and Gretel's had. But Hailey's stepmomma wasn't like that at all. She was funny and nice and gave big hugs.

"When I married your daddy," she had told Hailey, "God put a special place in my heart just for you. That's why I love you, even though you're not my own little girl."

Hailey thought about that as her stepmother finished the story and closed the book.

"Sweet dreams," she said, kissing Hailey's cheek. "I love you."

"I love you, too," Hailey replied. Ever since God had put that same special place in her own heart, she knew that she would take her stepmomma over seven dwarfs and a prince any day.

Lord, put a special place in my heart for my husband's children so that they never have to fear a wicked stepmother. Amen.

Day 84

Cut to the Heart

The LORD your God will circumcise your hearts and the hearts of your descendants, so that you may love him with all your heart and with all your soul, and live.

DEUTERONOMY 30:6 NIV

After months of attempting to bond with her stepchildren, Susan felt hopeless. She opened her Bible seeking encouragement. Deuteronomy 30:6 practically leaped off the page, and she sensed God had provided a life raft for her soul. *You're not through with my children, are You, God? When You circumcise their hearts, our relationship will improve. Maybe then we'll be like a "real" family.*

Susan fell victim to the "point a finger at others and three fingers point back at you" dilemma. Her life-raft verse included two heart circumcision promises—one for herself (parents) and another for descendants—but Susan focused on the hearts of her descendants. We often do the same. "Lord, change his heart!" is a far more comfortable plea than, "Father, change me!"

If you're discouraged over family relationships, look inward. Ask God to purify *your* heart and soul. It's a difficult prayer, but one God always seems to honor. Remember, it's safe to surrender to the Father who created you. As God removes every hindrance within you to loving Him fully, your relationships with others will improve. So ask Him to go to work on you, and trust Him with the results. You won't be disappointed.

Father, forgive me for constantly seeking change in others, assuming I'm fine as I am. Search my heart. Remove what offends You. I trust You to change me and to deal perfectly with the hearts of my descendants. Amen.

Fitly Spoken

A word fitly spoken is like apples of gold in pictures of silver.
Proverbs 25:11 KJV

Oh, how we love to impart our wisdom. The sound of good advice flowing from our lips is like an elixir that we crave. We want our children to listen in wonder, and we can become frustrated when they shuffle their feet, they edge toward the door, or their eyes glaze over as they focus their thoughts elsewhere. Then we become affronted because they aren't excited about learning all we have to teach them.

God encourages us to be ready to instruct our children at all times. We never know when those teachable moments will come: when we're standing, sitting, or walking. Often they come at a time that isn't as convenient as we would like. When they do happen, and our young ones are ready to listen, we must remember that their attention span is not as long as ours.

We should consider how God teaches us. He doesn't use long lectures. Even in lengthy sermons, God usually grabs us with a word or phrase that speaks to our heart and soul. Likewise, we must pray to have the right words in the right moments. Our thoughts should come from the heart, expressed in love as God's messages are to us. Then we will have imparted words like apples of gold.

Lord, please help me to follow Your example. Give me the words to speak, something that will touch the heart of my child. Amen.

Day 86

Marked

Having believed, you were marked in him with a seal, the promised Holy Spirit, who is a deposit guaranteeing our inheritance until the redemption of those who are God's possession—to the praise of his glory.

Ephesians 1:13–14 NIV

God's Word tells us, and our hearts testify, that we were given the Holy Spirit to indwell in us when we believed. The Father has marked us with His seal, guaranteeing our spot in heaven. If your faith is real, the presence of the Holy Spirit in your life will be evident. The Spirit works in us to transform us into all that God wants us to be. Is the Spirit of the living God at work in your life? If you have never accepted Christ as your personal Savior and asked Him to be Lord of your life, don't let another moment slip by without experiencing the freedom and peace that only He can bring. Ask God to forgive you and set His seal in your heart for all of eternity. You will begin to see evidence that God's Spirit is leading you and guiding you moment by moment and day by day. Reading God's Word will take on new meaning as the Spirit gives you discernment. You will learn how to listen for and hear that "still small voice." Have you been marked?

Dear Father, thank You for sending us Your Spirit to lead and guide us. Help me to hear Your "still small voice" in my life. Amen.

Day 87

Show, Don't Tell

But Jesus replied "Leave her alone. Why criticize her for doing such a good thing to me? . . . She has done what she could."

Mark 14:6, 8 NLT

Stepmothering has its ups and downs. Do you have a strong-willed stepchild or birth child? One stepmom, Patty, found ways to bond with her stepson. She went to all of her stepson Jared's baseball games. She washed his uniforms. She went to the football backers' meetings. Patty never missed an event.

Despite Patty's loyalty to her stepson, Jared often allowed his birth mother's anger toward Patty to fill him with rage. Patty admits that Jared's anger hurt. She spent a lot of time in prayer during those years, asking for God's wisdom.

Now, several years later, Patty and Jared have a very close relationship. Patty believes they are friends now because she never retaliated in anger when Jared lashed out at her. She chose to love him quietly. It's like the old adage says, "You catch more flies with honey than with vinegar."

Our stepchildren need mothers. And we might be surprised to know that all our stepchildren really want is a mother. So the next time you're scrubbing out grass stains and sterilizing mouth guards, remember that you are showing love to your kids. These quiet acts of love show your motherly devotion to them in louder words than you could ever say.

God, thank You for giving me practical ways to show my love toward my stepchildren. Please help them to see You in me. Amen.

Day 88

God Knows

I am worn out from groaning; all night long I flood my bed with weeping and drench my couch with tears.
Psalm 6:6 NIV

Exhausted and emotionally drained, she carried her newborn baby to the living room to sleep so their "night life" (crying, feedings, diaper changes) wouldn't disturb her husband. Collapsing in tears on the couch, she clutched her baby and her Bible and began to read Psalms. The words of Psalm 6:6 jumped off the page and into her heart. *God knows where I am!* she thought. *He knows what I'm going through. He hasn't forgotten me.*

This tired, overwhelmed, hormonal mother needed to know right then that God was with her *right then*. And the Most High God, who doesn't have to prove Himself to anyone, lovingly proved Himself once more to her. He reassured her that He knew where she was at that very moment: *drenching her "couch with tears"*!

Perhaps today you feel lost in confusion or trials or exhaustion and you just need to be reminded that God knows where you are. If so, read His Word and humbly expect Him to speak to your situation. While you won't find any verses that say "checking my e-mail" or "talking on my cell phone," you will discover that He does, indeed, know where you are. And if God knows where you are, then you are surely not lost.

Dear Lord, thank You for reassuring me that You know where I am and what I'm going through. Let that be enough for me today. Amen.

Bite Your Tongue

"Words are powerful; take them seriously. Words can be your salvation. Words can also be your damnation."
Matthew 12:37 msg

They noticed the added set of earrings soon after they picked up their teenaged daughter from her mother's.

"I thought I told you I didn't want you getting your ears double pierced," her father said.

"Well, Mom said if I wanted to get them done again, I had to do it just then." Then, in a quieter voice, "So I did."

Her dad glanced over at her stepmother, and a look passed between them. Neither said anything, but their thoughts were identical. Their daughter had been knowingly encouraged—again—to disobey her father. Her stepmother said nothing. Her father said, "I didn't want you to do that." The topic never came up again.

Sometimes children become pawns in a game of one-upmanship between the divorced parents. It's ugly all the way around. The stakes may be small (double-pierced ears) or large (birth mom verbally abuses her ex and his wife to the children caught in the middle). Some things stepmoms must let go. But even with name-calling and undermining of parental authority, retaliation in kind has no place.

When the teenager grew up, she let the second piercings grow closed. They were a hassle. Her bonds with her mom, her dad, and her stepmom have held. And though it may not always happen, often time and maturity bring an end to petty game-playing.

Father, keep me from criticizing my stepchildren's mom in front of them. Remind me to take my complaints to You alone. Amen.

Day 90

Find a Friend and Pray

The effective, fervent prayer of a righteous man avails much.
James 5:16 NKJV

Life wasn't meant to be lived alone. Throughout the Bible we read that we really do need each other; faith isn't a solitary journey. So finding an intercessor to help strengthen our prayer walk is certainly scriptural. We aren't to choose someone with whom we gossip or gripe, but someone who will exhort and uplift and pray.

Intercessory prayer is vital in a believer's life. Exodus 17 tells the story of Moses overlooking the battlefield when the Israelites fought the Amalekites. Moses promised to stand on the hilltop, holding his rod up so the battle would be successful. When he lowered the rod, the Amalekites had the advantage. When it was raised, the Israelites won. Within a matter of time, his arms grew weary. "So Aaron and Hur. . .stood on each side of Moses, holding up his hands. So his hands held steady until sunset" (Exodus 17:12 NLT). A victory ensued.

Who holds your arms up when you grow weary? Do you have a trusted friend you might turn to? Jesus is beside you, yet sometimes we need a flesh-and-blood partner to encourage us, support us, and pray with us. Ask Him to reveal a person who might stand by you.

Father, I thank You for Your mercy and grace.
Please place a trusted intercessor in my path. Amen.

Written on the Heart

Day 91

Do not let kindness and truth leave you. Tie them around your neck. Write them upon your heart.
PROVERBS 3:3 NLV

Imagine a beautiful necklace in the very back of your jewelry box, one given to you as a child by your father. The jewels sparkle, and the silver, though slightly darkened over time, still looks precious to you. Maybe you wear it to remember him if he's no longer with you. It means a lot to you simply because it is a gift from him. You take it out on special occasions. Wearing it close to your heart feels good.

Kindness and truth are like a necklace that never goes out of style. Treating people kindly is always in fashion, but it's not always easy, is it? So, who do you struggle with? A difficult stepchild? Your husband's ex-wife? Your spouse? Pull out that necklace, daughter of God. Let the "sparkles" of kindness and truth captivate you once again. Wear it close to your heart. And teach your children to do the same. In fact, you might actually consider giving your daughter or stepdaughter a real necklace to wear as a reminder.

Kindness is a gift—a precious gem. Fortunately, it's one you can keep—and give away. So share a little kindness today!

Lord, today give me the power to treat everyone with kindness, particularly those who don't treat me kindly. Soften my heart toward the people in my world who are the most difficult to love. Write their names on my heart. Amen.

Day 92

Reliable Love

And we have seen and testify that the Father has sent his Son to be the Savior of the world. If anyone acknowledges that Jesus is the Son of God, God lives in Him and he in God. And so we know and rely on the love God has for us.

1 John 4:14–16 NIV

John is not speaking from hearsay. He saw the Lord Jesus firsthand, in the flesh. John ate with Him, walked with Him, talked with Him, and listened to Him teach. He watched Jesus be crucified and then saw Him alive again after He had been dead! This apostle was a firsthand eyewitness to Jesus' life. He wrote the words we now read so that we could know, as he knew, that Jesus was God's Son.

Why in the world would God send His only Son to die for a cruel, wicked world? Only because of love. Only because of a love that is so far above our comprehension that our minds reel from the thought of it. Such a love goes far beyond anything we can imagine. And yet the very fact of it assures us that God's love is *reliable*. A God who would go to such lengths to provide a way of salvation will surely not withdraw His love for any reason. We can know that He loves us no matter what.

Dear Father, thank You for loving me enough to send Your Son to die for me. Thank You for Your reliable, unchanging, never-ending love. Amen.

You're Not My Mother

Day 93

Children, obey your parents in the Lord, for this is right.
Ephesians 6:1 NASB

Although Lauren's words cut her to the heart, Cindy didn't let it show as she replied calmly, "No I'm not your mother. But I do have parental authority over you given to me by God and by your father. And I love you too much to allow you to disobey me or disrespect me."

Fifteen-year-old Lauren was stunned by her stepmother's reply. "You love me?" she demanded. "I thought you only loved Dad."

"I wouldn't have married your father if I didn't love you, too," Cindy said gently.

Lauren stared at Cindy for a moment and then went to clean her room as she had been told to do. That moment marked the turning point in Lauren and Cindy's relationship. Love flourished between them. When Lauren graduated valedictorian from her high school, she thanked God, her father, and "Mama Cindy." It was a wonderful moment for her whole family.

We cannot allow our children's hurtful words to overshadow our love for them. God loves us no matter what we do. We need to love our children enough not to let them get away with being disobedient or disrespectful no matter how they react to us at any given time.

Father, please show me how to love my children like You love me; and help me to show that love to them. In Jesus' name, amen.

Day 94

A Kinsman

And the women said unto Naomi, Blessed be the LORD, which hath not left thee this day without a kinsman, that his name may be famous in Israel.

RUTH 4:14 KJV

To get the full effect of the story of Boaz and Ruth, you really ought to read the entire book. It's a small one, so it won't take that long.

Remember, Ruth had been married before. Her husband had died before they had any children. That is a very critical detail. Without children there was no one to carry on the family name or to claim the inheritance. According to the law, if Ruth were to remarry, the first child born of the union would be the heir of her late husband rather than of his biological father.

As you read this passage, you find Boaz, a man of great godly character, willing to step into this role. He does this lovingly and with great compassion regardless of what it will cost him personally. Boaz's situation is, in a sense, opposite of yours, but the implications are very similar.

How wonderful it is that Boaz filled his role so graciously, for it is through the bloodline of his firstborn son whom he had no legal right to claim, that Jesus Christ our Redeemer came. In his lifetime Boaz probably did not foresee the result of his kindness, but we should all be grateful that he was willing to act as the stepparent to his own son.

Heavenly Father, I can't see the whole picture, but I know You have a special plan for me. Amen.

God's Example, Our Commitment

Day 95

But you, O Lord, are a compassionate and gracious God, slow to anger, abounding in love and faithfulness.
Psalm 86:15 NIV

That "slow to anger" part always seems hard to master. Emotions are raw for the new stepmom, and even the seasoned pro lives in a world of surprises and upheavals. We look at our lives and see leaks and gaps all over, and the only boat to safety is a dingy tied to the ocean floor. How will we survive?

God sets the example for us. He lives boldly through us, not because we're always safe and un-leaky, but because He draws upon what we are to build us up to what He wants us to be. He is compassionate and gracious when we fail, when we display something far less than our spiritual breeding and get angry quickly. He has the control and discipline to operate out of love and faithfulness. And we can follow His example.

Those around us are no less perfect than we are, no less apt to fail, display unsettling behavior, or wrap themselves in anger. But we can make a choice. We can respond with compassion and grace—it's a choice God makes every moment of our imperfect lives. We can pause, wait, listen, understand. We can fight the anger with love and faithfulness, and we can rescue ourselves to the place of safety in our hearts where God's example reigns.

Father, I pray You will continue to work to make me compassionate, gracious, slow to anger, and abounding in love and faithfulness, just like You. Amen.

Day 96

Strength for Tomorrow Starts Today

"Be strong and courageous. Do not be afraid or terrified because of them, for the Lord your God goes with you; he will never leave you nor forsake you."
Deuteronomy 31:6 NIV

Many women become stepmoms at what just might be the hardest possible time: during their stepchildren's teenage years. Often taller, louder, and more opinionated than we are, teenagers can be jaded and difficult creatures. Their views on family, love, and marriage have begun to solidify during what were probably months or even years of family stress, turmoil, and heartache leading up to divorce.

When joining two families—each with the sharp, jagged edges of past hurts—seems both painful and nearly impossible, take courage from these words from the book of Deuteronomy and from the words of an old hymn: "Strength for today and bright hope for tomorrow, blessings all mine with ten thousand beside!" When we pray for what we need today, the strength we receive from God becomes ours for the next trial.

Teenagers may be taller than you, but they still need leaders. Take courage and say, as Joshua did when confronted by the "giants" in the land the Lord had promised the Israelites, "Fear them not!" For great is His faithfulness!

Dear God, thank You for the chance to prove Your faithfulness daily. Help me to be strong, loving, and courageous as I face the "giants" in my life. Amen.

Burning Love

Is not my word like as a fire? saith the LORD; and like a hammer that breaketh the rock in pieces?
JEREMIAH 23:29 KJV

The talk show speaker spoke about the divine goodness of man. Ellyn, folding never-ending laundry, wished she could meet him. Ellyn never had met her own dad, but this man's fatherly, resonant voice sounded exactly the way she'd always dreamed he would speak.

Ellyn glanced at the clock. Her husband's children would be here only an hour from now. She deserved a hot cup of tea and a little feel-good time watching her favorite TV host. But the man's words disturbed her like a buzzing mosquito. He seemed to ignore the obvious evil in the world. And when he insisted little children had to be taught to be selfish or violent, Ellyn almost laughed.

"Has this guy ever spent ten minutes with a two-year-old? Maybe I'll call him and invite him to share church nursery duty with me next Sunday!"

She found it difficult to halt his hypnotic voice, but she hit the OFF button.

Ellyn, a young Christian, often struggled with difficult passages in the Bible, especially those that spoke of God's judgment on evil.

"But You are always honest with me, Lord. And I can depend on You as my heavenly Father. I guess that's what I need most of all."

Holy Lord, Your powerful, flaming Word burns deep into my soul. Let it destroy every sin that would challenge Your love and wisdom. Amen.

Day 98

Fitting the Mold

Just as our bodies have many parts and each part has a special function, so it is with Christ's body. We are many parts of one body, and we all belong to each other.
Romans 12:4–5 NLT

Connor is driving me crazy," Mia complained about her fourteen-year-old son. "He's smart, but he doesn't care about achieving in school. He's a good athlete, but he doesn't like the intense competition of sports. And now he says that my husband and I are giving him stomachaches. He says we put too much pressure on him. We just want him to reach his potential!"

Mia and Doug are very high achievers. So are their other children. But Connor, their youngest, marches to his own drummer.

"It might help if you try to see that your family needs Connor, instead of cramming Connor into your mold," her counselor wisely told her. "His calm temperament helps all of you to slow down, relax, and focus on what's important."

Have you ever thought that your kids are in your life to help balance *you* out? One reason God created families is to help us understand that, day by day, our strengths can compensate for each other's weaknesses and create a complete, effectual unit. We need each other.

Loving Father, You have individually fashioned my children. Help me to stop trying to cram them into my mold, and allow You to help them reach their potential. Amen.

Day 99

Speed Bumps

"Peace and prosperity to you, your family, and everything you own!"
1 SAMUEL 25:6 NLT

Dalton's first visit to see his dad and stepmother since they moved from Texas to Arizona held a few surprises. Driving home from a trip to Walmart one afternoon, Dalton noticed a sign that said SPEED BUMPS AHEAD.

Curious, he leaned forward from the backseat to see what a speed bump looked like. His stepmother, Missy, slowed down to carefully maneuver the unusually wide speed bump. "Why are you going so slow?" Dalton asked.

Missy smiled. "If I go too fast, I could damage the car, and it would make for a pretty bouncy ride."

Problems in life offer the same choices as speed bumps. When you're faced with a problem, you either slow down and take your time or race forward and cope with the bouncing ups and downs. It's natural to try to solve what life throws at you as fast as you can. You might even feel as if you're helping God by holding your own.

Leaning on your own understanding and knowledge doesn't always get the answers God wants you to have. Slowing down and maneuvering carefully with God's help, you may find the speed bumps in life a little easier to handle. Take a breath, slow down, and see what direction God wants to take you.

Lord, I'm always trying to figure out the best way to handle the situations life brings. Help me to look to You for direction instead of racing through the challenges I face. Amen.

Day 100

Need Advice?

The plans of the righteous are just, but the advice of the wicked is deceitful.
PROVERBS 12:5 NIV

To whom do you go for advice? Your best friend? Your mom or dad? A television talk show host? One of the most important things we can do, if we want to be *wise*, is seek wise counsel. Foolish people consult with their foolish friends and make foolish decisions. Wise people seek out other wise people and make wise decisions.

Anytime we need advice, we should first seek the opinions of people who know more than we do. If we have money questions, we should seek the advice of a banker, a stock broker, or a financial planner. For fashion questions, we should ask the most fashionable people we know. And for life questions, we should seek counsel from those who have their lives together!

An important thing to look for when seeking advice is whether a person lives a *righteous* life. No matter how successful a wicked person may be in his or her area of expertise, that person cannot be trusted. A person who lies, cheats, gossips, slanders, and the like may choose you as his or her next victim! Righteous people, however, always try to do the *right thing*; and so we can trust that they will do their best to steer us in the right direction.

Dear Father, please give me wisdom as I seek advice in the many areas of my life. Guide me to people who will advise me in wisdom and truth. Amen.

I'm Telling Dad!

Don't worry about anything; instead, pray about everything. Tell God what you need, and thank him for all he has done. Then you will experience God's peace, which exceeds anything we can understand. His peace will guard your hearts and minds as you live in Christ Jesus.

PHILIPPIANS 4:6–7 NLT

Children intuitively acknowledge their vulnerability. They instinctively run to their parents when help is needed. "I'm telling Dad" becomes a familiar battle cry. They defer to someone whom they know and trust, believing that intervention will happen and their needs will be met.

Whom do you cry out to for help? Many times we phone a good friend or turn to our husbands. Friends and husbands may offer wise counsel or listen attentively. But they are unable to impart peace or intervene supernaturally. There is only One who can exchange our anxiety for His peace—Christ Jesus.

There is no problem we face that is either too small or too big for the Lord to handle. When anxiety grips your heart, tell your heavenly Father. Present your requests to Him. Share your needs. Then leave them in His hands and trust that He will intervene. He will come to your rescue. The circumstances in life will not instantly change, but peace will flood your heart and mind. Telling our heavenly Father enables us to say, "It is well with my soul."

Dear Lord, help me give You my anxious thoughts so I may receive Your peace. Amen.

Day 102

Spirit Friendly

Whatever good thing each one does, this he will receive back from the Lord.
EPHESIANS 6:8 NASB

As earth's resources dwindle, we are striving to become an environmentally-friendly society. At home we turn off lights we aren't using and recycle newspaper, plastics, and cans. At the supermarket we read the labels of cleaners to determine whether the products are harmful to the environment. We carpool to work in order to save fuel. Such an earth-friendly consciousness is commendable. But are we as aware of how we affect our spiritual surroundings as we are of how we affect our physical one?

Along with an earth-friendly mind-set, we would be wise to adopt a spirit-friendly mind-set, conscious of how our words and actions influence the spirits of others. Does what we say replenish or pollute the spirits of our friends and family? Can our words be recycled, or do we cringe when we hear them coming out of our children's mouths? Are our actions ones that enrich the hearts, minds, and attitudes of others? Or do they poison the very air we—and others—breathe?

Let's be spiritually friendly and reap the benefits of what we sow on the plot of "ground" the Lord has given us: the hearts, minds, spirits, and souls of family, friends, and strangers. For when we sow love, praise, and kindness to others, that is what we will reap.

God, I want to build up my family and friends. But I need Your help. Give me a spirit-friendly mind-set. Grant me the wisdom to say and do the right things at the right time to enrich the lives of others. Amen.

Freedom

Day 103

Is not this the fast that I have chosen? . . .and that ye break every yoke? . . .and that thou hide not thyself from thine own flesh?

Isaiah 58:6–7 KJV

Laying down rules for our children can seem so right, but we have to be careful not to get carried away. We have to allow a measure of freedom, or our children will feel so restricted that they rebel against the restraints. If they resist our authority because we've become too rigid, we can find it very difficult to regain their trust.

True freedom comes from being allowed a choice, not from being forced into certain behavior. Yes, we need boundaries to feel comfortable, but not rigid laws. God always gives us a choice. He tells us the right and wrong then leaves it up to us to determine what we will do. There are repercussions when our actions are not in alignment with the proper decision. Some of those consequences can be very difficult to endure.

We must give our children decent limitations while not burdening them with a heavy yoke. This can be difficult to know how to do. We should make sure our guidelines are biblical. Then we can take the time to talk this over with our children, just as God always gives instruction to us through His Word.

Lord, thank You for caring enough to allow me the freedom to make mistakes, and for loving me when I do. Amen.

Day 104

Kindness vs. Quarrels

And the Lord's servant must not quarrel; instead, he must be kind to everyone, able to teach, not resentful.

2 Timothy 2:24 NIV

A stepmom to several teenage children found she spent a lot of time quarreling with them. They were accustomed to doing things in a certain way and argued with her about everything she did. It didn't matter if it was the cooking, the laundry, or the way she dressed—they picked a fight over it. After one exhausting day, she picked up her Bible and realized there was a better way to handle the conflict.

She started making changes the next day, and when the teenagers criticized, she bit her tongue and smiled instead of arguing. It was difficult to do, but after a few days, she noticed an improvement in their attitudes. "You've been so much nicer to be around," one of them commented. "And I like the shirt you're wearing today."

Kindness is the oil of love that can remove friction from life and make life more pleasant. God instructs us to be kind to everyone and not to harbor resentment. If we live according to these standards, God uses our life as a lesson and we are able to influence those around us in a positive manner. Make a decision today to be kind.

Dear God, I want to be Your servant and show kindness to those around me. Please remind me of this when I'm tempted to argue and fight. Amen.

Day 105

My Stuff, Your Stuff

Each of you should look not only to your own interests,
but also to the interests of others.
PHILIPPIANS 2:4 NIV

Sometimes as moms we get too wrapped up in our own stuff. We lay claim to things. This is mine; that is yours. We're not keen on sharing. When you combine two families into one, there's sure to be some squabbling over stuff. Bedrooms. Furniture. Clothing. Even people. Yes, it's true. When you marry someone who has children from a prior relationship, he doesn't just belong to you; he belongs to his children. That doesn't sound like a big deal. . .until you're all living in the same house. Then suddenly your home can become a war zone!

Maybe you've been putting yourself first—focusing on your own interests instead of those in your household. How do you begin to go about sharing, not just "stuff" but attitudes, people, and even love? It's easy. Acknowledge that nothing belongs to you anyway. It's all the Lord's. He's the owner and the keeper of it all. And He's big on sharing.

Today take inventory. Is there anything that you've been protecting as your own? Anything that you could or should be sharing with others in the family? It's time to shift your focus!

Dear Lord, I'll admit I usually think of myself first. My interests. My plans. My hopes and dreams. My stuff. Help me to lay aside any selfishness and look after the interests of those in my family. Amen.

Day 106

Connection

Remember the days of old; consider the years of many generations.
Deuteronomy 32:7 ESV

As the oldest of the five of them, Kara would probably be the only child who would remember. She alone would have solid memories of their mother. When breast cancer took their mom, she was eight. Her youngest sibling was not yet a toddler.

Her father remarried. His new wife—her stepmom—came to the marriage with three children of her own. It wasn't long before Kara and her biological siblings were calling their new stepmom "Mom"—just like their stepsister and stepbrothers did.

Kara's stepmom never tried to supplant her birth mother. On the contrary, her stepmom went through old photographs. She had a photograph of Kara's mom and her framed. Kara kept it on her bedside table. Her stepmom encouraged that connection, even after she legally adopted her and her four siblings. With that connection encouraged and solid, Kara was able to develop a deep closeness with her stepmom.

Just as Israel needed to remember things from their past, we do, too. Whether we're adults or children, neither the present nor the future should displace the best of our past. As we build our blended families, we need to ask for God's wisdom and sensitivity. We know the importance of our own memories. Healing will come for our stepchildren when we encourage them to hold on to the best of theirs.

Father, show me how to help my children build on the good things of their past. Amen.

Love Never Fails

[Love] always protects, always trusts, always hopes, always perseves. Love never fails.
1 Corinthians 13:7–8 niv

Loving someone who doesn't love you back isn't easy. And becoming a stepmom means you place yourself right in the middle of that possibility. Not every stepchild will warm up to the fact that you are now an authority figure in his or her life. Not every stepchild will want another mother.

You and your new family will go through a time of adjustment as you learn to trust each other. For some, the process will be quick; for others, it will take time. No matter how long or difficult the process will be, God has given you this unfailing truth to hold on to through the ride: Love never fails.

This isn't a mushy love that comes and goes; it's an unconditional love that will always be extended, regardless of how it's received.

When you love someone unconditionally, you don't love that person based on his or her feelings for you. You aren't moved by rejection or a halfhearted response. You aren't moved by what you see. You are only moved by love. And that's what you have been called to do: love your family unconditionally. When you love them without regard to how they respond to you, you open the doors to let them love you back.

Lord, help me to love my family unconditionally. Remind me continually of Your promise that unconditional love never fails. In Jesus' name, amen.

Day 108

Bearing Fruit

But the Holy Spirit produces this kind of fruit in our lives: love, joy, peace, patience, kindness, goodness, faithfulness, gentleness, and self-control.
GALATIANS 5:22–23 NLT

If we have committed our lives to Christ and we are growing in Him, the Holy Spirit produces fruit in our lives. Wouldn't it be great to be a part of a family that is known for being loving, joyful, peaceful, and patient? Do you long to be in relationships that are kind, good, faithful, and gentle? And don't forget self-control! Wouldn't you love to be self-controlled and trust that your family members possess self-control as well? In John 15:5 (NIV) Jesus says, "If a man remains in me and I in him, he will bear much fruit." Come together in prayer as a family and commit to remaining *in Christ*! Choose to obey God and seek a personal relationship with Him each day. Make Christ the center of your family, not just at the top of a list of priorities. Then you will see the fruit of the Spirit begin to grow and ripen in your life and in those around you who have also made this commitment.

Dear Father, show me what it means to remain in You. Be the center of my life and my family. Let the fruit of the Spirit abound in my life and in my family. Amen.

Day 109

Mother's Day Blues

For God is not unrighteous to forget your work and labour of love.
HEBREWS 6:10 KJV

It was well after midnight when Marsha finally gave up and went to bed. She'd known hours ago that the call wasn't coming, but she'd waited up just in case. Sighing, she closed her novel and rinsed her teacup in the sink.

So, he didn't call, she thought as she climbed the stairs. *So, he didn't give me a card. So what?*

So it hurt, that's what. One more Mother's Day had slipped by without acknowledgment from the child she'd helped raise. She thought of the many years she'd cleaned up his messes, helped with homework, and driven him to practices. The gifts she'd lavished on him for birthdays and holidays. The emotional blows she'd taken.

"Dear God," she prayed through her tears. "You know how hard I've tried. . . ."

And He did know. Each time she bit her tongue instead of lashing back, each mile she went out of her way, each tear she shed over her husband's son—God saw it all. He understood her disappointment like no one else could, for He knew what it was to sacrifice for those who did not appreciate it. Such sorrow did not lessen His love; and like Him, Marsha knew she must forgive.

So, he forgot to wish me a happy Mother's Day, she thought, smiling ruefully. *At least I'm not still picking up his dirty socks.*

Lord, grant me a forgiving heart, and help me to remember that even though my stepchildren may not notice my efforts, You always do. Amen.

Day 110

Never Will I Leave You

"Never will I leave you; never will I forsake you."
HEBREWS 13:5 NIV

After tucking their young children safely into bed, a couple sat on their back porch to watch an approaching storm come in. Heavy rain began pelting the roof. Strong winds whistled through the trees. Suddenly, the screams of hysterical children could be heard. The children were frantically running room to room in search of their parents. Rushing inside, the concerned father asked what was wrong. The children cried in unison, "We thought you and Mom had left us!" As incomprehensible as that seemed to the parents, the children truly believed they had been abandoned.

What about you? Have you ever felt abandoned? Perhaps your world looks dark and stormy. Frightened, you cry out to God, but He doesn't appear to hear you. Fearing the Lord has left, you feel alone, forsaken. Although you are scared, do not rely on your emotions when searching for truth. Feelings can fool us. Instead, go to God's Word. He promises never to leave us nor forsake us. God cannot lie. He faithfully stands behind every promise He makes. As believers, God's presence is possible through the indwelling Holy Spirit. His presence is permanent. Leaving is never an option.

The parents couldn't imagine that their children would think they had left them. Similarly, God wants us to be confident of His omnipresence. Trust Him in your darkest moments. He is there. Cry out to Him in the storm. Your concerned heavenly Father will come.

Dear Lord, help me trust You when my world looks dark and stormy. Amen.

God's Goals

I guide you in the way of wisdom and lead you along straight paths.
Proverbs 4:11 NIV

Americans readily embrace goal setting. Deciding what we'd like to achieve and determining steps to attain goals makes sense. It's logical, orderly, and focused. But if we simply look ahead driven by our imaginations, will the goals we choose and the means to meet them align with God's plan for us?

God's purposes and ways rarely resemble man's. When God released Israel from Egyptian slavery, His goal for them entailed far more than arriving in the Promised Land. He chose a route and itinerary that defied human logic, keeping the details of the journey to Himself. God required Israel to duck, weave, and turn on a dime, constantly following His pillar of cloud by day and of fire by night. What a challenge! Israel never could predict how long they would stay in one place or what the next day would hold. They complained plenty and failed to enter the land the first time around; but through constant training, God changed the Israelites. Only then could they occupy the land of promise.

There's a lesson for us in this. Before we set goals, we should seek God's guidance. We never know what will happen in the next minute, much less in coming years. But God does know, and He has a plan! As we humbly pray and listen, we can trust Him to give us godly goals and lead us along perfectly chosen paths.

Father, my ultimate goal is to please You. Here's my hand. Please take it, and I will follow wherever You lead. Amen.

Day 112

Committed

Commit your way to the Lord, *trust also in Him, and He shall bring it to pass. . . . Rest in the* Lord, *and wait patiently for Him; do not fret.*

Psalm 37:5, 7 NKJV

Sandra woke up one rainy morning, her mind in a tumult. Doubts and worries filled her head: Have I done the right thing by remarrying? Are my kids getting along with their new siblings? Am I treating all the children equally?

As anxieties crept in, growing ever stronger, Sandra's thoughts grew as cloudy as the gray skies outside her bedroom window. Turning on her side, she spied a green index card filled with her own handwriting on the windowsill. *One word from You, God. . . ,* she thought as she reached for the card. There she read, "You will keep [her] in perfect peace, whose mind is stayed on You, because [she] trusts in You" (Isaiah 26:3 NKJV).

Clutching the card to her chest, Sandra repeated the verse to herself over and over again, knowing that before she faced the day, she had to set her heart and mind right, moving from fears and reliance on self to courage and trust in God.

Before your feet hit the floor, begin your day protected by God's Word and its mind-transforming power.

Abba, I trust in You, and You alone, to help me in this journey. Set my heart and mind straight, knowing that to rely on You is the only way to live in this world. Take away my fears and concerns. Fill me with Your courage and wisdom as I commit myself to You.

Plowing Hope

And now, God, do it again—bring rains to our drought-stricken lives so those who planted their crops in despair will shout hurrahs at the harvest, so those who went off with heavy hearts will come home laughing, with armloads of blessing.

Psalm 126:6 MSG

Stepmoms must be the most optimistic people in the world. We enter into unions the statistics tell us are long shots at best. We bring scars and wounds not yet healed while trying to be a sustaining pillar of an unstable enterprise. We come to understand drought and despair with the familiarity of hunger or sleepiness. Our lives grow out of control.

And yet God knows we continue to plant. Despite the forecast or the conditions, like a hummingbird blown to an alien land, we seek the best we can find and work with what we have. We may know little more than the next moment as we work, but we hope because God tells us to.

We're optimistic because it's His habit to supply what His children lack, to take their anemic efforts and gush forth blessings. If we continue to work the best we can, sometimes through the tears we can't hold back, we're plowing on His promise, not our production. We're trusting in His provision, not our predicament.

The harvest is coming, He says, and we'll barely be able to carry it all. That hope leads us out today for tomorrow's bounty.

Father, You know my weariness and worry, but You support me with hope and grace. Please help me never to doubt Your skills or fail to plant in faith. Amen.

Day 114

Battle Up?

He causes wars to end. . . . He breaks the bow and snaps the spear.
Psalm 46:9 NLT

"Why did a trip to the zoo sound like a good idea?" A frazzled mom had had it with blended-family bickering and fighting. This was supposed to be fun, but now she and her husband just looked at each other with narrowing glances. They'd agreed the night before to stay calm and help the kids to stay cool. Instead, dispositions, attitudes, and feelings were in a state of disrepair. Who could put them back together again?

Certainly not the royalty who tried to fix Humpty Dumpty! But the Lord could do it! He calmed a raging storm that had made His disciples fall to pieces. That means He's able to heal the cuts from stabbing remarks or piercing words. The Lord can relax the furrowed brow and put smiles back on faces. He can mend the broken heart and touch the wounded spirit. He alone can turn weapons of war into instruments of peace.

When your family mix has a Humpty Dumpty experience, will you ask God to help you put things back together again? He's the One who fashioned each of you in the first place.

O Lord, You know I fall apart when our family goes after one another. Please help us to surrender ourselves to You. Amen.

Day 115

Loving Your Children's Father

Each of the younger women must be sensible and kind, as well as a good homemaker, who puts her own husband first.
TITUS 2:5 CEV

Sometimes the busyness of life can become overwhelming. You have been trying to keep your husband happy, raise children, and maintain a household. Where does the time go? Suddenly, you realize that it has been awhile since you set time aside for your husband. *He understands that there just hasn't been enough time in the schedule to get away*, you reason. However, he does have the need to spend "alone time" with you.

Your schedule is not as free as it was in your earlier days, but take the initiative to set aside time to go out together. If you have a difficult time finding a babysitter, you could plan your date for a Saturday lunch, when babysitters are more readily available. Or perhaps you could find another couple to swap "date nights" with: You watch their kids when they go out; and they in turn watch your kids for your special time away. Your kids will benefit from seeing you set aside time for their daddy, putting him "first," as the verse above instructs. And your relationship with your husband can only improve as he recognizes the importance you place in growing closer to him.

Dear Lord, I ask for Your help as I prioritize spending time growing closer to my children's father. Amen.

Day 116

Don't Be Discouraged

So let's not get tired of doing what is good. At just the right time we will reap a harvest of blessing if we don't give up.

Galatians 6:9 NLT

One of the most common feelings of all stepparents is discouragement. When stepchildren are teenagers, they may become rebellious and resist all efforts of guidance and sound instruction. Even younger children learn to play the competition game between parents and wreak havoc with their demands and attitudes.

This is the time to turn to God and seek His guidance. He will encourage you and lift your spirits because you can rely on His promises to see you through. At age twelve, Marsha decided to see if she could get more from her stepmother by telling her that her real mother gave her things and let her go places that were not acceptable for the stepmother. Instead of giving in, the stepmother put aside her own animosity and called Marsha's mother.

At first the ex-wife didn't want to talk with the stepmother, but the stepmother persisted until Marsha's mother was willing to discuss the behavior. As both mothers talked, they came to an agreement that they would consult each other about the daughter's requests and ultimatums. Once Marsha learned she couldn't fool the two women any longer, she became much more willing to abide by the rules set by both parents.

This may not always work, but perseverance will pay off in blessings if you don't give up.

Heavenly Father, instill in me the patience to persevere and not become discouraged in guiding my stepchild. Amen.

Day 117

Dwelling in Unity

Behold, how good and how pleasant it is for brethren to dwell together in unity!
PSALM 133:1 KJV

Behold! Sit up and take notice. What David is about to say should deliver a big punch. It's a simple truth really, but it's often taken for granted.

We figure kids—and adults for that matter—are going to have spats. Sibling rivalry and even dissension are inevitable. But that doesn't mean parents should tolerate or encourage such behavior.

Instead, parents and stepparents must help their children work through these trying times. All children are different from one another; and this should be celebrated, not looked upon as some difficulty. It is the job of parents to guide their children—to show them how to use their uniqueness together to blend into a beautiful bigger picture. Adults must set the example. They must get along with one another, and they must expect their children to get along as well.

Find creative ways to blend your family. Accept that each person has something wonderful to contribute. With God's help, you will be a living, loving, beautiful family portrait.

Jesus, You've been through everything that You might better understand me. Thank You for even becoming a stepchild. Amen.

Day 118

A Prayer for Patience

Create in me a clean heart, O God; and renew a right spirit within me.
Psalm 51:10 ESV

The kids were at it again! Melanie walked into the kitchen to hear her daughter and stepson fighting over the last clean spoon. She took a deep breath before entering the room and was immediately bombarded with angry words. Jared said that Amanda took the last spoon, and Amanda rolled her eyes. "Why is there only one clean spoon?" Melanie asked. Immediately both kids blamed each other for not running the dishwasher. Losing her patience yet again, she sent both kids to their rooms in an angry huff.

Melanie and Amanda had been on their own for years, and she understood that having a stepfamily wasn't easy on her daughter who was used to being the center of her mother's attention. Melanie believed the experience of having a brother would be good for Amanda. But she had been spending a lot of time frustrated and angry, praying that the Lord would change her family. She soon found, however, that He wanted to transform her own heart. Melanie, once again, found herself before the Lord in prayer, surrendering all to Him, asking for wisdom and an attitude of grace as she climbed the stairs to their rooms.

Dear Lord, give me patience when I feel frustrated. I want to honor You with my actions and please You with my heart. Help me to be an example to my family. Amen.

God's Delight

Who is a God like You, pardoning iniquity. . .of the remnant of His heritage?. . . He delights in mercy. He will again have compassion on us.
Micah 7:18–19 NKJV

Every parent makes mistakes. Sometimes daily. Sometimes hourly. When we realize what we've done, we grieve. The pain we've wrongfully caused our children is something that is uncomfortable to admit or face. Even though we ask forgiveness from our children, and from God, the repercussions can weigh us down. We find it hard to let go of the lapse in judgment.

When we don't let go of the faults that haunt us, we are refusing to accept God's forgiveness in full. Our guilt can become a painful lash that serves no good purpose. We have to realize that all parents stumble. We are not perfect. When we accept God's pardon, we are free to try again with the idea of working toward being more like Him in our parenting.

One of our greatest joys can be coming to the realization that God delights in showing mercy. As we come to accept His love and forgiveness, we are abler to demonstrate the same for our children when they make mistakes. God displays compassion beyond our ability to understand so that we can find a small measure of His charity for our family.

Father, please help me to be more like You. Show me how to consider my words and actions and not cause hurt. Amen.

Day 120 Stepmother to the King of Kings

But Ruth said, "Do not urge me to leave you or turn back from following you; for where you go, I will go, and where you lodge, I will lodge. Your people shall be my people, and your God, my God."

RUTH 1:16 NASB

Ruth is one of the shortest and sweetest books in the Bible, the story of an unlikely adoption by a somewhat unwilling stepmom! When Naomi—along with her two daughters-in-law—becomes a widow, she decides to return to her hometown. One daughter-in-law elects to remain in Moab. Naomi urges the other, Ruth, to go back to her own people and her own gods; but Ruth weeps and pleads until Naomi relents.

The two women travel together—now more like mother and daughter—to a land that is, for one of them, completely unknown. Whether it was their shared history or the strength of Naomi's trust in the power of this unknown God she called the Lord, something in Naomi drew Ruth. And Naomi took on this girl, not knowing whether she would be a blessing or a burden.

We all know how the story ends: Ruth marries Boaz and bears a son, who eventually becomes the grandfather of King David. Ruth, the foreigner, becomes to Naomi "better than seven sons" and the great-great-great-great grandmother of the greatest king of all: Jesus. All because Naomi was willing to open her heart and her home to a girl who wasn't her responsibility.

Dear God, You can tell the most awesome stories with and through our lives. Help me to be willing to be used by You. Amen.

Grade A People

I will give them an heart to know me, that I am the LORD: and they shall be my people, and I will be their God: for they shall return unto me with their whole heart.

JEREMIAH 24:7 KJV

The ax finally fell. Nebuchadnezzar, king of Babylon, conquered Jerusalem and carried off Jehoiachin, king of Judah, as a captive, along with his officials and many educated and skilled citizens. Jeremiah the prophet warned the king and his people many years before disaster struck, urging them to repent and turn to God. Now hope seemed like a foolish dream. Jeremiah probably did not expect positive messages from God. But the Lord gave him a vision of two baskets of figs, one delicious and one inedible. Although He compared Jehoiachin and his supporters to rotten figs, God affirmed His deep love for His people by likening them to the basket of lovely fruit. He intended to watch over them, build them up, and help them grow while they lived in Babylon. Even in their darkest hour, He saw the exiles as His beloved children whom He wanted to heal and bring home.

We may find ourselves in miserable situations, but God does not forget us. We may see ourselves as defeated, alone, or hopeless, but God sees us through His Son—whole, perfect, and beautiful.

Lord Jesus, I do not feel worthy to return to You, but You call me back to Your side. I can't run there fast enough! Thank You. Thank You. Amen.

Day 122

The Best Reward

[She] provides food for her household. . .she reaches out her hands to the needy.
PROVERBS 31:15, 20 NKJV

Stepparenting can have some great rewards. CeCe, a stepmother of six, decided to remember that Tom's children were not her children. She allowed Tom to handle his children's battles. She found this very freeing, and it allowed her stepchildren to continue seeing their father as the authority figure.

But she found ways to work with Tom toward creating a happy home. CeCe learned that her stepchildren had come from a noisy household, one where competition, fighting, and yelling were a lifestyle.

So CeCe provided a quieter household for her stepchildren, one that felt like a refuge. She provided healthful meals and insisted on eating dinner as a family. She made games out of baking cookies with Tom's kids. She made sure their hair was combed and their clothes matched. She taught Tom's daughter how to style her hair. CeCe provided peace and love.

In the end, CeCe made her stepchildren feel loved by spending time with them. She didn't try to whip them into shape; she patiently nurtured them. She now feels the peace of seeing her stepchildren grow into happy, productive adults. CeCe thinks this is the best reward she could ask for.

Father, thank You for helping me to love my husband's children. In Jesus' name, amen.

Day 123

Godly Contentment

But godliness with contentment is great gain.
1 Timothy 6:6 kjv

Have you ever felt totally, completely content? Just happy to be who you are where you are? We seem to go through seasons of contentment, don't we? And often those seasons morph into seasons of great discontent! One minute we love our lives and feel completely blessed. The next minute we're fretting over this or that, wondering if anyone else has it as hard as we do.

God loves a contented heart. He doesn't want us striving for things we don't need or taking our eyes off Him. In fact, His idea of contentment involves resting in Him, even when we're in seasons of want—and that's not always easy!

So where are you on the contentment scale today? Are you doing pretty well in this area, or are you struggling? Wishing your house, your car, your kids, or your husband were more like your neighbor's? Wonder if you'll ever stop striving for more, bigger, and better? Watch out! To be truly content, you can't play the comparison game. And godly contentment—having a heart after God and trusting Him in every area of your life—will come only if you lean on Him and not on yourself.

Heavenly Father, thank You for reminding me that You are in control. Help me to trust in You and to not play the comparison game, even during seasons of lack. May my striving cease, and may I be truly content in You. Amen.

Day 124 Walking on Eggshells

A fool shows his annoyance at once, but a prudent man overlooks an insult.
Proverbs 12:16 NIV

Have you ever been around a person who is easily annoyed? It's like walking on eggshells—even the smallest pressure causes him or her to crack! It's easy to spot this undesirable trait in others, but God wants us to look inward. How many times have we been easily annoyed? How many times, because of a bad day or week or month, have we unleashed the stress of our lives on those we love most?

Just think of the shape we'd be in if God chose to show His annoyance at us every time we messed up! But God is patient. His Word tells us time and again that He is slow to anger. Aren't you glad He overlooks so many of our character flaws? Instead of condemning every little mistake, He looks at our hearts. He sees when we are trying to please Him. He sees when we're sorry for our mistakes, many of which are not on purpose. He lovingly wraps His arms around us and says, "I forgive you."

Let us strive to be like the prudent man who overlooks the faults in those around him. For the day will surely come, and probably soon, when our faults will surface. If we are quick to overlook the flaws in others, they will be quick to overlook the flaws they see in us.

Dear Father, please forgive me for showing my annoyance too easily. Please help me to have a loving and patient heart. Amen.

Day 125

Great Expectations

Wait patiently for the LORD. Be brave and courageous.
Yes, wait patiently for the LORD.
PSALM 27:14 NLT

Waiting in line, waiting for an appointment, waiting for your husband to come home, waiting for a baby to be born. You spend a lot of time waiting. But in all of these instances, you expect something to happen. The very nature of waiting is expectation. You *expect* to get to the front of the line, you *know* your doctor will eventually get to your file, you *believe* your husband will show up with a good reason for being late, and you *trust* the day will come when you can hold that baby in your arms.

In more serious circumstances, though, waiting can be a grueling test of faith. Waiting for a financial breakthrough, a relationship to be repaired, or medical test results can cause your rock solid faith to crumble and blow away like sand. Today's verse says, "Be brave and courageous," because it's tough to wait, especially to wait *patiently*. Remember, though, that waiting is expecting something. You must *expect* the Lord to work, look forward with hope to His answer, and even *believe* that He is already working, regardless of what your eyes see. Faith—believing in what you cannot see—transforms your waiting from mundane to miraculous. And His miracles are always worth the wait.

Dear Father, help me to be brave, courageous, and patient while You bring about Your miracle. I trust that You are already working on my behalf. Amen.

Day 126

Jesus' Gaze

One thing I ask of the Lord, this is what I seek: that I may dwell in the house of the Lord all the days of my life, to gaze upon the beauty of the Lord and to seek him in his temple.

Psalm 27:4 NIV

As soon as the rooster began to crow, Jesus, who was standing nearby, "turned and looked straight at Peter" (Luke 22:61 NIV). Like a blazing arrow that found its mark, Jesus' penetrating gaze touched his soul. Luke uses a specific word for Jesus' glance. It is, interestingly enough, the same word John had used to describe the very first time Jesus looked at Peter. It's a Greek verb, *emblepo*, translated "to look straight at." It means to see with your mind, to understand.

That thoughtful gaze of Jesus could not have been one of disdain or condemnation. That was simply not Jesus' way. So, then, what kind of look was it? What look could have broken Peter's heart so completely? Only one of love and forgiveness. That is what we can expect from our Savior.

The slightest glance can speak volumes. What kind of look do we convey when we gaze at our children? Too often it is filled with frustration, annoyance, or impatience. Starting today, let's practice a look of love.

Lord Jesus, one day I will stand before You, face-to-face. I long to experience that intent gaze of Yours, to see in Your eyes what Peter saw. Until then, remind me to reflect Your gaze to others. Amen.

I Like You and Love You

Day 127

Go after a life of love as if your life depended on it—because it does.
1 Corinthians 14:1 msg

"Crystal, do you like me?" blurted ten-year-old Hannah. Crystal was shocked at her stepdaughter's question.

"Of course I like you, Hannah! Why would you ask that?"

"You're always talking to Halle and Justin about memories they were a part of. I don't feel like I'm a big part of your life, because you and I don't have much to talk about. With you and Dad getting married last month, I feel like you know your kids and my dad well, but you don't know me. We don't have much in common, I guess."

"Oh, Hannah," Crystal said, giving her a brief hug, "we have two *big* things in common. We both love Jesus, and we love your dad very much and want the best for him. I don't want to take over your part in that—I just want to share it with you so that together we can make him the happiest he can be. And I not only like you, I love you. You are a part of him, which makes you extremely special to me. I know Halle, Justin, and I have made memories together, but I'm looking forward to the memories I'm going to make with you and your dad. I love you, sweetheart."

Dear heavenly Father, help me to show my love to all of my children. Help them each to realize how special they are to me. Amen.

Day 128

A Little Yeast

"A little yeast works through the whole batch of dough."
GALATIANS 5:9 NIV

Have you ever made your own bread? It's a rare thing to do in this day and age! However, if you try it just once, you'll find that a little packet of yeast causes an entire batch of dough to rise. This verse in Galatians is also found in 1 Corinthians 5:6. Both times the writer is trying to get this message across: one person can negatively influence a lot of others. The opposite is also true: One person can positively influence a lot of others. A little bit of love, kindness, and respect can go a long way—especially in your family relationships. You may not have a great relationship with your stepchildren. Take small steps toward building a loving relationship by the little acts of kindness you can show along the way. Ask the Lord to give you the wisdom to know how to show love to each individual in your home. And speaking of making your own bread, why not invite the whole family into the kitchen and make this a fun learning project? Include a little lesson about yeast from God's Word while you're at it!

Dear Father, help me to be a mother who positively influences my family. Help me to show Your love to each person in my home. Amen.

Day 129

Imperfection

For we know in part and we prophesy in part, but when perfection comes, the imperfect disappears.

1 Corinthians 13:9–10 NIV

An Amish quilt may appear flawless. Every block looks impeccably stitched. All the colors are skillfully matched. The quilt seems perfect to the casual observer. Yet upon close inspection, a slipped stitch or imperfection can be detected somewhere on the quilt. Apparently, Amish quilters purposely leave a mistake in every quilt as a subtle reminder of our human imperfection.

Life is full of imperfections: cracks in driveways, scratches on furniture, leaky faucets. Admittedly we live in an imperfect world; yet why do we sometimes expect perfection from ourselves or others? We inadvertently yell at the children. Our husband forgets to call. Our child loses his homework. Mistakes happen. Accidents occur. No one is perfect. Give yourself and those around you a break. Cut them some slack. Show compassion and mercy. Be quick to forgive.

Jesus was the only person who was sinless and perfect. He does not require perfection from us. He was the Lamb without blemish. That is precisely why He could become the atoning sacrifice for our sin. Someday He will return. All things will be made new. Perfection will appear. Until then, remember the Amish quilt. We all have flaws, and that is why we need a Savior. Accept His forgiveness. Then you can extend it to others who are imperfect, too.

Dear Lord, thank You for loving me in spite of my imperfections. Help me extend that love to others. Amen.

Day 130 Garden-Variety Motherhood

O Lord. . .be our strength every morning, our salvation in time of distress.
Isaiah 33:2 niv

Just how many kinds of mothers are there?

Mothers-to-be. Birth mothers. Foster moms. Mothers-in-law. Surrogates. Those-who-are-like-a-mother-to-me. Adoptive moms. Stepmoms.

Of all those moms, probably the last one alone carries a stigma. And that's where we live.

If we have our own children who go to spend time with their dads and stepmoms, we're less than excited at the prospect. We may feel a little threatened. When it's our turn and we wear the mantle of stepmom, those same emotions—plus the unflattering memory of Cinderella's stepmother—come home to us. We want to be loving and fair, but it's demanding, exhausting, and sometimes unrewarding work.

On those tough days when we're weary of not quite measuring up, we can take comfort from our Father—the One who chose to adopt us into His family. Just as He chooses to make us His own, we too can choose to make a difference for good in the lives of our children and stepchildren. It is work—hard work. Heartbreaking work sometimes. But all mothering is work. God's help won't be exhausted in an hour or a day. We need it day by day. He will give it as we go.

Father, in areas where I failed yesterday, help me not to fail today. Thank You for the strength You give for each new day. Amen.

Oops! I'm Sorry

Day 131

The LORD *is more pleased when we do what is right and just than when we offer him sacrifices.*
PROVERBS 21:3 NLT

Because we're human, we make mistakes. We overlook an important event; we blame one when it's another's fault; we're too quick to judge. Not intentional errors, but slipups and blunders. When we take a misstep, it's only natural to make excuses. But excuses might cause more harm than good. The words "I'm sorry" often ring truer than any explanation or defense.

One desire of a God-given heart is to make things right with an injured party. It's not easy to pay back a debt or give an apology, but it's worth it to know that our lives reflect God's presence. "I'm sorry" can become more precious than gold to the recipient.

Let's consider where we might have erred. Is a sincere apology needed? We need to pray for God's guidance in the situation and ask Him for the right words and timing. When we choose to obey, He will honor our act of restitution and give us a clean slate. When we pray as Jesus taught His disciples in Luke 11 (NLT), "Forgive us our sins as we forgive those who sin against us," He will forgive us. Is it time to say, "I'm sorry"?

Dear Lord, show me where I've sown seeds of unkindness and help me apologize. Amen.

Day 132

Choosing Words, Repairing Hearts

Set a guard over my mouth, O Lord; keep watch over the door of my lips.
Psalm 141:3 NIV

Sometimes it can seem as if we've worn the hinges off the doors of our lips, can't it? We're quick to criticize and quicker to defend ourselves. We hurt, and we often add to our pain with the words we use that come back to haunt us like too much chili late at night.

We may strike out with bitterness, ridicule, blame, or—one stepmom's personal favorite—sarcasm. She was good at it, but her husband recoiled and bit back harder. The kids just looked hurt. It was reflective of her feelings but a poor choice when tensions were high. She was slow to see what she was doing, but finally she understood the damage.

So she chose to restrain the words that would fly out like shrapnel from a deadly bomb and, with God's help and lots of practice, replace them with calmer and more mature methods of communication. She found that her feelings could still find mechanisms to bring them to life without the barbed attacks, while her listeners stayed closer and seemed to wince no more.

She learned to submit her words for God's approval and direction, to open that door only with His blessing and guidance. And she found that when she was silent, He never withheld His words to her heart. He provided every word she needed, with not a hurtful one among them.

Father, please monitor my words from my heart to my family's hearing, and let Your Word be the last word on all I think or speak. Amen.

Day 133

Heritage

Lo, children are an heritage of the Lord: and the fruit of the womb is his reward.

Psalm 127:3 KJV

What is your heritage? What has been passed down to you from family members? Perhaps your grandmother's wedding dress with the beautiful lace. Maybe some jewelry, a picture, a treasured recipe, the color of your eyes, or a personality trait.

No matter what is passed on to us, we want to keep the item safe, to give it special care in order to preserve the legacy that is now ours.

How many of us consider that children are a heritage given to us by the Lord? The fruit of the womb is a reward, and that doesn't have to be the fruit of our own womb. God believes all children are worthwhile. He has entrusted us with his precious gift, not without thought, but after careful consideration. He knows the trials and difficulties that might be ahead, but He also knows the wonderful moments and shared joys that are in store for us.

We are God's children. He loves us beyond measure and considers us worth His all. How can we think any less of those He's given to us? We need to treat each moment with the same awe we would that precious heirloom passed down for generations in our family. Every child is worth that devotion.

Lord, thank You for considering me worthy of this child. Thank You for Your wonderful gift. Amen.

Day 134 Building Security in Your Home

"Behold, God is my salvation, I will trust and not be afraid; for the Lord *God is my strength and song, and He has become my salvation."*
Isaiah 12:2 NASB

Every new relationship takes time. You and your husband invested hours and hours together getting to know one another. Sometimes that desire to be married conflicts with giving his children time to know you and your children time to know him.

Trust doesn't always come easy—especially when children are insecure in their relationship with their parents after death or divorce. They need time to get to know you, and first impressions are everything. Children are looking for security. Sometimes they feel left out or feel that their father can't love them as much if he loves you. It takes time to develop trust in new relationships with your stepchildren.

Everyone has a need to feel secure, and true love eradicates fear. When a stepmother tells her stepdaughter, "I love you. I want what's best for you. I'm here for you," it's seldom enough. Children have to learn through your actions.

Offer security by affirming everyone in the home verbally. As they come to know you and begin to feel comfortable with you, you can offer hugs and kisses to them. Affirming words and acts of love no matter whom you're expressing your love to builds great security in your home.

Dear God, help me not to push the kids away by trying to make them accept me. Show me how to speak to them with Your love through my actions and words. Amen.

Multiple Blessings

"The Lord will command the blessing upon you in your barns and in all that you put your hand to, and He will bless you in the land which the Lord your God gives you."

Deuteronomy 28:8 NASB

He was everything she had ever wanted—except for one thing. He came with a ready-made family. Realizing it was all or nothing, she put aside her fears and embraced them as a whole. When difficult times came, she persisted in loving them, trusting that God had placed her there and would continue to bless.

This woman grasped the truth that God desires to bless us in every area of our lives: in our finances, our work, and our family. The land He gives us is not just the physical place where we live, but the family that surrounds us and the friends we socialize with.

Our daily lives are often filled with caring for our family, and it can be tiring. Running a household, doing the same repetitive tasks, and being taken for granted may not seem like much of a blessing. Like this woman, we need to embrace our situation and look for God's hand. In the midst of the mundane, God gives health and good school reports, fresh food and times of fun and laughter. We just need to open our eyes and look, right where we are.

Dear Lord, help me to see my family with different eyes and appreciate the marvelous way in which You bless us every single day. Amen.

Day 136

Fightin' Words

She openeth her mouth with wisdom; and in her tongue is the law of kindness.
PROVERBS 31:26 KJV

"You're not my mom!"

The words struck Maureen like a blow. How swiftly a simple discussion had turned into a power struggle! She stared at the insolent girl before her and felt the color rise in her own cheeks. She had done nothing to deserve this blatant rebellion, and her first impulse was to strike back.

I'm glad I'm not your mom, you cheeky little brat! she thought. But no. Engaging in a battle of words was foolish and destructive. Maureen's parental role would never be established by mimicking an unruly teenager, and reacting to her stepdaughter's childish excuse for disobedience would only encourage her to use it again.

"No, I'm not your mom," she said, gazing steadily into the girl's eyes. "But I may as well be for as much as I care about you. In this family the rules are the same for everyone. Including you."

She watched as the fire in her stepdaughter's eyes flickered out. The girl shrugged in typical teen fashion and muttered that she had homework to do. Maureen nodded and watched her retreat to her bedroom. Then she licked the tip of her index finger and made an invisible mark in the air. *Score one for the stepmom*, she thought.

Lord, guard my tongue against hasty words that wound and scar. If my speech must be firm, let it also be kind. Amen.

Priorities, Plans, and People

We can make our plans, but the LORD determines our steps.
PROVERBS 16:9 NLT

Brenda looked at her watch as she hung up the phone. Two o'clock, and she still hadn't even scratched the surface of the work piled on the desk in her home office.

Her day was not going as planned. So far she'd had three calls—one from a friend facing a crisis, one from a woman who just needed someone to listen, and one from her stepson who needed her to run his saxophone over to the high school. *I'll have to stop answering the phone*, Brenda thought. But of all the people who'd called her that day, who would she have ignored?

Many days our schedules suffer from "life *interruptus*." But we're not alone. Consider the apostles Peter and John who, while on their way to prayer, were interrupted by a lame beggar sitting at the temple gate. Instead of entering the temple as planned, Peter stopped and prayed, then ended up delivering a sermon and being put into custody. The next day, he and John were brought before officials, admonished never to teach of Jesus again, and finally released.

Although their day was not going as planned, Peter and John calmly allowed God to have His way, resulting in the healing of a beggar, the preaching of God's Word, and—later, as they prayed with their companions—a house-shaking encounter with the Holy Spirit (Acts 3:1–4:31).

Your day not going as planned? Relax. God is in control, walking with you every step of the day—for the good of the Way.

Dear Lord, give me the patience to let You have Your way in every moment of this day. Amen.

Day 138

The Rights of the Firstborn

"But he shall acknowledge the firstborn, the son of the unloved, by giving him a double portion of all that he has, for he is the beginning of his strength; to him belongs the right of the firstborn."

DEUTERONOMY 21:17 NASB

She couldn't wait until he turned eighteen. That would have been obvious enough by her behavior even if she hadn't worked it into every conversation involving her stepson. Family portraits were sent out at Christmastime with one face conspicuously absent; birthday parties were organized for the two children she and her husband had had since their marriage, but not for the son her husband had brought into their marriage. Though he had blond hair, he was clearly the black sheep of the family. And as he grew older, the divide only intensified.

In reading the book of Deuteronomy, one is often struck by God's powerful sense of *fairness*. His all-encompassing mind seems to touch on everyone and everything: slaves, unmarried women, donkeys, oxen, foreigners, even firstborn sons of unloved wives. This last one is a powerful message to women—and men—in a stepfamily situation not to play favorites. We may be tempted to give precedence to the children of our body, but God's Word clearly cautions us that this is wrong. A son is a son no matter who his mother may be.

Dear heavenly Father, thank You for being so loving, merciful, and fair. Help me to be more like You, Lord, when dealing with my children. Amen.

Making the Un-Move

Day 139

Lord, through all the generations you have been our home!

Psalm 90:1 NLT

Trying to get settled the first night in a new place, the eight-year-old rousted up in bed and said, "I'm scared, Mom!" Changes unnerve everybody, whether it's a different house or a new blend of people under the same roof. So how can you stay settled amid the moves or changes of life?

Not a stranger to change, Moses declared God to be his forever dwelling place. Maybe because, as a baby, the Nile River was home before the bathing princess rescued him. With her permission, Moses' own family sheltered him under their roof until he went to live in the palace. As a fugitive, he called the desert home while he tended sheep. God then moved him back to Egypt, only to return to the desert later with a huge number of "stepchildren"—the children of Israel. In the process, Moses also moved in and out of a variety of family structures.

No wonder Moses claimed permanent residency in God who is the only unchangeable dwelling place. God will also be your permanent residence amid change.

God has an excellent reputation for housing residents who are always on the move. Fill out your "unchange-of-address" card today. You can settle down no matter where your next move takes you.

Thank You, God, for the permanent residence You offer me. Thanks for being my constant in a world of change. Amen.

Day 140

Good or Bad?

But solid food is for the mature, who by constant use have trained themselves to distinguish good from evil.
HEBREWS 5:14 NIV

Few things are by nature inherently good or bad. Take kudzu, for example. Brought to America in 1876 from Japan, this rapidly growing vine seemed nearly perfect. Its ornamental leaves and sweet-smelling flowers provide food for wildlife, livestock, and even people. The vine helps prevent erosion as well. No wonder from 1935 to the mid-1950s, kudzu's benefits were touted, especially to farmers.

However, when kudzu is planted in the Southeast, it grows up to one foot per day. Without the controlling forces of cold weather and pests, it scurries up trees and shrubs, breaks off branches, uproots plants, and blocks out sunlight. Clearly it needs restraint!

The "good" things in our lives also require restraint. Striving for excellence taken too far is perfectionism. Excessive relaxation breeds slothfulness. Both spending and saving are useful activities, but extremes create spendthrifts or misers. Almost anything—exercising, eating, working, socializing, hobbies—can become an obsession if left unrestrained.

We need discernment if we're to live godly lives. Scripture points out danger to those who read it. The Holy Spirit counsels those who ask for illumination. The good things in life won't ensnare us if God trains our senses. Relying on Him, we can distinguish good from bad!

Father, help me make good choices each day. Sound a warning in my heart and mind when an otherwise good thing is becoming a snare, and set me free. Amen.

No Worries

"Therefore I tell you, do not worry about your life, what you will eat or drink; or about your body, what you will wear. Is not life more important than food, and the body more important than clothes?"
Matthew 6:25 NIV

Maintaining a family puts strains on the budget like nothing else. At times it can require juggling skills that many of us lack. As we sit with the bills stacked on one side and the checkbook on the other, we wonder how on earth we'll be able to stretch the dollars. We wish that the dollars would multiply like the loaves and fishes did when Jesus fed the five thousand. Or that the food in the cupboard would never give out, as was the case with the widow's oil and flour in Elijah's day (1 Kings 17). Or that our children's clothes would never wear out, like the clothes of the children of Israel in the wilderness (Deuteronomy 8:4).

Jesus tells us that we don't need to worry about these things. He is able to provide all we need. Instead, we should focus more on our relationship with Him, on our eternal life, not only for ourselves but also for our children and husbands.

The next time you're faced with a deficit in the checking account, use that circumstance to teach your children about God's provision. Allow them to help you pray for the needed funds to keep the family eating and clothed. Teach them the importance of depending on Him for all their needs. And rejoice when God provides.

Father, thank You for Your provision. I know that I can count on You to give us just what we need. Amen.

Day 142

Seize the Day

I do one thing. I forget everything that is behind me and look forward to that which is ahead of me.
PHILIPPIANS 3:13 NLV

When driving down the road of life, we can become distracted by past hurts, failures, and shortcomings or sidetracked by the words others have spoken into and around our lives, playing their lines over and over in our minds.

Preoccupied, we begin steering erratically. Our vision is no longer on what is before us, but on what is behind and around us. In such a state, how will we ever reach our goal? For in looking back, we are apt to face defeat—or drive into a brick wall.

Christ tells us to keep our eyes and our lives moving forward: "No procrastination. No backward looks. You can't put God's kingdom off till tomorrow. Seize the day" (Luke 9:62 MSG).

Are you still reeling from the hurtful words addressed to you yesterday? Put them out of your mind, and step forward into today. Afraid you're going to fall short this month like you did last month? Keep your eyes on Jesus and forget about past mistakes.

Don't wait. Don't become frozen with inhibitions, fear, and anxiety. Make today the first day of the rest of your life. Drive forward with God, reaching out to build up His kingdom one road at a time.

Oh, Jesus, my eyes are set on You. In Your strength I can do anything. Be by my side as I reach forward today, forgetting what lies behind. Amen.

United in Love

My purpose is that they may be encouraged in heart and united in love, so that they may have the full riches of complete understanding, in order that they may know the mystery of God, namely, Christ, in whom are hidden all the treasures of wisdom and knowledge.

COLOSSIANS 2:2–3 NIV

A young woman married a man whose first wife had passed away from cancer. His children, though young, were terribly wounded by the loss of their mother. They went through the motions of adapting, sure, but everything was such a struggle. The woman worked daily to teach them the things of God and prayed with them at night. Still their grief continued. Though she tried to relate to their pain, she had nothing in her life to compare. How could she be like-minded, united?

Her answer came in looking at the grief her heavenly Father experienced when His Son died on the cross. Suddenly, she had a clear picture of grieving. She was then able to completely relate to what the children were going through.

Do you struggle when it comes to being united with everyone in your family? Is there one child you just can't seem to connect with? Is there some issue you can't see eye to eye on? Today ask the Lord to unite your hearts in love.

Heavenly Father, I want to be "one" with those in my life—particularly my spouse and my children. Join our hearts, Lord. Unite us. Remove any divisions today, I pray. Amen.

Day 144

The Taste Test

Wise friends make you wise, but you hurt yourself by going around with fools.
PROVERBS 13:20 CEV

A neighbor brings you garden-fresh veggies. A friend drops by with a dish of apple cobbler. Then a well-meaning woman offers you advice on dealing with stepchildren. How can you receive the "genuine" without falling prey to the "questionable"?

When it comes to advice, ask yourself if the words passed on to you will make you wiser. Obviously, you don't want to become "foolisher." If the one passing advice on to you is growing in the rich soil of God's Word, her advice may nudge you to trust God more in your greatest stepmother challenges.

But more than listening to her words, watch this stepmom in action. Her stepteen gripes about *never* getting to use the car. The stepmom refuses to go down the road of quarreling. Instead, she says kindly, "If you simply let me know your request, we'll see what we can work out." Rather than going in circles and getting nowhere, she moves forward with a plan. "I can't control my stepson's reaction," she tells you later, "but I know God wants me to act, not react."

Wise friends pass on the right amount of wisdom—like the veggies or tasty dessert—not so much to overwhelm you but so you, too, can benefit from the cream of the crop. Whatever you're doing when wisdom knocks, be sure to answer the door.

Dear God, help me to take my stepmom cues from those who take their cues from Your holy Word. Amen.

Day 145

There's Fear, and Then There's Fear

"Make the Lord of Heaven's Armies holy in your life. He is the one you should fear. He is the one who should make you tremble."
Isaiah 8:13 NLT

When we talk about God, we might describe Him as loving, all-powerful, just, compassionate, strong, mighty, majestic, and gracious. We feel blessed to serve a God who embodies all of these characteristics. We also feel awe and gratitude. One emotion that we may not feel immediately, though, is fear. Fear primarily has negative connotations in our world—we have fears about losing our jobs, about harm befalling our families, and about where our world is heading. It seems strange that Isaiah would tell us to fear the Lord.

The fear that Isaiah demands, however, is different. We are commanded to fear the Lord Almighty, meaning that we should be filled with awe and reverence. We should stand amazed at how powerful He is. God alone is the Holy One. Isaiah tells us that if we are filled with reverence for the Lord, we don't need to be afraid of anything else. Fearing the Lord—knowing in our hearts that He is the God of all creation and that He loves each one of us—takes away our fears, because we know that God will take care of us, no matter what the world brings our way.

Dear Lord, I worship You with fear today, knowing that You alone are the Holy One. When my eyes are upon You, I will not fear anything else. Amen.

Day 146

New Clothes

Therefore, as God's chosen people, holy and dearly loved, clothe yourselves with compassion, kindness, humility, gentleness and patience. . . . And over all these virtues put on love, which binds them all together in perfect unity.

COLOSSIANS 3:12, 14 NIV

Have you ever stood in your crowded closet, staring at piles of clothing, but felt you had nothing to wear? That happens daily in countless closets around the world.

We end up wearing the same tired things again and again, when truly, if we'd just take the time to scoot those hangers to the side and really look at our clothes, we might rediscover something "new" and fresh.

Sometimes we wear the same old attitudes instead of taking the time to rediscover the treasures that God has placed in our hearts. They are there, for God has already given us everything we need to live for Him. But for some reason, we hang on to our old self-centeredness. We are easily annoyed. We feel miffed at the world for things we can't even explain, and we respond to others with our dingy old standbys.

But if we dig deep and examine the treasures that God has provided, we'll find *compassion, kindness, humility, gentleness, and patience.* And as the crowning glory of it all, we will find *love.* When we wear these things, we'll look beautiful to everyone who sees us! It will be like having a shiny new outfit, because God's glory will surround us.

Dear Father, thank You for caring about what we wear. Please help me to wear an attitude that will please You. Amen.

Mighty to Save

Day 147

"The Lord your God is with you, he is mighty to save. He will take great delight in you, he will quiet you with his love, he will rejoice over you with singing."
Zephaniah 3:17 NIV

Some days are pure chaos. Murphy's Law is in effect: Anything that can go wrong does. Seemingly before we can even get out of bed, the plan for the day is drastically changed. A child is sick. Another lost his homework. A heavy snowfall or windy rainstorm makes everyone late for school and work. The plumbing backs up. The washing machine breaks. The car won't start. You get the idea. Any one or all of them at the same time can have the same effect: disaster. You wonder when the day will be over.

Yet through it all, we can know that our God is with us. He's not surprised by anything. He's not ruffled by a problem followed by more problems. Instead, He takes great delight in being near, ready to hear our cry for help, for wisdom, for relief. He's delighted when we call on Him.

An old chorus says, "God specializes in things thought impossible." When you are faced with impossible circumstances, difficult days, and children or teens who seem to thrive on conflict, it's good to remember that God delights in you. His love will quiet you, calm you, help you to think and come up with creative solutions to work through each problem. Nothing ruffles God. In fact, right now He's "rejoicing over you with singing." Gain strength and renewed purpose from His love song to you.

Father God, thank You for being there for me—even when days are difficult. Amen.

Day 148

Service with a Smile

Charity. . .seeketh not her own.
1 Corinthians 13:4–5 KJV

Everyone needed something. A ride to the mall, help with homework, clean laundry, and most of all, dinner. Rachel sighed at the enormity of her family's demands. *Does anyone care about what I need?* she wondered. What if, just once, she put herself first?

"Take the bus," she could say to the one begging for a ride. "Do your own laundry, fix your own dinner, ask someone else about that homework. . .I'm busy taking care of *me*." She imagined their facial expressions—surprise, confusion, panic—and chuckled. Her family would fall apart without her.

And I would be miserable without them, she thought.

She loved each member of her hodgepodge family—the children she had birthed as well as those that came with her marriage. Taking care of them was overwhelming at times, but she knew she wouldn't have it any other way. Motherhood—especially stepmotherhood—was a sacrifice, but it was also a blessing. And just as she would never complain about the blessings, she refused to mope about the sacrifices. Her family trusted her with their lives, and she would lavish them with her love.

Everyone needed something, but they also needed *someone*; and Rachel was glad that someone was her.

Gracious Lord, help me to see beyond the sacrifices and demands of stepmotherhood so that I can remain a cheerful giver of myself. Amen.

Little Foxes

Catch for us the foxes, the little foxes that ruin the vineyards.
Song of Solomon 2:15 NIV

Most parents face a time when the misbehavior of their child is overwhelming. From rudeness or minor infractions to major offenses, we feel battered by the assault. During a difficult period like this it is easy to justify letting some areas slide. We seem to be constantly badgering or disciplining, and the relationship suffers.

When we let down our guard, those little foxes can creep in and destroy the connection we've established with our child. Resentment begins to build. Anger takes root. Bitterness grows. Before we know it, the little annoyances have become major problems. Explosions of temper can occur. Words can be spoken in haste that hurt everyone involved.

We must recognize the foxes who are trying to ruin our vineyards. We can't hide them in the dark inside us but need to bring them to the light. Prayer is our greatest hope. God can show us which transgressions we need to confront and which can be forgiven and forgotten. He will guide us and get us through the tough times of parenting. God can help us talk with our child about the problem. When we do it with His guidance, there will be healing and strengthening between us. Our child will be more open when he doesn't feel attacked but loved.

Help me, Lord, to rid my home of the little foxes that destroy.
Fill me with Your love. Amen.

Day 150

As Long as It's Black

Children, obey your parents because you belong to the Lord, for this is the right thing to do.
EPHESIANS 6:1 NLT

"You can have any color you like, as long as it's black." So said Henry Ford, perhaps mythically, about his quintessential Model T automobile.

Have you ever found yourself parenting children the way Ford tried to spin sales for the automobile? It's a clever strategy, especially if we are conflict avoiders. Rather than have a head-on confrontation because we are telling our children no, we dance around it. Soften its edges. Attempt to camouflage it. We try to make our kids think that they're really in charge of some choices when, in truth, they aren't. There are some choices our kids just don't get to make—like having a curfew or obeying the driving laws. Some things in life just are what they are. When you need to say no, you need to say no.

Sometimes, the kindest word a parent can say is *no*.

Lord, give me the chutzpah to say a clear no to my kids and stick to it when I need to. Even if the results of a no make me unpopular, I need to do the right thing for my kids. And when You say no to me, help me remember that the reason is because You love me enough to say it. Amen.

Hang in There

Day 151

Perseverance must finish its work so that you may be mature and complete, not lacking anything.
James 1:4 NIV

Every checkout line is stacked five deep with people who apparently haven't bought groceries for a month. With your mouth propped open unnaturally wide, you tolerate the shrill whine of the dentist's drill. You're stuck as hundreds of cars slow to a crawl amid road construction at rush hour. What do you do? You hang in there; you tolerate; you endure.

That's perseverance: patiently enduring until you "get there." And remembering the final result makes the enduring possible. To patiently endure the long checkout line, you remember you like having food in the pantry. To survive the stint in the dentist's chair, you remind yourself of the benefits of healthy teeth. To get through the traffic jam, you keep in mind your destination.

Whether you are experiencing difficulties with the "blending" of your family or wondering how you can even face another day, remember your destination. In Christ's power, you can keep going; you can persevere so that you will "be mature and complete, not lacking anything." Consider today your starting line, look ahead to your finish line when you are "mature and complete" in Christ, and determine in Him to stay in the race and finish well. The prize will be more than worth the price.

Faithful Father, please help me to keep on going, to keep my eye on the prize of spiritual maturity and completeness in You. Thank You for running this race with me. Amen.

Day 152

Too Hot to Handle Alone

"Let us acknowledge the Lord; let us press on to acknowledge him. As surely as the sun rises, he will appear; he will come to us like the winter rains, like the spring rains that water the earth."

Hosea 6:3 NIV

Kara's life felt like one long, dry summer. Her husband, Gabe, had surgery and was off work for weeks, and the family finances were being drained. Sam, Gabe's teenage son, hated remedial summer school. Three-year-old Danielle suddenly decided she didn't want to sleep at night. Even the dog ran away. Kara, searching for the dog in the afternoon heat, felt like doing the same.

She tried not to think how she and Gabe had neglected their relationship with Christ. They went to church, but they hadn't even prayed at meals lately. Kara missed her husband's Bible reading at breakfast. But she didn't feel like talking with the Lord; in fact, Kara avoided Him.

When did she first hear Him calling? Maybe it was the song on the car radio. The simple words refreshed her like cool water. Later Danielle asked if she could pray at supper. She, Gabe, and even Sam bowed their heads. That night Kara and her husband sat on their front porch welcoming the rain's music as it watered their parched yard. Together they decided to get reacquainted with the One who could revive their souls and help them grow again.

Father, I find it so easy to forget You. But You never forget me. How I appreciate Your faithful, refreshing love! Amen.

Day 153

Getting to Know You

Better to be patient than powerful; better to have self-control than to conquer a city.
Proverbs 16:32 NLT

"But I don't *like* tomato sauce!" Abby wailed. Amanda, standing at the stove, willed the tears not to come. She tried hard to keep the home running smoothly, but she was still learning things about her stepchildren. She had spent the afternoon making Rob's favorite—lasagna. But she had totally forgotten that Abby didn't like tomato sauce. Should she just make Abby eat it anyway? The transition had been hardest on Abby, Amanda was sure.

"Abby," Amanda began. "I remembered how much your daddy likes lasagna, and I wanted to make him happy. You know how much fun it is to make him happy, right?"

Abby smiled. "You mean like when I give him a great big hug when he gets home?"

"Exactly!" Amanda agreed. "And because you are so special to both of us, we want to make you happy, too. I'm sorry I forgot that you don't like tomato sauce. How about this time I make you a grilled cheese sandwich?"

"Yes!" shouted Abby. "Thank you!" After giving Amanda a squeeze around the thighs, she skipped away to play.

Amanda smiled at the outcome of this crisis. She knew there would be more compromises to come, but she also knew that she could depend on her heavenly Father to give her the strength she would need.

Heavenly Father, please give me the insight I need to make fair compromises. As I learn more about my stepchildren, bless us all with tolerance and love. Amen.

Day 154

The Greatest News

How beautiful upon the mountains are the feet of him that bringeth good tidings, that publisheth peace; that bringeth good tidings of good, that publisheth salvation; that saith unto Zion, Thy God reigneth!

Isaiah 52:7 KJV

God reigns. How awesome that is! When we stop and acknowledge that God is in complete control, it should drastically improve our outlook on life.

Not only does God reign, though. He saves. He pulls us from the depths of our disgusting sin-stained lives and makes us fit for His kingdom. There's nothing we as humans can do to rid ourselves of our guilt. God, through Jesus' death and resurrection, can reconcile us to Himself. Our only part is to recognize this—to ask His forgiveness and to accept Him as Savior.

With Christ as our Savior, what wonderful news we will have to proclaim. Think about it. Life can be like a steep, rugged mountain. Trying to reach the summit on your own is dangerous at best. But with Christ by your side, you will arrive victorious.

Though weary and bruised from the journey, from the top of the mountain you can triumphantly proclaim, "My God reigns. He brings peace to the troubled and hope to the destitute. Won't You accept Him, too?"

Oh God, You are great! I will share Your good news with all those I meet. Amen.

Thick-Skinned

Day 155

"You have been weighed on the scales and found wanting."
Daniel 5:27 NIV

When God examined King Belshazzar's life and reign, He declared him "wanting." Belshazzar didn't make the grade, and he was judged accordingly.

One stepmom says she doesn't make the grade in her stepkids' minds, either. Her stepchildren forever compare life with their dad and her, their Christian stepmom, with life at the home of their (non-Christian) birth mom and her husband. The children find the Christian home "wanting" with its rules, expectations, and accountability. That mom comes to grips with one sad fact: Her stepchildren seem to look for any reason not to like her. She knows her home is not the popular one but says, "Being a stepmom has made me very thick-skinned."

Christ called living the Christian life "hard work" (Revelation 2:2 NIV). Paul said Christians know what it's like to be "hard pressed" (2 Corinthians 4:8 NIV). The apostle John claimed we shouldn't be surprised if the world hates us (1 John 3:13). To be Christian requires a tenacity to persevere in the exercise of right. It may not endear us to those in our charge, but God calls us to a high standard. His ways are right and beneficial—for us and for our stepchildren.

Lord, help me to want to please You first of all. Make me both thick-skinned and tenderhearted. Amen.

Day 156

Different Needs, Equal Love

I want you to think about how all this makes you more significant, not less. A body isn't just a single part blown up into something huge. It's all the different-but-similar parts arranged and functioning together.

1 Corinthians 12:14 msg

The first summer that Bonnie and Todd were married, all six of their children played baseball. Todd coached baseball, and his three children had played for years. They loved it. Bonnie signed up her three kids, too. Her oldest daughter and son liked playing, but her youngest daughter, Laura, seemed indifferent.

One afternoon about five years later, Bonnie found a notebook that Laura had written in. Laura wrote, "I'm sitting on the bench at the ball field during practice. It's raining, and I'm cold. And I don't like to do this. I wish I could just be at home with my mom instead of having to play ball just because that's what Todd's kids do."

Bonnie learned a good lesson that afternoon, even if it was a late lesson. She learned that she needed to remind herself, especially once her girls got to be teenagers, not to get so caught up in buying Todd's daughter a beautiful prom dress that she forgot to get excited about her daughters' choir concert and dance recitals.

Leaving her heart open to her daughters' needs helped keep Laura's and Bonnie's relationship strong. Why not think of ways to strengthen your relationship with your children today?

Dear God, please remind me to love my own children as much as my husband's. Please don't let me neglect them. In Jesus' name, amen.

Spirit Renewed

A Message from the high and towering God, who lives in Eternity, whose name is Holy: "I live in the high and holy places, but also with the low-spirited, the spirit-crushed, and what I do is put new spirit in them, get them up and on their feet again."

Isaiah 57:15 MSG

New spirit. How wonderful would that be? How refreshing and strengthening would a new outlook, a new hope, a new optimism be?

God knows. He knows when getting up and on our feet to face the woes and worries of another stepmom day seems equivalent to fighting our way to the top of a mountain—from the inside. He knows when we feel alone and removed from His care and oversight, when hopelessness and defeat begin to define who we are. So wrapped up in the demands and disappointments of every day, we need help, encouragement, peace, and renewal—a message to keep us going.

And so God provides. He reminds us that He is never removed from us, despite our lapses into that delusion. He understands our pain, desperation, and despair; and He promises it won't last. He promises to replace all that with an injection of His wisdom, strength, and peace, with the power to carry on because we realize He is carrying us. And we're on our feet again, ready to walk with Him close enough to touch, removed no more.

Father, thank You for Your wisdom and willingness to take me in any condition and create me anew with Your Spirit. Help me up so that we may walk together. Amen.

Day 158

Facing the Giants

But we are not of those who shrink back and are destroyed, but of those who have faith and preserve their souls.
HEBREWS 10:39 ESV

It has been said that courage is not the absence of fear, but taking action in spite of it. Moses sent twelve spies into the Promised Land. They all acknowledged that the land was flowing with milk and honey. But ten spies shrank back in fear, reporting that the people looked like giants. In contrast, Joshua and Caleb believed that God could give them victory. Had it not been for their courageous faith, the Israelites never would have entered the Promised Land.

Fear causes us to shrink back. Fear convinces us to retreat. Fear defeats us. God had given the Israelites the Promised Land. But they had to trust Him by stepping into the unknown. We may face similar giants. Yet, as we trust God by stepping out in faith, we can conquer our fears and experience victory.

Do you sense the Lord calling you to a new job, location, ministry, or relationship? What is your response to the unknown? Like Caleb and Joshua, we need to trust the Lord wholeheartedly and courageously take steps of faith. Ask the Lord to give you courage. Face your fearful giants in the Lord's strength. Trust Him to provide. Believe that He is able. With the Lord on our side, we have nothing to fear. May your faith enable you to trust the Lord and not shrink back!

Dear Lord, thank You for giving me courage to face the giants of the unknown. Lead me down Your path. Amen.

Faith and Love

The only thing that counts is faith expressing itself through love.
GALATIANS 5:6 NIV

We've heard the saying that "people don't care how much you know until they know how much you care." You can argue and debate with someone all day long about what you believe, but your knowledge isn't going to change anyone's heart. Only by loving and caring for someone do we see our faith at work in someone else's life. When we build personal relationships with people and let them see our faith in action, we can then begin conversations to find out where other people are in their own spiritual walk with God. This applies to your own family members as well. You might have a stepchild that is very far from God. If you want that child to open up to you, you will first have to show her or him that you care and that you can be trusted. If the child isn't comfortable talking with you yet, let the child know that you are available if and when she or he needs you. Find little ways to start building a relationship. If you want to win a loved one to Christ, don't try to do it with words only. Show that person Christ's love through you.

Dear heavenly Father, help me to truly care about others. Show me how to love as You love. Amen.

Day 160

The Listening Ear

Hear my prayer, O Lord; let my cry for help come to you.
Do not hide your face from me when I am in distress.
Turn your ear to me; when I call, answer me quickly.
Psalm 102:1–2 NIV

The Psalms are cries to God from the depths of the human heart. They are cries of joy, of pain, of fear; they are cries of confusion, of loss, of despair. Though they were written thousands of years ago, the voices that echo in these songs are our voices, too.

Children feel all these emotions, often more poignantly because they haven't yet had the life experiences that will teach them that "this, too, shall pass." Whatever they feel right now seems to them to be how they will feel forever.

They need us to ask them how they are doing, and they need us to be there to listen to the answer. Their desire for communication will not always be convenient. It may come in the middle of the night. It may come when we are trying to juggle a dozen other competing demands. But God is never too busy to listen. We need to extend to them the same gift and grace God gives us: Be there. Listen.

And most importantly, we need to point them to the God who is always there and whose ear is always listening for the cries of His children.

Dear Father, help me to be a listening ear to my children. Help me to teach them to cry out to You, Lord, knowing that You will answer. Amen.

Sturdy Stuff

Through wisdom a house is built, and by understanding it is established.
PROVERBS 24:3 NKJV

Its days of livin' are over—the old farmhouse, that is. The front porch sags and the squeaky swing no longer has family sipping lemonade on it. The house still stands, but the home has moved out. With due respect to improving your house, it's wiser still to use only the best materials to build your home.

First, go after the wisdom of Jesus Christ to undergird your blended home. Christ is eager for you to apply His wisdom to your blended family issues. Used generously, this wisdom is proven to hold homes together.

Also, pick up a generous supply of understanding to better grasp what each one in your family brings to the table. Whether yours, his, or "our" children, value each one's strengths, and accept or deal with individual weaknesses. It'll keep dispositions from sagging and outlooks from drooping.

So, are you ready to go on a shopping spree? It's not cheap to build a home, but it is the wisest investment you'll make. And you never have to worry about a short supply—God has everything you need on hand. Building instructions are in the manual, God's Word. These tried and true materials are sure to keep a home in your house!

O, Lord, I want to toss materials that cause our home to disintegrate. I want to go to Your storehouse to build our home well. Amen.

Day 162

Martha's Hands and Mary's Mind

"The King will reply, 'I tell you the truth, whatever you did for one of the least of these brothers of mine, you did for me.'"

MATTHEW 25:40 NIV

When Dorcas died, the disciples at Joppa immediately sent two men to Peter begging him to come. What was so important about Dorcas? She wasn't an apostle. She wasn't a prophet. She wasn't an evangelist. Yet the people of Joppa didn't know how to live without her.

Dorcas was a minister in the verbal sense of the word—she ministered to people's physical needs. No one could accuse her, as James accused some, of saying, "Keep warm and well fed" (2:16 NIV) while not doing anything practical for the needy. Dorcas combined Martha's busy hands with Mary's mind set on Jesus. The result was—as Acts 9:36 (NIV) says—she was "always doing good and helping the poor."

The world around us is full of people in need. We not only need to open our eyes, our hearts, and our purse strings, but we also need to teach our children to be responsive to the needs of others. God loves cheerful givers who spread His bountiful goodness among all His children. We need to teach our children how to respond to the needs of God's children.

Heavenly Father, please open my eyes and my heart to the needs of those all around me. Help me to show them Your love and Your care. Amen.

At Heart and Hand

"You have great mercy, so you did not leave them in the desert. The pillar of cloud guided them by day, and the pillar of fire led them at night, lighting the way they were to go. You gave your good Spirit to teach them. You gave them manna to eat and water when they were thirsty."

NEHEMIAH 9:19–20 NCV

In troubled times, we may feel as if we are in the wilderness without food, water, or guidance. When the world seems to be crashing down around us and money seems tighter than it's ever been, we find ourselves wondering if we'll have to choose between investing in straightening our stepdaughter's teeth, buying the trombone our son needs for the school band, or paying this month's mortgage. Amid such dire straits, where can we turn for comfort, help, guidance, and peace?

To God. No matter what situation we are facing, He is with us. Like the Hebrews in the desert, we are not without help. God is here to lead us in the way we should go—night and day. His Holy Spirit is at hand to teach us. His Word is at our fingertips to feed us. His Spirit is within us, quenching our thirst. How wonderful to have a God so loving, so caring, so close at heart and hand.

Oh, God, there is no one like You. I am overwhelmed with love, knowing that You care so much about me. Thank You for always being with me—night and day. You are the One I can always count on, to lead, comfort, and help me, and fill me with peace. Amen.

Day 164

No Pain

And Jabez called on the God of Israel, saying. "Oh, that You. . .would keep me from evil, that I may not cause pain!"
1 Chronicles 4:10 NKJV

How easy it is to hurt someone with a sharp word, a snide comment, or a teasing jab. Frequently, the words are out of our mouths before we even think about what we're saying. By the time we see the hurt reflected on the other person's face, it is too late to retract what we've said.

Too often our children bear the brunt of our thoughtlessness. We make remarks about their poor grades, their friends, or their abilities. As mothers we are trying to encourage them to do their best, but we may do it in a way that attacks who they are instead of building up what they are capable of doing.

We must constantly weigh our words. We need to learn to ask God to show us those times when we have said things that are hurtful, and to protect our children from any insensitive words we might say. When we do realize we've done harm, we need to ask forgiveness and try to do better the next time.

God is faithful to help us turn away from wrongdoing. He is merciful and will answer our prayers. As we learn to turn to Him for help, He will be faithful to help us guard our tongues.

Lord, thank You for helping me to speak wisely so I don't cause pain. Amen.

Master Builder

Day 165

The wise woman builds her house, but with her own hands the foolish one tears hers down.
PROVERBS 14:1 NIV

Does a wise woman build her house with hammer and nails or skillfully sew together an elaborate tent? Fortunately, this verse has nothing to do with bricks and sticks. A woman's *house* is really her household, her family.

The wise woman builds with her words. She builds up her husband and tells him how blessed she is to be married to him. She builds up her children, encouraging, teaching, and telling them she is proud of them. She is quick to praise but slow to criticize.

The foolish woman tears her household down. She criticizes, always ready with some type of correction or reproof. Seldom do positive, uplifting words leave her mouth. While the wise woman *builds up*, the foolish woman *tears down.*

It's human nature to focus on what is not perfect. But the godly, Christlike woman will allow God's love to so fill her heart that her own negative tendencies will be pushed out. The wise woman will build up her family no matter what—even when she is having a bad day, even when she feels neglected and taken advantage of, even when she is *right.* For the wise woman knows something the foolish woman has not learned: She will reap the rich benefits of the lovely household she builds!

Dear Father, please help me to become like the wise woman, never tearing down but always building up my family. Amen.

Day 166

Ceaseless Prayer

Let your hope make you glad. Be patient in time of trouble and never stop praying.
ROMANS 12:12 CEV

Prayer and patience are important in all phases of life. When stepchildren come into the picture with a blended family, patience sometimes goes by the wayside. New habits, new attitudes, and new ways of doing things need to be learned. Leaning on the old standby, "We have always done it this way," will bring problems most of the time if the children are school-age or older.

No one guaranteed that stepparenting would be easy. Trouble will come no matter how careful you may be to meet needs and adapt to different feelings. Those times are when patience comes to the forefront. Prayer is the action that will lead you through the times of turmoil and uncertainties.

Ceaseless prayer doesn't mean to be literally on your knees at all times, but it does mean to have a heart and mind-set that are in tune with God and seeking His will. A prayer breathed in time of conflict will calm the spirit and help tame the words. Continual prayer for the children in your care will lead to times of peace and harmony. Be constantly in prayer for them to follow God's will for their lives and to love Him with all their hearts.

Patience and prayer go hand in hand when seeking to do God's will in all aspects of your life.

Father God, give us the patience we need to handle all troubles that may come our way, and give me an attitude of ceaseless prayer. Amen.

Plug Back In

Anyone who speaks should speak words from God. Anyone who serves should serve with the strength God gives so that in everything God will be praised through Jesus Christ.

1 Peter 4:11 NCV

The stress of going with her husband, Michael, to his daughter Maria's birthday party at his ex's house weighed heavily on Sharon. Michael was already in bed, but Sharon had needed a few more minutes to unwind. She slid off the sofa, turned off the television, and poured the last drops of water remaining in her glass into the sink before turning off the light.

She grabbed her cell phone on the island and thankfully remembered to plug it into the charger. The battery hadn't been charged in a few days, and it was low. *Come to think of it, that's how I feel, Lord,* Sharon thought.

Do you ever feel as if you've been left unplugged from the presence of God for several days? It's easy to get so involved in daily activities that we miss our quiet time one morning. . .then two. . .then for a week, and we haven't recharged. Our spirits are sluggish, and we don't seem to have answers for the decisions we need to make.

Take a few minutes right now to recharge your battery. Get alone with God and sit in His presence. Open the Bible and drink in His Word.

Dear God, I need to plug into Your presence and Your Word. When I get so busy, remind me to take a time-out with You. Amen.

Day 168

Always

We give thanks to God always for all of you, making mention of you in our prayers.
1 Thessalonians 1:2 NASB

What does the word *always* bring to mind? You know that God's love for you will remain—always. And surely you vowed to love your husband—always. There will always be bills and taxes to pay, always be rainy days, and always be laundry to wash. (Funny how this *always* thing works both ways, right?) Always brings to mind forever, and in all circumstances.

Do you give thanks to God for the people in your life—always? If you're like most women, the days rush by and you forget. You mean to do it but get busy. Sure, you always remember to brush your teeth, wash the dishes, and feed the dog. You'd never skip out on bathing or watching your favorite TV show. But, thanking your heavenly Father for the people in your world? Sometimes that gets overlooked.

Today pause long enough to thank God specifically for each person in your family, even the difficult ones. Enter His throne room and lift each name before Him. This will do two things: It will deepen your love for that person, and it will be a daily reminder that God loves each of you as individuals.

Dear Lord, I'm so grateful for my children and my husband. I probably don't thank You enough for all of the family members You've entrusted to me. Bless them and watch over them, I pray. Amen.

The Right Kind of Mother

But ye, brethren, be not weary in well doing.
2 Thessalonians 3:13 KJV

Anne felt tired and frustrated as she watched Davie stomp off to his room. Anne had met his father and fallen for him within a few months of dating. But there had been one catch: William was a dad. William had custody of his son, which meant four months ago when they had married, Anne had inherited a stepchild.

Anne thought about Davie up in his room on *another* time-out for disobeying her. She thanked the Lord for the love that was growing in her heart for this boy. The transition of her joining their family had not been easy. When she and William had been dating, Davie had loved her, but now that she had to be a mother, he was rebelling. She used to be all fun, playing with him and leaving the disciplining to William. But once she had moved into the house, they both realized things needed to change. Right now Davie didn't like her new role of stepmom and neither did she; and no matter how hard it was or how weary she grew, she needed to trust God to give her the wisdom and strength to be the kind of mother Davie needed.

Dear Lord, some days it is hard to be the kind of mother You want me to be. Please give me the strength, love, and courage I need to be the parent You would want me to be. Amen.

Day 170

Power Source

. . .and he strengthened me.
DANIEL 10:18 KJV

In 1982 *The Electric Grandmother*, a television movie based on a short story by Ray Bradbury, was released. It was a heartwarming tale of a widowed father who purchased a humanlike robot to care for his young daughter and two sons. The automated grandma performed her daily duties then retreated to a rocking chair each evening, where she plugged herself into a wall outlet to recharge.

Much like the electric grandmother, you have been tasked by your Creator to care for someone else's children. Such tremendous responsibility can test the limits of your physical and emotional endurance. Even the most stalwart heart needs frequent recharging, and only one Power can fortify you for the struggles of every day.

God knows what makes you tick. He understands the inner workings of your heart, how your mental wheels turn and what parts need repair. He knows when your circuits are overloaded and when your battery needs charging—and so do you! God offers limitless grace and strength, but only if you tap into them. Take a tip from the electric grandmother. Find a private place to "plug in" to God. Let Him renew your spirit and prepare you for the daily duties of stepmotherhood. Don't wait until every nerve is frazzled to ask for help. Seek Him early, and you'll never have to worry about blowing a circuit.

Dear Father, no matter how hectic my schedule is, remind me to take time for soul-renewing, strength-recharging prayer. Amen.

Just Knock

"To him who knocks, the door will be opened."
MATTHEW 7:8 NIV

Lucy is a persistent cat! When a door is closed and she is separated from her master, she puts her tiny paws to work. Rising onto her hind legs, Lucy paws the door, stroking up and down, up and down—faster and harder—until someone takes notice. Separation cannot be tolerated! Lucy refuses to rest until the door opens and she's allowed to enter.

Jesus would approve of Lucy's persistence. But when we desire to be ushered into His presence, there's no need to beg, plead, or beat down the door. A light knock—a simple prayer—is all it takes. As believers, we have constant access to our Savior and Lord!

Our problem is that, unlike Lucy, we're often content to live in self-imposed separation. We get caught up in the cares of the world, busy schedules, self-sufficiency, human solutions, and pride. We underestimate our need and sometimes doubt Jesus' desire to be involved in our daily lives.

The truth is Jesus wants us to knock! He knows we need Him, and He's waiting to throw open the door and welcome us inside. When we enter, we find that He is ready, willing, and able to meet all our needs. What a privilege! Just knock. A simple prayer will do.

Father, help me understand how much You desire to be pursued. Remind me to knock on Your door throughout every day. May I never be content to live in this world with any separation between You and me. Amen.

Great Side Effects

Pleasant words are a honeycomb, sweet to the soul and healing to the bones.
PROVERBS 16:24 NASB

Oh, for a medication without drowsiness, nausea, or cottony mouth. That's rare enough. But rarer still is a prescription that has only positive effects on the whole family whatever its blend may be. You don't need a pharmacist to fill this order—you fill it! What is this rare find?

With the possibility of an outbreak of harsh words always lurking nearby, it's best to keep an ample supply of pleasant words handy. Use generously at mealtimes, bedtime, chore time; and this prescription has also been proven effective when traveling. If restless conditions persist, take immediately. By the way, what wonderful effects do pleasant words have?

Your stepchildren, along with everyone else, will feel better inside (the soul) and outside (the body). Observe what happens to muscles or nerves when someone says, "What did you go and do that for?" Contrast that posture with what happens with a prescription change: "You really look nice today."

Winnie the Pooh might say it like this: "Pleasant words are like crawling into the honey pot for a good dose of sweetness."

Dear God, may others receive the great benefits of pleasant words that You enable me to speak to them. Amen.

Day 173

Wise Choices

Be happy [in your faith] and rejoice and be glad-hearted continually (always).

1 Thessalonians 5:16 AMP

Many fairy stories and movies include a stepmom in the cast of characters. Think of tales such as *Cinderella* and *Snow White* where the stepmother is portrayed as evil, jealous, and bad-tempered. It's no wonder that in today's society, the word *stepmom* often conjures up a negative image.

One way to fight against this misconception is to follow the words Paul wrote to the church in Thessalonica. He emphasized his point by repeating it three times in one sentence—be happy, rejoice, and be glad-hearted. Having faith in God is something we can always celebrate. In fact, our relationship with Him should be a source of great joy that overshadows any difficulties in life. He desires that we live victorious lives that bring honor to Him.

The stepmothers in the fairy stories were miserable people, but we can choose our attitude. We are the ones who decide if we're going to be grumpy and miserable or cheerful and happy. We can willingly put aside bad attitudes and live positive lives, especially when times are tough. Never forget that people are watching, and our behavior can set off ripples that ultimately affect many lives for the better.

Loving God, help me choose daily to rejoice and be happy in my faith. Let my life send positive ripples into the lives of those around me. Amen.

Praying Friends

Then Daniel went home and told his friends Hananiah, Mishael, and Azariah what had happened. He urged them to ask the God of heaven to show them his mercy by telling them the secret, so they would not be executed along with the other wise men of Babylon.

Daniel 2:17–18 NLT

Daniel was facing a serious, life-threatening crisis. King Nebuchadnezzar of Babylon had ordered the execution of all of his advisers, including Daniel and his friends, because they failed to reveal the meaning of a troubling dream. Unlike the other advisers, Daniel sought God. First, he asked his friends for prayer support. In modern-day parlance, he went to his small group. Then he went to the Lord for guidance. God mercifully answered their prayers and revealed the dream to Daniel.

Most likely, you have friends you can call when you are facing a crisis. Good friends can be a wonderful comfort. But praying friends who will drop to their knees before God on behalf of you and your family are a rare and wonderful gift. Imagine if Daniel's friends had only empathized with him or offered to bring a casserole for dinner. No—they stopped and prayed until the crisis passed.

If you have a friend like that, praise God for her. If you don't, pray that God will open your eyes to such a friend. She's out there! And seek to become that kind of a friend to others.

Thank You, Lord of life, for placing friends in my life. Thank You especially for my praying friends. They show the world that You are real. Amen.

Mother's Day Doldrums

Day 175

"For you, you only, know the hearts of all the children of mankind."
1 Kings 8:39 ESV

She dreaded Mother's Day at church. Every year it came, and every year it played out the same.

"All mothers in the congregation please stand so that we can recognize you." Applause. Corsages for the oldest mom, the youngest mom, the mom with the newest baby, or the mom with the most grandchildren. More applause with some "oohs" and "aahs" thrown in.

She never knew what to do. She was a stepmom but had not been able to have her own children. Should she stand? Sit? Would her stepdaughter resent her standing? ("You're not my mom!") Or would she be hurt if she remained seated? ("What am I to you—sliced bread?" Why didn't she just stay home from church that day?

Fortunately, most pastors now qualify their announcement with "All you moms here: stepmoms and adoptive moms, too." But for many stepmoms, Mother's Day is bittersweet—a struggle with how we fit in as moms.

No matter our maternal status, the Lord knows our hearts. He knows our desire to be good mothers whatever our "label." It may not make Mother's Day any easier, but our mother's heart can be at peace.

Lord, help me be the best mom I can be to the children You've brought into my life. In Jesus' name, amen.

Day 176

Some Days

Work with a smile on your face, always keeping in mind that no matter who happens to be giving the orders, you're really serving God.

Ephesians 6:7 MSG

A young woman faced the bathroom mirror early one morning. Her hair was uncontrollable despite the products she used. "I have bed-head," she murmured, as she stumbled into the kitchen to make breakfast. The coffee was bitter, the eggs too runny, and the toast burned. The children turned up their noses, and her husband made a disparaging remark. "I'm not having a good morning," she replied. Pointing to her hair, she said, "I even have bed-head." The nine-year-old boy stared at her for a moment then said, "You must have bed-heart, too, you're so grouchy." Brought up short, the mom sought a few moments of privacy in the bathroom and talked with God. Her attitude brightened after a time of prayer and praise.

Some days are just like that—things aren't going our way, life's too difficult. How do we manage? The apostle Paul encouraged believers to give up their lives, to choose an attitude of thanks, to work with smiles on their faces because they are serving the Lord. That's not necessarily an easy outlook every day, but as we mature in Christ, we find that way of thinking draws us closer to Him.

Prayer and praise—two methods of bringing our hearts and mind-sets nearer to the risen Savior.

Dear Lord, forgive me for the bad attitudes I've displayed. Help me walk closer to You this day. Amen.

Lighthouse Living

"I am God. I have called you to live right and well. I have taken responsibility for you, kept you safe. I have set you among my people to bind them to me, and provided you as a lighthouse to the nations."
ISAIAH 42:6 MSG

Lighthouses are necessary to the safety of fishermen and sailors along any coastline, especially in times of bad weather and rough seas. The boom of the foghorn and the beam of the light illuminating rocky shores and entrances to safe harbors keep those who are out in the storm assured that they will be safe if they heed the warnings.

God has called us to be lighthouses, sounding the warning of rough waters, dangerous tides, and treacherous rocks to our families. Illuminating the way by example. Drawing them to the safety of our homes by creating an atmosphere of unconditional love and acceptance. Teaching them the precepts and principles of God's Word. As God has taken on the responsibility for keeping each one of His children safe from the enemy, so we are to take on the responsibility of showing our children the way to God through Jesus Christ.

How is your light? Is it dulled by dirt and grime built up on the lens? Or is it shining brightly from daily polishing in God's Word and prayer? Do your family members know that they can trust you to point out the pitfalls and dangers ahead? Or have you neglected your responsibility to them by letting your light fade away? If the latter, take time today to get with your Lord and make the necessary repairs.

Father, please help me to let my light shine brightly for You. Amen.

Day 178

Getting a Grip

Stalwart walks in step with God; his path blazed by God, he's happy. If he stumbles, he's not down for long; God has a grip on his hand.

Psalm 37:23–24 MSG

As they walked to the park, Becky kept a firm grip on the hand of her four-year-old stepson, Jason. And it's a good thing she did. For not only did it keep the boy from falling flat on his face whenever he stumbled, but it kept him heading in the right direction—out of traffic and en route to the park. Because Jason was assured of Becky's love, care, protection, and guidance, he happily skipped along as they walked. The traffic didn't frighten him, nor did the strangers passing by. Without a care in the world, Jason and his stepmom were heading to his favorite place. And he couldn't help but smile.

Like Jason, we, too, have someone who has a firm grip on our hand: God. When we walk in step with Him, we're happy as a child on the way to the park. And if we stumble upon our pathway, He is there to pull us back up. With our hand in God's, He'll lead us to the right place and protect us along the way.

Want to be carefree? Get a grip and walk with God. He'll never let you down.

Lord, with You holding my hand, life is like a walk to the park. As I stroll in step with You, I may stumble, but I know I won't be down for long. For You have a firm grip on my hand, my soul, my spirit, and my heart. I can't help but smile. Amen.

Promises in Ink

"This is what the LORD, the God of Israel, says: 'Write in a book all the words I have spoken to you.' "
JEREMIAH 30:2 NIV

God spoke to Jeremiah about restoring His people: bringing them back from captivity and returning to them what was theirs. Write it down, because you can count on it, God says.

Let us write down God's promises, too—those in His book and those He speaks to us in our own captivity of fear, insecurity, and confusion. Let's try it for just a month and see what happens.

Get a small notebook and number thirty days. Perhaps get up a half hour earlier or take your lunch break and focus for a while on His tender promises. Read His Word and look for all the times He promised His followers, "I will be with you." Write that each day in your notebook, along with other promises you discover.

And pray. Then be keenly aware of all the ways He may speak to you—through His Word, family and friends, circumstances—and take note. Listen for the promises He makes about your concerns and your future. And then look for how He works it all out. You may not see big changes in your life in just a month, but you'll develop a valuable habit and come to see your life in the hands of God's promises. And that's something worth writing down in ink.

Father, thank You for promises new and powerful and uniquely made for me and my family. Help me to trust You to keep them and sustain me as they come to pass. Amen.

Day 180

What We Will Be

Dear friends, now we are children of God, and what we will be has not yet been made known.

1 John 3:2 NIV

This verse should bring a huge sigh of relief. Yes, we are God's children, and He's not finished with us! We can quit beating ourselves up over all of those little things about ourselves that are so far from what they should be. God is still working on us, perfecting us, making us more of who He wants us to be.

Although we shouldn't make excuses for our sin, we can feel good about knowing that *what we will be has not yet been made known!* Becoming like Christ is a process, and we can be confident in knowing that "he who began a good work in you will carry it on to completion until the day of Christ Jesus" (Philippians 1:6 NIV). Our Father, who created us and knows us better than we know ourselves, will never give up on us!

Healthy children, when given proper nutrition and exercise, will grow into healthy adults. As God's children, we must feed ourselves on His Word and be obedient to Him. Then, because of God's grace, we will grow to spiritual maturity. None of us have reached our goals yet—to be exactly like Christ—but we will! Praise God, as we continue in Him, we will.

Dear Father, thank You for providing everything I need to grow into the person You created me to be. Amen.

The Trust Factor

But those who wait upon God get fresh strength.
They spread their wings and soar like eagles.
Isaiah 40:31 msg

A brand-new stepmom, Jenni glanced out the window to catch her breath. She also caught a glimpse of a biker whirring past. At that moment, Jenni recalled her first bike with training wheels. Then she thought about learning to keep her balance on a bigger bike. What a challenge that was! She had wondered if she would ever catch on. Then, somewhere along the way, Jenni no longer had to try so hard to make it work. She simply enjoyed riding her bike.

Will it be like that with stepparenting? But how could she get the hang of caring for another mom's child? So, Jenni thought about "balance" at every turn. In fact, she concentrated so hard on being a good stepmom that she could never relax. Then, somewhere along the way, she began taking her eyes off of "trying" and began "trusting" the God who made her and her stepchild.

The load on Jenni's shoulders lightened now that God carried the load she had tried to bear. Oh, yes, there were plenty of bumps along the way, but she could actually glance up now and then to catch the beauty in her stepchild. Could it be she was actually starting to enjoy the ride?

Are you ready to move from trying to be a good stepmom to trusting the Lord with the journey ahead of you?

O, Lord, as a stepmom, may I trust You more and try
less to make things work on my own. Amen.

Day 182

Patterns

In all things showing yourself to be a pattern of good works. . .
Titus 2:7 NKJV

Any of us who has ever used a pattern to make something knows that the directions may look easy but can turn out to be more involved than they first appeared. When we're learning something new—whether sewing, knitting, or any other craft—we must start at the beginning and take one step at a time. If we begin with the first step and then skip to the last, our project will be unrecognizable from what it is supposed to be. Our actions must follow the directions.

God gives us wonderful instruction on raising children. Throughout the Bible, He demonstrates the concepts, from His loving preparations in the Garden of Eden to His discipline, mercy, forgiveness, and ultimate sacrifice of His Son, Jesus. God understands we aren't perfect. He is patient with us as we learn and grow.

Likewise, we must take on these same attributes and apply them to our child rearing. We need to lovingly prepare our hearts and our homes. Our expectations should be realistic. Most of all, our discipline should be surrounded with mercy, forgiveness, and love. Time after time, we will be called to sacrifice for our children. That may be hard, but it is God—who understands more than we ever can—who will give us the strength.

Father, thank You for establishing the perfect pattern for me to follow. Help me as I do this, Lord. Amen.

The Best Way

Who is wise, and he shall understand these things? prudent, and he shall know them? for the ways of the LORD are right, and the just shall walk in them: but the transgressors shall fall therein.

HOSEA 14:9 KJV

Claire checked her calendar. Six more days before Andrea arrived! They'd been roommates in college then shared an apartment before Claire married.

So much had happened since then. Claire sighed. Greg soon left her for someone else. In her loneliness, Claire began to attend church and eventually accepted Christ. There she met and fell in love with Justin and his two kids. Would Andrea believe how much her life had changed?

Years ago, they partied every weekend. Andrea's occasional letter reflected more of the same, with a string of brief relationships. She'd find Claire's new lifestyle pathetically boring!

Claire felt a sudden longing for days when her top concerns involved what she would wear when she and Andrea hit the bars. She'd been so carefree—no worries about children or budgets. And Andrea never considered what God wanted in her life.

Claire shook herself. What was she thinking? Jesus had given her a loving husband, fun, crazy kids, and, best of all, His forgiveness and promise He would never, ever leave her.

She and Andrea had shared lipsticks and shoes. Now Claire couldn't wait to share her new wealth with her old roomie.

Lord, You are so good to me! Help me show my gratitude by blessing another poor person with Your loving truth. Amen.

Day 184 No Stepmartyrs Allowed

The joy of the LORD is your strength.
NEHEMIAH 8:10 KJV

All work and no play makes Mom a stressed-out grouch. Sure, it takes a lot of work to run a household, but you don't have to be a martyr. Make one of the most taxing vocations in the world easier on yourself by taking some time out for fun.

The same God who created the universe made your funny bone, and He expects you to use it! Wearing yourself to a frazzle every day isn't healthy for you or your family. Take a break from the crazy realm of his kids, her kids, ex-spouses, and child support. Show your stepkids how cool you can be! Dust off the board games, air up the bicycle tires, spend an afternoon at the park. Fly a kite, play ball, toast marshmallows over an open fire. Allow the weighty duties of stepmotherhood to slide from your shoulders for a day and relax. The world won't stop spinning because you took some time off, but your head just might.

Laughter is still the best medicine. There are no adverse side effects, and no one ever died from an overdose. Give yourself and your family a well-deserved break. After all, if Mama ain't happy, ain't nobody happy.

Dear Lord, we both know that grumpy stepmoms don't suffer alone. So remind me of the healing qualities of laughter. Help me to take time out when my spirit is overwhelmed. Amen.

Morning Mercies

It is of the LORD's mercies that we are not consumed, because his compassions fail not. They are new every morning: great is thy faithfulness.
LAMENTATIONS 3:22–23 KJV

New crayons, new shoes, new cars—ahhh, can you smell them? Something about "new" excites our noses. Remember when you were little and got that brand-new box of crayons for school? Somehow it signified a new beginning, a fresh start, a chance to get the next school year right. (Or maybe it was just fun to have unbroken crayons for a day or two.) Similarly, when we get new, especially comfortable, jogging shoes, they put a spring in our step and maybe even motivate us to stay with our exercise program. And that new car smell! Who can explain its particularly rejuvenating effect?

We tend to like new things, things that have never been used by anyone else, new things that aren't broken, that still work right, and, yes, smell *new*. Guess what! When you awoke this morning, God blessed you with a brand-new supply of compassion for this day. You never get leftover or broken or "preowned" compassion from God. No, you get the brand-new, out-of-the-box, specially-made-for-you kind of compassion. Whatever you are facing today, remember that His faithfulness is great and "[H]is compassions fail not." He gives them every single morning. That's something worth getting up for!

Lord, thank You for blessing me with new compassion every morning. Great is Your faithfulness! Amen.

Day 186

No Exceptions to the Rule!

Summing up: Be agreeable, be sympathetic, be loving, be compassionate, be humble. That goes for all of you, no exceptions. No retaliation. No sharp-tongued sarcasm. Instead, bless—that's your job, to bless. You'll be a blessing and also get a blessing.

1 Peter 3:8–9 msg

Isn't it funny how we never think about breaking a rule until someone makes one? If a road sign tells us not to drive over sixty-five, we immediately want to drive seventy. If the doctor tells us to cut back on sweets because our blood sugar is elevated, we crave sugar. There's such a temptation to do the wrong thing. But rules are there for our good, our protection.

The same is true when it comes to spiritual truths. God has laid down some ground rules to make our lives—and our relationships—better. Take a look at the scripture above. Do you see how many things made the list? The Lord has called us to be agreeable (always!), to be sympathetic (even when we don't feel like it), to be loving (even to the unlovable), to be compassionate (reaching out to those who are difficult or complicated), to be humble (when our instinct is to be proud).

Are there any exceptions to these rules? No. We're not to retaliate or be sarcastic. Instead, we're called to bless. So stick to the rules and you'll not only bless others, you'll receive a blessing in return!

Lord, today make me a blessing to those You've placed in my life. May I be found agreeable, sympathetic, and loving. No exceptions! Amen.

Day 187

God's Will

The world and its desires pass away, but the man who does the will of God lives forever.
1 JOHN 2:17 NIV

How many Christians are struggling and searching to find God's will for their lives? We want God to show us His plan for our lives all at once. Many get carried away looking for that "one big thing" that God has for them to do. Sometimes the Christian life isn't like that. We tend to make things way more complicated than they are. What is God's will for you and your family? It is simply to obey. God wants us to obey Him moment by moment. It's not just "one big thing," it's obeying in all of the little things, too. That might lead some into great acts of Christian service, or it may lead to a simple and quiet life of love. Both of those paths are of great value to God and have eternal impact on the lives of others. Psalm 119:35 (NIV) says, "Direct me in the path of your commands, for there I find delight." Ask God to direct your path. Keep your eyes focused on Christ and obey Him one moment at a time. In doing so, God's will for your life will become clear.

Dear Father, give me the desire and the strength to obey You moment by moment. Amen.

Day 188

A Gentle and Quiet Spirit

Clothe yourselves. . .with the beauty that comes from within, the unfading beauty of a gentle and quiet spirit, which is so precious to God.

1 Peter 3:4 NLT

Gentle and *quiet* are not words that are typically in the forefront of moms' minds. In fact, some days are spent trying to block out the noise of "outdoor voices" or quelling quarrel after quarrel. To attempt to convince children to be gentle and quiet seems most often an impossible task, but it can start with us.

As we read in God's Word, we are to focus on the beauty within us—a "gentle and quiet spirit" with a beauty that will never fade. What a blessing it would be to be known by our family—and others around us—as someone who has a gentle and quiet spirit. But even beyond that, we are "precious" to God! Very few things hold the label of "precious" these days, but that's how God views someone with a gentle and quiet spirit.

The next time you go about getting ready for the day, remember also to "clothe yourself" with the inner spirit of beauty. The more we invest in developing a gentle and quiet spirit, the easier those days will seem when we need to remind our children to turn down the music or finish up with computer time.

Lord, with all of the activity around me, help me to put on a "gentle and quiet spirit." Thank You for reminding me that I am "precious" to You. Amen.

Someone Else's Baby

Day 189

But while he thought on these things, behold, the angel of the LORD appeared unto him in a dream, saying, Joseph, thou son of David, fear not to take unto thee Mary thy wife: for that which is conceived in her is of the Holy Ghost.

MATTHEW 1:20 KJV

It certainly wasn't the way Joseph had planned on beginning his marriage. Imagine the emotions that tumbled through his mind. Feelings of rejection, humiliation, and betrayal must have haunted every waking moment; yet he would not publicly cast off and have stoned this woman he held so dear. Still, the thought of being married to a woman who was carrying another man's child was too bitter a pill to swallow. So Joseph chose to end it all quietly. Until the dream. "Take Mary to be your wife, Joseph. The baby she is carrying is God's Son."

So Mary hadn't lied! The tale had seemed so preposterous that he'd almost been disgusted that Mary would take him for such a fool. Yet here was this angel letting him know that Mary had been faithful. His sweet, pure Mary was so good in fact that God had chosen her to be the mother of His Son.

Suddenly, another realization hit him. God had amazingly chosen him to be the Messiah's stepfather. The thought was humbling.

God, I give You praise for all You are doing in my life. Amen.

Day 190 Using the Tools We Have

For this God is our God for ever and ever; he will be our guide even to the end.
Psalm 48:14 NIV

As stepmoms, sometimes we focus so hard on our children's needs that we neglect our own. How many times have we served dinner for our kids and our husband before we get a bite of food? How often have we served our kids seconds of cereal and wiped their sticky hands before we drink our cold tea and eat lukewarm oatmeal?

Sometimes stepmoms need extra help. One stepmom felt she needed counseling. If you feel you need to try this route, don't hesitate. It's not a sign of weakness.

We can't take care of our children if we're too sick to take care of ourselves. Divorce, remarriage, widowhood—these all take their toll on our emotions and on our minds. Good counseling and proper medications can help us heal so that we can help our families heal.

Abraham Lincoln once said that we need to use the tools we have. We're blessed to live in a time when antidepressants and trained psychologists are available to us. Pray for God's guidance in choosing a psychologist, and ask her or him to help you determine if you need to go on medication. Why not thank God for these tools and put them to good use today?

God, thank You for Your guidance. Thank You for Your perfect answer in Your perfect time. Amen.

When Love Becomes Enough

Hope does not disappoint us, because God has poured out his love into our hearts by the Holy Spirit, whom he was given us.
Romans 5:5 NIV

God's desire for relationship continues to draw you to Him as He pursues you with unrelenting passion. Love is His essence; His character and love would never allow Him to give up on you.

He created Adam and Eve in His likeness—for their spirits to rule their minds, wills, and emotions, and to direct their bodies in what was right. When they disobeyed God's command, their relationship with Him was severed; and the physical and natural became dominant over their spirits.

Before you accepted Christ, your spiritual senses sat in darkness, allowing your physical senses to interpret your life. When you accepted the sacrifice Jesus made to bring you back to God, His life and light immediately illuminated your spirit.

That's why Paul reminds us that we are new creatures. The old person—ruled by the physical world—dies, and we become alive in Christ to forever be led by our spirit (2 Corinthians 5:17).

God's design is to bring every man, woman, and child back into fellowship with Him. As the ultimate Father, He doesn't want to be separated from us. He loves us more than we could ever fathom.

Dear heavenly Father, help me to become Spirit-led. May all of my decisions and actions come directly from who I am through my relationship with You. Amen.

Day 192

I Didn't Sign Up for This!

"You must influence them; do not let them influence you! They will fight against you like an attacking army, but I will make you as secure as a fortified wall of bronze."

JEREMIAH 15:19–20 NLT

Jeremiah's years as a prophet before and during Judah's captivity were full of frustration. His people turned a deaf ear to his warnings. They turned on him like wild dogs. He never stopped speaking against their wickedness, but he never stopped loving them, either.

One stepmom's sentence about the trials and rewards of shared parenting of her preteen stepson sums it up well: "It's the hardest thing I've ever had to do."

When we're stepmoms, we face many dilemmas. Like Jeremiah, we can't walk away from the people to whom we're most closely connected. We have to deal with the hard stuff, cry our way through the hurt, and hold on to God with everything we have. We can identify with Jeremiah in the heartbreak of Lamentations 3 but find hope in verses there like "The LORD is good to those who depend on him" and "No one is abandoned by the Lord forever" (Lamentations 3:25, 31 NLT).

Just like the stepmom above and Jeremiah, we, too, may not have signed up for all the headaches and heartaches our position has brought us. But maybe—just maybe—we can come to the same conclusion that young mom did: "There have been many, many low points, but the high points make up for them."

Thank You, Lord, that You bring joy and laughter even when I've had lots of tears and hard days. Amen.

The Cock Crows Many Times

Not that I have already obtained all this, or have already been made perfect, but I press on to take hold of that for which Christ Jesus took hold of me.
PHILIPPIANS 3:12 NIV

Could anyone on earth have felt worse than Peter when the cock crowed for the final time? At that moment, he remembered the words Jesus had spoken to him: "Before the rooster crows, you will disown me three times!" (John 13:38 NIV). In one quivering and heartrending moment, Peter's panicky fear turned to shame. He slipped out of the high priest's quarters and "wept bitterly" (Luke 22:62 NIV). He knew he had failed the Lord miserably.

Though this was Peter's lowest point, he didn't allow Satan to keep him in a state of despair, as Judas had done. Peter reached out to Jesus to be restored, just as he had done when he walked on water, started to sink, and grasped for Jesus' hand. A fresh start once again.

As stepmoms, we're faced with our imperfections on a daily basis. Humility is not hard to swallow; we're accustomed to its taste. Yes, we make plenty of mistakes, even with the best of intentions. But God does not want us to remain stuck, dwelling on our shortcomings. He wants us back on track, ready for a fresh start.

Lord Jesus, the rooster crows many times in my life to warn me not to sin. Teach me to be like Peter and turn to You immediately to be forgiven and restored. Amen.

Day 194

A Gentle Mother

As apostles of Christ we could have been a burden to you, but we were gentle among you, like a mother caring for her little children.
1 Thessalonians 2:6–7 NIV

Have you ever watched a young mother oohing and aahing over her baby? She treats that little one with great love and care. They share giggles and smiles, butterfly kisses, and tummy tickles. That mother can't imagine the road ahead could be rough or that her baby will ever give her any grief. She only sees the fragile, needy infant in front of her.

Maybe you once were that mother. You cradled that baby in your arms and planted kisses on her soft little cheeks. Now time has passed. You're frazzled—at your wit's end. You're caring for your own children and your husband's, as well. Your days are filled with squabbling, chauffeuring, and working. And the exhaustion that follows is almost unbearable at times.

Looking for an escape route? There's only one for the Christian woman. When you reach the end of your rope, let go and let God. Give it to Him. He's the One who can take your troubles and turn them around, and He can give you peace in the process. He can return that joy you once knew when your babies were little; and He will show you once again how to treat those children with a renewed tenderness.

Heavenly Father, today I ask that You return the joy that I once knew when my children were babies. May I treat them with that same gentleness, love, and self-control. Amen.

Day 195

The Complicated Life

I will instruct you and teach you in the way you should go;
I will counsel you and watch over you.
Psalm 32:8 niv

Who's picking up Nancy after school today? Is this our weekend to have the kids? Did you remember to call Rob on his birthday? Let's face it, the life of a stepmom can be quite complicated. There are so many balls to juggle, so many people to keep track of. How do we handle the balancing act without going crazy?

Trying to schedule life on our own can leave us frustrated, frazzled, and frantic. We desperately need the Lord's wisdom and discernment. Seeking Him before the day gets under way helps put life into proper perspective. Ask the Lord to show you His priorities: What things should you let go of, what things are a must-do? Learn to say no without feeling guilty. Although you might yearn to do it all, that is not God's will. Utter exhaustion and weariness are not fruit of the Spirit! Love, peace, patience, and self-control will be exhibited when you walk through the day in the power of the Holy Spirit.

There's a lot to juggle in our lives. Why not willingly hand over the juggling balls to the Lord? Seek His wisdom and counsel to sort through your agenda. Then your activities will be purposeful and you won't feel like you're running in circles. Go to Him. Let Him speak and show you the way to go.

Dear Lord, thank You for instructing and teaching me the way I should go each day. Help me come to You each day. Amen.

Day 196

A Bright Red Snowsuit

She fears not the snow for her family, for all her household are doubly clothed in scarlet.
Proverbs 31:21 AMP

The woman had a full house: husband, three children from his first marriage, two children from her previous marriage, two dogs, and herself. They lived in the desert, with rocks and cacti instead of trees and grass. If it had ever snowed here, she had never heard about it. She laughed as she read the passage in Proverbs about the woman dressing her household in thick scarlet clothing; hers would have died of heat prostration!

But when she thought about it, she realized that warm fabric and bright colors weren't the point. The point was the care and love that this proverbial paragon lavished on those in her care. And not just her own children, but all those of her "household." The word translated "household" in this passage is the Hebrew word *bayith*. Used more than two thousand times in the Bible, *bayith* often refers to a house or dwelling place and to the people who live in it, not just the members of a family. The use of this word here greatly broadens the scope of people for whom the Proverbs 31 woman was responsible.

There is no distinction in this passage: servants, children, stepchildren, cousins, visitors. All deserve the care and protection only we can offer them. Even if it's a hundred degrees outside!

Dear Father, thank You for all those in my care. Help me watch over them with equal love and attention, as You watch over me. Amen.

I'm Sorry

Fools mock at making amends for sin, but goodwill is found among the upright.
Proverbs 14:9 NIV

Sometimes, saying I'm sorry can be almost impossible! Our foolish pride convinces us that no matter how wrong we've been, we were justified in our behavior.

But when we refuse to make right something that is wrong, when we refuse to make amends for sin, the Bible calls us fools. Our foolish pride won't give us the peace and joy that we seek. We can only have those things when we live righteous, upright lives. And part of being righteous is making things right, or making amends.

As Christians, we need to focus more on *doing right* than on *being right*. It's always right to try to live peacefully with others. If someone has hurt our feelings, chances are pretty good that we've hurt him or her as well. We should always remember that God is love and He wants His love to be made complete in us. Part of showing love involves spreading goodwill and keeping the peace.

So walk next door today and tell the neighbor you're sorry for the mess your dog made on his lawn. Apologize to your sister for the catty remark you made about her burned casserole. Ask the Holy Spirit to show you the things you've done to hurt others and the ways you can make them right. Then do them!

Dear Father, please give me the courage and the discipline to say I'm sorry, to make things right, and to spread goodwill. Amen.

Day 198

Making It through Each Morning

He giveth power to the faint; and to them that have no might he increaseth strength.
Isaiah 40:29 KJV

Sometimes waking up in the morning can be difficult. Dragging yourself out of bed to respond to a child's cry, head to a morning meeting, or simply get breakfast ready for your family can be a chore.

On those days, remember God's strength. When you've run out of your strength, He will come and take care of what you need. For example, if the president of the United States told you, "I will completely remove any debt in your name," you would walk a little lighter throughout your day, wouldn't you? You'd tell your neighbors that you received grace right when you needed it most to change your way of living.

God wants to do the same thing. He wants to take the burden of your care. He wants to take the things you worry about and lighten your load. He wants to be your strength and power when the cares that life brings are beyond what you can handle.

Life on its own is draining. But life by God's strength is rewarding. At the moments we are the weakest, He comes by and says, "With My strength and power in your life, you will be made perfect."

Lord, help me to rely on Your supernatural power and strength to make it through each day. In Jesus' name, amen.

Day 199

Unafraid and at Work

"I am giving you a promise now while the seed is still in the barn. You have not yet harvested your grain, and your grapevines, fig trees, pomegranates, and olive trees have not yet produced their crops. But from this day onward I will bless you."
HAGGAI 2:19 NLT

The Israelites returned to Jerusalem after the Babylonian captivity to rebuild the temple that had been burned. They worked hard, but they faced great opposition and soon lost their focus and strength, giving in to fear and giving up on their job. God would have none of that.

He sent Haggai the prophet to reassure them of His presence and control and tell them not to be afraid. We need the same reassurance, because we can easily feel like the Israelites that all is lost and hope is futile. But God will have none of that.

He told the Israelites to notice the seed still in the barn, the promise of growth and possibility that only He could limit, and He never will. He tells us we also still have "seed in the barn." Regardless of the failures or setbacks we've suffered, we still have a job to do and His strength and presence in which to work. The seed in our barn is everything in this life that is expanded beyond our imaginations.

If the Israelites would trust Him, work, and be unafraid, God promised His blessings on them forevermore. The harvest awaits for us, too.

Father, thank You for the never-ending seed in the barn, the possibilities and promises of a life lived trusting in You. Make me unafraid. Amen.

Day 200

Stand Firm

My dear friends, stand firm and don't be shaken. Always keep busy working for the Lord. You know that everything you do for him is worthwhile.
1 CORINTHIANS 15:58 CEV

All parents, whether biological or by marriage, must stand firm in their discipline and guidance of the children entrusted to them. Sheila loved her father and stepmother but didn't always like the rules and regulations they set down. As a teenager, she felt that her father and stepmother were much too rigid and didn't understand her needs. As she grew older, she began to see that their stand on her activities really meant they loved and cared for her. When she graduated from high school, she wrote a letter to her stepmother thanking her for being firm and consistent in her restrictions.

As much as they complain about following rules, most teens much prefer that parents take a stand and set firm guidelines. Many times they may be thankful when peers try to push them into a situation and they can say no because it would break a rule.

Don't be shaken by a teen's stubborn will or anger toward the guidelines you have set. Stand firm with love and encouragement to guide them down the path that will keep them out of harm's way. When they rebel, let them know you love them but expect them to follow the rules you have set for them. Occasionally, those rules can be bent or relaxed for special occasions. If they know that, most teens will not mind being obedient.

Heavenly Father, guide me today. Help me stand firm in love and discipline for our children. Amen.

Day 201

Tongue Troubles

"No weapon forged against you will prevail, and you will refute every tongue that accuses you. This is the heritage of the servants of the LORD, and this is their vindication from me," declares the LORD.

ISAIAH 54:17 NIV

The Sunday school teacher asked her class to name the deadliest weapons they could think of. The answers poured out as each child tried to outdo the other. "Guns," cried one. "No, tanks and grenades!" shouted another. "I think it's bombs and knives," offered a young girl. They were all surprised when the teacher suggested that the tongue is the deadliest weapon of all. In fact, the tongue has sparked off feuds and wars and led to great bloodshed throughout the course of history.

The tongue will always be a potential source of strife. A word of criticism, a harsh comment, or an unfounded judgment can deeply wound the people around us. The pain is even deeper if the attack is from a family member.

The good news is that God has given us a wonderful promise that any weapon used against us will not be effective in the long term. More specifically, He gives us the ability to deal with any words spoken against us. We are active participants in this process and must pray that these words will not reach their mark. God will protect our families and restore broken hearts as we trust in His Word.

Dear Lord, thank You for Your wonderful promise of protection. Help me to negate any evil words by taking them to You in prayer. Amen.

Day 202

Perfect Weakness

And he said unto me, My grace is sufficient for thee: for my strength is made perfect in weakness.
2 Corinthians 12:9 KJV

How children love superheroes! They love to wear costumes and pretend to fly or fight. They have action figures or computer games and spend hours making up scenarios where their favorite superhero saves the day. Our children may try to emulate these comic book characters, but the truth is that we are all human.

We want to be strong and capable, undefeatable and always right. Our excitement grows as our superhero fights injustice and saves the powerless while the music swells in the background. We are filled with weakness, unable to fly or perform great feats of strength. To ground our children in truth, we must teach that true strength comes from God, and only through Him are we able to do anything mighty.

God doesn't expect us to be superheroes. His desire is that we allow Him to work through our weakness that He would be shown to be strong. We shouldn't be afraid to feel unworthy of a task that He has given us, because we will be amazed at what He brings to pass through our surrender. When we do the work He has given us, even if the outcome isn't what we expected, we can know He is pleased with what we've done.

Lord, help me be content with my place in Your work. Please be strong in my weakness. Amen.

Feast for Famine

"The threshing floors shall be full of wheat, and the vats shall overflow with new wine and oil. So I will restore to you the years that the swarming locust has eaten."

Joel 2:24–25 NKJV

Mark kissed Lauren and left for work, head tilted because his neck hurt. Their doctor had traced Mark's aches and pains to everyday pressures. Lauren popped Tylenol to soothe her splitting headache. She made lunches for her son, Val, and Mark's daughter, Kia. Lauren would need to pick up more bread before she bagged the meal she'd eat on her 11–7 shift.

Lauren sighed. She and Mark worked so hard and got nowhere. Val's father had moved out of state, conveniently forgetting to give Lauren his new address. Kia's mother, who shared custody, demanded "only the best!" for her daughter.

Lauren and Mark struggled with their difficult financial situation. But they also had to deal with the consequences of their sinful past—as did the children. Now the frightening statistics on blended families she'd read in a magazine haunted her.

Lauren grabbed her Bible like a life preserver and began to read God's promises. Tonight she and Mark would pray together. They agreed: Even when life had looked hopeless, Jesus always came through. He was bigger than their mistakes!

Years later, as they watched their adult children and grandchildren grow in Christ, Lauren felt as if God had kept every promise—and more.

Lord Jesus, only You can change spiritual famine into a feast. I can't thank You enough! Amen.

Day 204

Pass the Grace

Let your speech always be with grace, as though seasoned with salt, so that you will know how you should respond to each person.
Colossians 4:6 NASB

Have you ever wished you would have kept your mouth closed rather than let loose a torrent of harsh words you didn't really mean? Or have you ever kicked yourself for saying nothing when you really should have had the courage to speak? Gulp. We've all been there, and, unfortunately, our family members usually take the brunt of our verbal outbursts or cold silence. Thankfully, the Lord not only forgives our conversational shortcomings, but will also teach us to respond to others graciously and wisely.

The key to gracious speech is grace itself. If we remember the grace (i.e., unmerited favor) extended to us by Jesus Christ, then we will desire to extend that grace to others—not only through our actions but also by our words. And those words are to be "seasoned with salt."

In cooking, a pinch of salt can transform a nondescript dish into a flavorful experience. Likewise, a touch of grace will make your conversation more loving and kind. This doesn't mean you have to be sappy and sweet without really addressing pertinent issues. Rather, it means to speak the truth with wisdom and with an undertone of kindness, mercy, and humility. If you do this, you will pass along the grace that Jesus has given you. Would someone please pass the grace?

Gracious Lord, please season my speech with grace and give me wisdom to know how to respond to every person. Amen.

A Perfect Blend

Day 205

Clothe yourself in love. Love is what holds you all together in perfect unity.
Colossians 3:14 NCV

If you like to bake or cook, you well know that different flavors must combine in order to produce a palatable dish. For example, flour plays a significant role in making a delicious loaf of bread. When it's added to the recipe, the outcome is quite appetizing.

So it is with anything that is blended, including your family. You have taken several individuals, each with a different personality, and blended them to make a new unit. Each person is unique and has a special contribution he or she adds to the group. One may be the eternal optimist, seeing everything in a ray of sunshine. Another may be contemplative, thinking long and hard through a decision before making it. These are great attributes in themselves, but sometimes certain "blends" don't mix quite so well. However, we were each made by God to have a certain function in our environment.

Take some time as a family to form a circle and have each member make one positive statement about a certain family member. For example, the first time around, everyone will say an encouraging word about Dad. You may need to establish a few ground rules to avoid comments such as, "I'm thankful my sister wasn't as annoying today as usual."

This may be an eye-opening exercise as heartfelt sentiment spills out. What a way to celebrate your own special blend!

Lord Jesus, thank You for our specially blended family. Help us to encourage one another and be thankful to You for bringing us together. Amen.

Day 206

The Cure for Drought

"He will be like a tree planted by the water that sends out its roots by the stream. It does not fear when heat comes; its leaves are always green. It has no worries in a year of drought and never fails to bear fruit."

Jeremiah 17:8 NIV

Few things are more beautiful than a well-watered, healthy tree. But when nourishment is withheld due to drought, severe damage occurs. The damage doesn't show up immediately—it appears over time, usually from the top of the tree downward, and from the outside inward. Once-shiny leaves become dull, turn brown, roll up, or become misshapen. Leaf-drop occurs prematurely and branches are left bare. A weakened tree, vulnerable to both diseases and pests, may be toppled by a strong wind.

Our spiritual lives are similar. We need nourishment from the Lord. If we ignore Bible reading, prayer, confession, praise, and other forms of communion with God, we enter into a spiritual drought. Busyness may conceal the effects at first, but in time we notice we've become dull to the Lord. Like browning leaves, we lack godly vigor, and our priorities are misshapen. We feel alone and barren—left open to Satan's attacks.

Thankfully, spiritual drought is curable. Jesus says, "Come to me and drink" (John 7:37 NIV). When we thirst, all we have to do is go to the Lord and receive His nourishment.

If you're feeling dull or dry, don't wait. Just go!

Father, forgive me for ignoring my need for You. I am thirsty! Please restore me—draw me to Your side and nourish me with Your living water. Amen.

Day 207

Make It Real

This is now bone of my bones, and flesh of my flesh.
Genesis 2:23 KJV

You're not a figment of anyone's imagination, and the last time you checked, you weren't made of plastic, so why do you keep hearing, "She's not my *real* mom"? What makes a mom "real" anyway? And when do you achieve "real" status in the eyes of your stepchildren?

Relationships can be tricky, especially those where children are involved. Your stepkids probably remember you before you became their mom, and their biological mother may play an active role in their lives. But just because you didn't birth them doesn't mean you don't care about them. Proving that is your greatest task.

Show your stepchildren through your actions that you aren't simply tolerating them because they came with the wedding package. As much as possible, be involved in their lives. Don't allow yourself to be shoved into a corner, dismissed and forgotten because the Real label hasn't been attached yet. The only way to earn bona fide mom status is to act like one. Be available. Be interested. Be. . .motherly! Eventually, your love and commitment to your stepchildren will make you just as real to them as if you were their own flesh and blood.

Dear Lord, let my actions prove my care and devotion to the stepchildren who are a very real part of my life. Amen.

Day 208

An Open Door

I know your [record of] works and what you are doing. See! I have set before you a door wide open which no one is able to shut; I know that you have but little power, and yet you have kept My Word and guarded My message and have not renounced or denied My name.

REVELATION 3:8 AMP

Kay hesitated outside her stepdaughter's bedroom door, wondering if she'd be welcome. As she clutched the Veggie Tales storybook in her hand, its title blurred.

Kay and Elliot had just gotten married. Overnight Kay had become not only a wife but a full-time mother to Emma.

Oh, God, she cried in her heart, *give me wisdom. Give me strength and guidance. I don't know what I'm doing, but You know my heart. Help me welcome Emma into my life and give her the love she needs. Show me a way to teach her about You.*

With a new resolve, Kay stepped through the doorway.

Emma looked up from her toys, saw Kay, smiled, and hopped into bed. "Oh, boy! Are you going to read me a story. . .Mama?"

Kay smiled, walked to her daughter's bed, and reached down to give her a hug.

God knows what's happening in your life. He knows the challenges you face. He's given you an open door, an opportunity to influence a child's life for Him. Don't hesitate. Walk through that door. He'll give you the strength to carry on.

Dear God, You know the challenges before me.
Help me not to hesitate, but to step forward into the
lives of my stepchildren and love them to You. Amen.

Day 209

That Magical Word

He maketh the barren woman to keep house, and to be a joyful mother of children. Praise ye the LORD.

PSALM 113:9 KJV

For over fifteen years their relationship as stepmom and stepdaughter had been a good one. Minimal issues with cross-family differences and no emotionally charged confrontations. The stepdaughter called her by her first name, which was fine—natural. The stepdaughter lived with her mom, but her time in both households was equally divided and enjoyed. Then it came time for the stepdaughter to get married. The event was out of state for everyone—for both families and for the bride and groom.

The stepdaughter called her stepmom and asked if she could meet her in the city where the wedding would be held. Her mom couldn't afford to make the trip. The bride-to-be wanted some help with decisions for the accommodations and more. So stepmom and stepdaughter met at the distant airport. They had a fun-filled three days lining up everything that would make the wedding happen seamlessly.

Much of it all blurs now as the stepmom recalls their wild weekend together. Yet one sweet memory stands out. At the baker's, the stepdaughter introduced the two of them saying, "My mom and I. . ."

Such a "happily ever after" conclusion may not be every stepmom's story. But what a blessing to have isolated moments to hold in our hearts.

Father, You created the family. Thank You for the bonds You strengthen as we grow up and grow together in our blended family. Amen.

Day 210

No More Darkness

But if we walk in the light, as he is in the light, we have fellowship with one another, and the blood of Jesus, his Son, purifies us from all sin.
1 John 1:7 NIV

Is there someone in your family who still lives in darkness? Is it negatively affecting your family life? The Bible tells us that if we will walk in the light of the Lord, we will have true fellowship with one another. True biblical fellowship is impossible unless each family member has committed his or her life to knowing and following Christ. How can you remove the darkness in your relationships? Reach out to your unbelieving family members and share with them the light of Christ. Live your everyday life in a way that pleases God. In doing this, you may actually draw loved ones into a closer relationship with Christ. If Christ is truly making a difference in your life, other people will begin to take notice. Pray for your unbelieving family members and ask God to shine His light into their hearts and bring you together as a family. Only the light of Christ can remove all darkness and create true and meaningful fellowship with God and with one another.

Dear Father, please continue to shine Your light into our hearts. Open the doors that I might share Your love and Your light with my loved ones. Amen.

Hard to Love

Day 211

If anyone says, "I love God," yet hates his brother, he is a liar. For anyone who does not love his brother, whom he has seen, cannot love God, whom he has not seen. And he has given us this command: Whoever loves God must also love his brother.

1 John 4:20–21 NIV

Sometimes, it is easier to love God, whom we can't see, than it is to love the people we must deal with face-to-face on a daily basis. People are flawed. They can be mean. They can be annoying, and loving them is really hard. But God is invisible, and we can just say we love Him and then go on about our business. Right?

Wrong! If we love God, we must love others. Period. When we *really* love God, then His love is born in us. And His love is perfect and complete. His love does not withdraw from us when we are unattractive. It is stronger than steel, more permanent than concrete. And when we love God and He lives in us, then we take on His nature, which is to love—no matter what. If we cannot love the people standing right in front of us, then we do not have the love of God in us!

Dear Father, thank You for loving me in spite of my many flaws. Please teach me to love others the way You love. Amen.

Day 212

Merciful

There will be no mercy for those who have not shown mercy to others. But if you have been merciful, God will be merciful when he judges you.
James 2:13 NLT

A mother caught her stepson in what appeared to be a lie. This wasn't the first time. She'd extended mercy several times in the past—even withheld discipline—only to be lied to again. She wanted her stepson to love her and had bent over backward to try to win his love. But this time was different. She caught him in the act and knew he needed consequences for his actions.

It's hard to know how to balance mercy with discipline, isn't it? God is merciful, but He's also a God of justice. If you're struggling to know how to handle a situation such as this, remember He's the one who decided mercy and justice had to work hand in hand. You really can't have one without the other. Judgment is unavoidable—whether it's from God or from a parent when a child misbehaves. How you dish it out—well, that's something worth praying about.

So take a deep breath, Mom. This is a balancing act, and you're going to need the Lord's help to see you through.

Heavenly Father, it's so hard to know how to balance discipline and mercy. I'll admit I swing back and forth between the two sometimes. One minute I'm all mercy. . .the next minute I'm all judgment. I need Your help to find that healthy place in the middle. Amen.

Your Piece of the Pie

Day 213

The Lord is my portion or share. . .therefore will I hope in Him and wait expectantly for Him.

Lamentations 3:24 AMP

When the proverbial pie is cut into pieces, what happens if you're left out? Maybe you didn't get the cut of time for your much-anticipated coffee date with your husband. You had highlighted it on the calendar, but it still got eaten up by errands he had to run for *his* kids. But just when you think you're getting the short end of the deal, is it possible that the best is straight ahead?

The tribe of Levi, too, may have thought it unfair when they didn't get a portion of land divided up among the tribes of Israel. *What do you mean* "none," *not even an acre?* But that's not the whole story. Instead of going away empty-handed, this priestly line got a portion of everyone else's offerings: animals, grains, meal, and oil. In other words, the Levites got their fingers in every piece of pie! God also blessed them with Himself—He was their portion.

God loves it when He is more satisfying to you than any cut of the pie. Besides, He has a way of providing for another coffee date in a way you'd never expect!

Dear God, if I get grabby about getting my piece of the pie, help me to know that in You I have all I need. Amen.

Day 214

The Right Heart- and Mind-set

I would have lost heart, unless I had believed that I would see the goodness of the Lord in the land of the living.
Psalm 27:13 NKJV

As stepmoms, there are days—sometimes weeks—when we feel as if we are being pummeled by the slings and arrows of misfortune. From meeting the demands of the kids' and our own hectic schedules, to dealing with the other sets of parents, to breaking up arguments between siblings, at times we may begin to lose heart. Our minds become filled with despair as we lose hope of having even one good day.

Yet God's Word, firmly fixed in our minds and hearts, can turn this land of the living upside down—or rather, God-side up! As God's children, daughters of the King Himself, we have the comfort of hope that even in the midst of our present trials we *will* see the goodness of the Lord in the land of the living.

Suffering day- and nightmares? If so, write these words on your heart: "I *will* see the goodness of the Lord—in this day, in this moment, in this life." Believe it. Claim it. Act it.

If we walk in the *faith* of that promise of God's goodness, in due time we will be walking in the *sight* of that goodness. There is no better hope-inducing formula than the words of Psalm 27:13 on our lips, in our mind, and on our heart.

When I feel faint, Lord, bring Your Word into my mind. Keep the thought in front of me that no matter what is happening, I will see Your goodness in my life. Thank You, God, for that assurance, that peace of mind. Amen.

Rest in Jesus' Arms

"Come to me, all of you who are weary and carry heavy burdens, and I will give you rest. Take my yoke upon you. Let me touch you, because I am humble and gentle at heart."

Matthew 11:28–29 NLT

Stepfamilies are wounded. One of the comforts of stepmothering is finding comfort in your husband's arms. One stepmom, Cheryl, remembers that during the early years of their marriage, when she was weak, her husband, Steve, was strong. And when Steve was weak, God gave Cheryl the strength to pick up the slack. The early years of marriage and of starting a new family with Steve were tough.

But Cheryl and Steve ultimately drew their strength from God. He was their source. God never allowed both Cheryl and Steve to falter, and He won't allow both you and your husband to falter, either. Cheryl now says that if she had not had her strong relationship with God, her marriage never would have survived.

If you don't have a relationship with Jesus, why not ask Him into your life today? Jesus knows all about pain and suffering. He promises to give you rest in Him.

Jesus, I ask You into my life today. Please take away my weariness and give me Your strength. Please take over my life and help me live for You. Amen.

Day 216

The Reality of the Wicked Stepmother

For all have sinned and fall short of the glory of God, being justified as a gift by His grace through the redemption which is in Christ Jesus.

Romans 3:23–24 NASB

We've all heard the stories. *Snow White*, *Cinderella*, *Hansel and Gretel*, and dozens of others that are less familiar. What do these stories have in common? A woman raising children she doesn't love, who tries to make their lives as miserable (and as short) as possible: a wicked stepmother.

To women who are trying to raise their stepchildren with love and care, this perennial characterization may seem a bit unfair. But the reality behind this stereotype is found in Romans 3:23: we all sin. We sin against our stepchildren; we sin against our husbands; we sin against perfect strangers. But what the wicked stepmothers in all these fairy tales are missing—which we have—is Jesus. They can't change; after all, their stories have been told, with only minor variations, for centuries. We, however, have the supreme gift of being made new by the power of God's Holy Spirit. Sure, we will still sin; but through repentance and the cleansing power of Jesus' blood, we don't have to keep on living that old, sinful story. We can turn the page and start a new tale.

Without Jesus, we all are wicked stepmothers!

Dear God, thank You that Your mercies are new every morning. Help me to turn from sin and seek righteousness. In Jesus' name, amen.

Rebuffed Affection

Be kindly affectionate to one another with brotherly love, in honor giving preference to one another.
ROMANS 12:10 NKJV

The stepmother put her arms around the child to give a hug. The girl stiffened, not lifting her arms to return the gesture. Hurt filled the mother. Once again she'd been turned away.

How many times have we been hurt by our children? We want to wipe away a hurt or reach out in comfort, only to be rejected by their words or attitudes. This feels very personal, as if they don't care for us at all. In fact, children often don't know how to react to certain situations. They are still learning how to handle hurt. They often react in a way that's inappropriate without meaning to wound anyone.

Our response is not to lash out to cover our emotional injury, but to love, pray, and continue to show affection. If our love is genuine, we can have the hope that the child will understand someday.

Think of all the times when God has reached out to us, yet we have been so hurt that we haven't accepted His offering in a receptive manner. God doesn't turn His back on us. He doesn't give up. He continues to reach out to us, to be there when we need Him the most, even when we aren't grateful. We must allow Him to continue to help us love our children.

Thank You, Lord, for loving me when I've been unlovable. Help me to do likewise. Amen.

Day 218

A Real Perspective

Let us constantly and at all times offer up to God a sacrifice of praise, which is the fruit of lips that thankfully acknowledge and confess and glorify His name.
HEBREWS 13:15 AMP

A Women of Faith conference was overbooked, so the staff brought in narrower chairs to accommodate the crowd. Many women grumbled at the cramped conditions. The presenters turned to Joni Eareckson Tada, a quadriplegic, to address the crowd. "I understand some of you don't like the chair you're sitting in. Well, neither do I! But I've a thousand handicapped friends who'd gladly trade places with you." An immediate hush fell over the group.

Gratitude is an attitude often difficult to express. We're accustomed to comfort. The women at the conference had paid good money to attend, and their expectations were high. But when a comparison was made, few could grumble. We read in scripture about the apostle Paul chained in jail, singing praises to the Lord. How did he do that? He focused on the goodness of God. He made a choice to glorify His name.

Life might be difficult at the moment, but choose to be grateful today. Choose to give thanks to the One who created you. Choose Jesus' way.

Dear heavenly Father, thank You for all You've done for me. I choose to be grateful this day. Amen.

And the Winner Is. . .

Day 219

Words from the mouth of a wise man are gracious,
while the lips of a fool consume him.
ECCLESIASTES 10:12 NASB

"But Dad said I could go to the mall with my friends," Marge's stepdaughter told her. For a moment, Marge wasn't sure what to do. *Should I stick with my initial no, or should I allow her to go? I'm not sure that Clifton really did say that she could go. Besides, she has that book report due tomorrow. But I've had such a difficult time getting close to her, and this might score me some points.*

"Beth," said Marge, "can I ask you something? Did your dad tell you that you could go to the mall with your friends today?"

"Well. . . ," began Beth, "he didn't exactly promise that I could go today."

Marge prayed a quick silent prayer then said, "How about this: I'll drive you to the mall on Friday so that you can shop with your friends. But for now, I remember you said you have a book report due tomorrow. If you need any help, I'd be happy to help out. If not, I can at least keep you supplied with snacks."

Beth gave her a weak smile. "Thanks," she said as she sauntered toward her room.

Marge smiled to herself. She knew this wouldn't be the last time that she and Clifton would be pitted against each other. But somehow, with time, it might get a little bit easier to handle.

Dear Lord, please give me wisdom in making decisions. Help me to remain unified with my husband so that we can together raise our children for You. Amen.

Day 220

An Intimate Relationship

If ye abide in me, and my words abide in you, ye shall ask what ye will, and it shall be done unto you.

John 15:7 KJV

Isn't this a beautiful promise? It is one of those conditional statements that is entirely dependent on the relationship between the two parties involved. Intimacy is implied here.

Jesus knew that the cross was just hours away. He realized that the apostles' faith would be tried in ways they could not begin to comprehend. He wanted them to be prepared when the time came, so He offered this encouragement.

You don't just spend time with the Lord so you get your way. Instead, you love Him so intensely that all you do—your words, desires, actions—are centered around Him and what He knows is best for your life.

Sure, Jesus understands your humanity. He became human so that He could understand. However, when your goal is Christlikeness, He is excited to help you on your journey.

Are your desires the same as Christ's desires? He knows what is going on with your life and with your family, but He wants you to share it with Him. He wants you to love Him so deeply that you begin to acknowledge that He really does know what is best for you.

I surrender all to You, Lord. Let Your will be my desire. Amen.

Clothed with Compassion

As God's chosen people, holy and dearly loved, clothe yourselves with compassion, kindness, humility, gentleness and patience.
Colossians 3:12 NIV

April's face was downcast as she gazed blankly at Prince Caspian, her little hand gripping a red crayon, frozen above the coloring book page.

Wendy watched her stepdaughter, a little girl who'd recently been abandoned by her birth mother. Mentally stepping into April's shoes, Wendy found her mind drifting back to her own childhood. *Perhaps April feels like I did when my father died: alone, abandoned, wondering if I'd done something wrong for things to turn out that way. Wondering if anyone would love me like he had.*

As light dawned in her mind, compassion warmed her heart. Quietly, Wendy closed her book and rose from her chair, careful not to startle her stepdaughter from her reverie. Once lying on the floor beside the child, Wendy picked up a crayon and began coloring the adjacent page of the Narnia book.

Feeling April's eyes on her, Wendy stopped coloring, put her arm around April, and looked into her eyes. "Sweetie, you are God's perfect child and my precious little girl. And you know what? Nothing will ever keep Jesus and me from loving you to bits. You can count on it. 'Kay?"

April gave a little smile, nodded, and began coloring again.

Sometimes, all a child needs is your love and compassion. Give them today.

Lord, fill me with Your love to overflowing. Help me to understand my children, to look upon them with compassion, and to shower them with the love they so desperately need. Amen.

Day 222

Jesus Climbing In

They all saw him and were terrified. Immediately he spoke to them and said, "Take courage! It is I. Don't be afraid." Them he climbed into the boat with them, and the wind died down. They were completely amazed.

Mark 6:50–51 niv

Jesus announced His presence to the disciples in the boat and encouraged them to be courageous because their fear was threatening to keep them away from their Savior. When does our fear do the same thing? When steplife winds are blowing fiercely and paddling farther away seems the preferable choice? Or when a cloud of anger, disrespect, distrust, and hostility hangs over our home and sucks all the joy away into a dark, unreachable place? We might see Jesus, too, but be as terrified as the disciples were.

Maybe we'll see Him in the mirror, revealing to us a stepmom still strong and capable despite the conditions. Maybe we'll see Him in the softened eyes of a stepchild or the understanding of a friend. Maybe we'll see Him in our efforts to forgive and reach out where we've been rejected before, refusing once again to give up.

We can be sure that in our most frightening storm is where Jesus will be. We may not recognize Him at first because of our fear, but He will be there to encourage us, to strengthen us, to climb into the horror with us, and to amaze us with His grace and power. Let's not miss it.

Father, thank You for being unafraid to weather my storms with me. Please help me find the courage You supply and steer this craft where You choose. Amen.

The Highest Priority

Christ is faithful as a son over God's house. And we are his house, if we hold on to our courage and the hope of which we boast.
Hebrews 3:6 NIV

Is God on your list of things to do today? When our days fill up with life's busyness, we can be tempted to look at our quiet time with God as a task instead of a desire just to be with Him. Everything He has ever done, He did with you in mind and with one purpose: to spend His time with you.

Prayer is as easy as intimate conversation with a very close friend. The things that are important to you are important to Him. He wants to know you and you to know Him. He wants to hear about your days—the great ones as well as those that are difficult.

Friendships that mean the most in our lives take priority. You make time for those who are closest to you. God wants you to make Him a person of priority in your life. The more time you spend with Him, the greater your desire grows to get to know Him better. Suddenly, you'll find that you can't wait to talk to Him, to tell Him just how much He means to you.

Dear God, help me to know You intimately. Show me how to open up to You and share my life with You. I want to know You and hear Your voice. I will make You a priority in my life today. Amen.

Day 224

Peace in Troubled Times

"I have told you these things, so that in me you may have peace. In this world you will have trouble. But take heart! I have overcome the world."
JOHN 16:33 NIV

Escalating gas prices. Housing slumps. Rising food costs. Today's world reflects troubled times. Front-page news highlights murders, poverty, and war. Television coverage echoes more of the same. Jesus warns us to expect trouble in this world. That is not what we want to hear! We yearn for calm waters, not turbulent ones. Local and world events may leave us feeling overwhelmed, helpless, and defeated.

But there is good news! Jesus tells us to take heart. He reminds us of truth: He has overcome the world. What reassurance and hope! Although we live in this world, heaven is our permanent home. Because Jesus has overcome death, we will, too. We must keep our focus on Jesus as we walk through troubled times on earth. He will walk with us *through* the valleys—implying that we will make it to the other side. It is possible to experience peace amid the turmoil. Jesus is the Prince of Peace. Bring your burdens to Him. Receive the peace He promises. Take heart by embracing the eternal victory He has won for you!

Dear Lord, may my eyes remain focused on You through these troubled times. Impart peace to my heart. Amen.

Old Testament 101

Day 225

"I will pour out my Spirit on all people. Your sons and daughters will prophesy, your old men will dream dreams, your young men will see visions. Even on my servants, both men and women, I will pour out my Spirit in those days."
Joel 2:28–29 NIV

Since Ashley knew little about the Old Testament, she studied every day.

At first the prophet Joel scared her. He declared sinners could expect severe punishment from God. But she also read how God pleaded with His people to repent so He could bless them. God wanted to pour out His Spirit on the old and young, men and women alike. When Ashley realized the disciple Peter quoted the above passage during his Pentecost sermon, she felt excited. It applied not only to Old Testament Jews, but to her, Ashley Simmons! But both passages mentioned the sun darkening and the moon turning to blood. When would these and other strange events occur? She wondered if her future would bring the scary times Joel described. And what was that about locusts?

When Ashley asked her pastor these questions, he agreed some parts of the Old Testament are difficult to understand. But he said bottom line is that both the Old and New Testaments teach us that God wants to forgive us and pour out His Spirit on us. Although we don't understand His time frame, and we may live through frightening times, God loves us and will take care of us.

That Ashley understood very well.

Father, as I read Your Word, help me comprehend Your heart! Amen.

What Seems Right

There is a way that seems right to a man, but its end is the way to death.
Proverbs 14:12 ESV

Have you ever noticed how the *wisdom* of this world changes? Some of the most knowledgeable scholars of every age have given lectures and advice on everything from child rearing to marriage to education. It's interesting to see how the "next new thing" in each area will soon be old, tired, and outdated.

Take education, for example. One year the open concept classroom was all the rage; the next year fully enclosed classrooms were the thing. When giving parenting advice, some experts insist on strict schedules and rules, while others preach independence and creativity. And while many experts make good points, not one of them will ever have the complete truth. The advice of this expert or that one may seem right today, but just wait awhile. Things will change.

Human wisdom is always incomplete, always fallible. But God's wisdom is perfect and will never fail. When we base our lives on the wisdom of this world, we will always end up flat on our faces, for man's wisdom will shift under our feet. God's wisdom, on the other hand, is unchanging, steady, and strong. When we build our lives on His proven, perfect Word, we will always have the stability that comes only from God. Man's way leads to destruction—every single time. God, and God alone, will lead us to the peaceful, joyful, abundant lives we desire.

Dear Father, please help me to recognize faulty, worldly wisdom. Help me to base my life on You alone. Amen.

Tough Love

That they may teach the young women. . .to love their children.
Titus 2:4 KJV

How interesting that the Bible would command that women be *taught* to love their children. Surely such a thing comes naturally! But as a stepparent, you know that loving someone else's child as your own can be very complicated. Some days you don't even like your husband's kids, let alone love them; and you have a sneaking suspicion that the feeling is mutual. Times can be difficult; and after a particularly trying event, you may find yourself wondering why you even bother.

The truth is that love doesn't always come naturally. When your efforts are held at bay by prickly rejections, you may feel like washing your hands of the whole mess. But children need loving the most when they deserve it the least. And like God, you must overlook unlovable behavior to see the greater need within.

Love is the essential ingredient to a happy relationship with your stepchildren. It is the difference between enjoying and merely enduring them. No matter how difficult it seems, keep trying. Nurturing loving relationships with your stepchildren may not be easy, but it will be worth it all someday.

Lord, teach me to love my husband's children whether they return love or not, and remind me that You loved me even when I was unlovable. Amen.

Day 228

Dark and Dreary Days

Create in me a pure heart, O God, and renew a steadfast spirit within me.
PSALM 51:10 NIV

Moms often face tough situations, not only with stepchildren, but also with our biological kids. It's tempting to glamorize families that don't have to deal with the same problems that blended families do, as if sharing DNA makes them immune to conflict. It helps to remember that everybody's household faces its share of problems. Even Jesus' Nazareth home was not untouched by difficulties.

Raised in a modest household in a poor village, Jesus slogged through days that felt as though they would never end. He acted as referee to His bickering brothers. He witnessed the despair on His mother's face when Joseph, His earthly father, passed away. We don't know much about Jesus' childhood and young adulthood, but what we do know is that He held on, steadfast. And as a man, we see even more evidence that Jesus persevered through the tough stuff. It was His way.

When we hit tough times, it's easy to want to strike back or to quit. But if we hang in there through the tough stuff, the rewards eventually come.

Lord Jesus, You know. You've lived in a family, You've felt the sting of being unappreciated, You might even have felt like an outsider among Your brothers. Right now, I lift my heavy thoughts and overcast feelings to You. Give me Your strength to "hang in there." Amen.

Day 229

Do I Hear a Tap at the Door?

Mary got ready and hurried to a town. . .where she entered Zechariah's home and greeted Elizabeth.
LUKE 1:39–40 NIV

When "stepping" into a new family blend, you may need, more than anything else, a friend who is also in the process of stretching beyond her comfort zone. Perhaps that's why Mary, the expectant mother of Jesus, went to visit her cousin Elizabeth, also pregnant.

Mary, a young teen, brightened the day of this woman old enough to be her grandmother. From the town of Nazareth to the Judean hills, encouragement traveled right to Elizabeth's door. Beyond simply "girl" talk, their even greater bond was a mutual desire to trust and magnify the Lord. With each pregnancy being a story of its own, they surely took comfort in knowing there'd be somebody else going through major adjustments, someone else experiencing bumps in the road.

When you think you're the only one stretching to the *n*th degree, God may well send a stepmom your way. Not only will her presence lift your spirits, but long after she's gone, her fragrance of hope and encouragement will linger.

Wait, do I hear a tap at the door?

Dear God, help me to believe that You will send me the stepmom brighteners that I need. Amen.

Oneness

"Holy Father, protect them by the power of your name—the name you gave me—so that they may be one as we are one."

John 17:11 niv

As Jesus made preparation for leaving this world physically, He prayed one of the longest recorded prayers in the New Testament. He didn't ask His Father to protect His disciples and future followers from hard times, broken relationships, or even martyrdom. He asked God to protect them so that they would be one.

When we pray for the children God has brought into our lives, we pray for many things. Have we ever thought to invoke God's protection so that we might be one as a family? Could it be that the greatest warfare being waged against us as a family unit has—at its core—the dismantling of our oneness? Is the realm of the spiritual world where our biggest battles originate?

Christ knew that if His small band of men didn't have a sense of oneness from the beginning, Christianity would not last until His return. The disciples would never be men who "turned the world upside down" for good and for God's glory (Acts 17:6 kjv). For Christianity to take root, they had to be one. It wouldn't just happen. It would take the power of God's name to pull it off.

We need to pray for unity and oneness in our blended families. Only in the protective name of our holy God will it happen.

Dear Father, protect us as a family. Protect us from discord and infighting. In the powerful name of Jesus, amen.

Everything We Need

Day 231

His divine power has given us everything we need for life and godliness through our knowledge of him who called us by his own glory and goodness.

2 Peter 1:3 NIV

God is so good! He has given us everything we need to live a godly life on this earth. He has given us His Word to follow. He has given us the Holy Spirit to dwell in us, to guide us, and to speak truth to us through the reading of the Word. He didn't leave us here to flounder around on our own. He knew that we wouldn't be able to carry on without Him, so He made provision for that. We have everything we need to live a life worthy of the Lord. We can be all that He wants us to be, because of His power at work in us!

Because of His power at work in us, we can get through any problem we face. Because of His power at work in us, we can share His love and hope with others. Because of His power at work in us, we have everything we need for life and godliness!

Dear heavenly Father, thank You for providing everything I need to live a godly life. Help me to be dependent on You in every situation. Amen.

Day 232

His, Mine, Ours

Therefore, as God's chosen people, holy and dearly loved, clothe yourselves with. . .patience.
Colossians 3:12 NIV

When you blended with your husband's family, many changes happened immediately. You may have been thrust into instant motherhood, or you may have added to your brood. Perhaps you needed to find employment or you ended your job in the workplace to stay at home and run the household. All the while, you wanted to make your man the happiest, most fulfilled male on the face of the planet. That's no small undertaking!

In addition to the physical toll, you added some mental and emotional stress, for certain. High expectations—whether self-imposed or imposed by others—can be draining. You may have determined to win over your husband's kids, parents, extended family, and friends immediately. Although that would be ideal, unfortunately it isn't always realistic. Changes in family dynamics take some time to process.

Allow time for everyone to work through the transition. Some may welcome you overnight. Some may take a little longer. Pray daily for those who seem to be having a more difficult time adjusting. Remember, God has made them and has you in their lives for a purpose. Praise Him for this opportunity He has provided for you to show His love.

Dear Jesus, thank You for each new person in my life as a result of my marriage. Above all, help me to point others to You. Amen.

Day 233

Steel Magnolias

This is how we know what love is: Jesus Christ laid down his life for us. And we ought to lay down our lives for our brothers.
1 John 3:16 NIV

Wow. Love holds a pretty high standard. Jesus died for us because He loves us. Does this mean He wants us to die for others?

Probably not. As a matter of fact, He wants us to do the opposite. He wants us to live for others. Sometimes, dying would be easier! Living for others often means giving up our own personal desires and letting others have their way.

Does that mean He wants us to be doormats? Of course not. A doormat is weak and flimsy. Jesus wants us to have the steel kind of love—beautiful and solid. It carries the kind of strength that will endure hardship and discomfort so others will not have to. It is the kind of strength that goes without food so another can eat, sleeps on the floor so another can have the bed, stands in the shadows so another can shine. The love Jesus wants for us is the kind of love that will give life to other people and, in the process, will truly set us free from bondage to our own selfish desires!

Dear Father, I want the love I have for others to be strong and solid, not weak and flimsy. Please help me to love like You love. Amen.

Sweet Waters

Doth a fountain send forth at the same place sweet water and bitter?
James 3:11 KJV

Do you ever feel like Dr. Jekyll and Mr. Hyde all rolled into one person? You're sweet, innocent Dorothy one minute and the Wicked Witch of the West the next? Maybe you return home from a Bible study on a spiritual high. Nothing can get to you. You walk in the door to discover the kids left the house in a mess and forgot to feed the dog—again. Immediately you snap. Oh, you don't mean to, but you do. All of that sweetness goes sailing right out the window.

It's hard to be even-keeled, isn't it? Life moves at a rapid pace, and our situations change quickly. We make up our minds to be one way, then something comes along to change all of that. We do—or say—the very thing we promised ourselves *not* to do or say.

Today, focus on the words that come from your mouth. Make sure the water is sweet! But remember, it's really the heart that's speaking. So you might need to spend a little time with the Lord to deal with those heart issues.

Dear Lord, my tongue gets me in trouble so often! I want to tame it, but I know it's really my heart that needs the taming. Lord, I know that no bitterness comes out of You. May my heart beat like Your heart—not just today, but always. Amen.

Part of the Process

Work willingly at whatever you do, as though you were working for the Lord rather than for people. Remember that the Lord will give you an inheritance as your reward, and that the Master you are serving is Christ.

COLOSSIANS 3:23–24 NLT

As overwhelming as the job of stepparenting can sometimes be, there is one truth that takes some of the pressure off: The children God puts in our care are not truly ours; they are the Lord's. Like us, they are His children (1 John 3:1), His unique, precious creations. We, as parents, are merely God's servants, people He uses to work His will.

Our goal is to serve God as best we can by loving, protecting, guiding, and providing for our children—spiritually, emotionally, and physically. We are only their guardians for a season. But they are His—mind, body, spirit, and soul—forever.

There will be times when our kids may not like us—or even love us. But that cannot dissuade us from setting a godly example. Bestow that unconditional love, show them the path to God's door, and leave the rest up to Him. He has His eye on them. He already knows their past, present, and future. He even knows how many hairs they have on their heads! Amazing.

So do your best, thank God for allowing you to be a part of His process, and leave the rest to the Father.

Thank You, Lord, for blessing me with children. Help me to set a godly example, love them as You love me, and leave the rest in Your hands. Amen.

Day 236

God Who?

And these words, which I command thee this day, shall be in thine heart: and thou shalt teach them diligently unto thy children.
Deuteronomy 6:6–7 KJV

The story of our great Creator has been told since Adam and Eve first began tucking their children in at night. Handed down through the generations, it is the single most important inheritance that parents can give, and it is the reason that God gave you to your stepchildren.

Choosing to become a stepmom affords you the same duties that women all over the world are given at the birth of their babies: to love, nurture, protect, provide for, and prepare them for life and eternity. As a Christian, you bear the responsibility of teaching your stepchildren to discern good from evil and right from wrong. To foster morality and values that don't come instinctively.

Whether your husband's kids came to you as infants or adults, you have an obligation to teach them about God. Show them through your actions what it means to be a follower of Christ. Lead them by example, and let your deeds consistently match the Word. You don't need a soapbox or a pulpit to spread the message. Living the life before them speaks volumes more than any flowery sermon could. In all of the busy responsibilities of stepmotherhood, don't neglect to pass the torch of God to the next generation.

Dear Father, let my life be a godly example to my stepchildren so that I might guide them to the Way of Life. Amen.

Broken Vessels

Day 237

"Can I not, O house of Israel, deal with you as this potter does?" declares the Lord*. "Behold, like the clay in the potter's hand, so are you in My hand, O house of Israel."*

Jeremiah 18:6 nasb

She kept a certain vase in a corner of her desk, filled with pens and pencils, a ruler, and a pair of scissors. Once it had been shiny, new, and perfect, but time had marred it. Now it was scratched and chipped and laced with the glue lines of repaired cracks. Over the years, friends and relatives had noticed it and given her lovely new vases for birthday and Christmas presents, but she had never replaced it. She kept it as a reminder to herself that what looks like brokenness to others may be the hand of the Master Potter.

We become stepmoms through brokenness. Whether through death or divorce in our own lives or the life of our spouse, new stepfamilies join together with the cracks of previous loss. Death and divorce are often ugly and very far from what God had in mind for us when He gave Eve to Adam in the Garden of Eden. It is hard to get over the loss of that marital ideal. But God can—and *is*—using our experiences for His purposes.

Give thanks for the brokenness. Let God use it to glue you and your family into a shape that truly glorifies Him.

Dear Father, I praise You for how You are working in my life. Help me remember daily that You are the Potter and I am the clay. Amen.

Day 238

Encourage One Another

But encourage one another daily, as long as it is called Today, so that none of you may be hardened by sin's deceitfulness.

Hebrews 3:13 NIV

No one in Sherry's mother's family thought she should attend college. No one else in the family had gone, and her mother said Sherry didn't have what it took to be a college student. Discouraged, Sherry sought advice from her father and stepmother. They both encouraged her to do what she wanted to do and to follow her dreams. They promised to help in any way they could.

Her father arranged for Sherry to interview for a scholarship. She was accepted, and her tuition was paid for. Her stepmother encouraged Sherry in her dream to become a teacher by helping with college applications and paying her room and board. With their support, Sherry went on to earn her bachelor's degree and her master of education degree. Their encouragement built a trust between Sherry and her parents that lasted through the years.

Words can build or destroy. When you encourage your stepchildren when they have self-doubts, you build a bridge. You help build their confidence and their self-esteem, which will lead to trust. It is not an overnight thing, but something you will need to do every day the son or daughter is with you. Building trust takes patience and endurance. As you are helping your child, you keep your own heart open and ready for God's guidance.

Heavenly Father, may our words spoken today be those that will build bridges and encourage our children to be the best they can be for You. Amen.

A Time for Everything

A time to tear and a time to mend, a time to be silent and a time to speak.
Ecclesiastes 3:7 NIV

This passage from Ecclesiastes teaches that there is a time for everything under the sun. As families blend, it is often a time for tearing down. Routines change, housing arrangements change, family structures change, and nothing feels stable or familiar. The best way to deal with this is to recognize that a tearing is taking place and accept and understand what is happening.

Tearing is often a process that cannot be rushed, but discussing it together as a family can be helpful. Initially, it may seem to cause more tearing as grievances are aired, loyalties are tested, and anger expressed. Don't give up, because out of this process the mending will begin. It may be slow at first. A stitch here, a building block there, but with open communication, new routines and relationships will begin to grow.

The best thing to do as mother in the household is to be available. Take time to listen and embrace family members with loving arms. If this is not acceptable, hold them up in prayer. Ask God to bring peace as feelings settle and the tearing process is worked through, and ask Him to bring wholeness to each person involved.

Dear God, the process of tearing can be painful and uncomfortable. Use me as a vessel to bring healing to the hearts of my family. Amen.

Day 240

Redeemer's Hope

For I know that my Redeemer lives, and He shall stand at last on the earth; and after my skin is destroyed, this I know, that in my flesh I shall see God.

JOB 19:25–26 NKJV

Raising children can be tough. At times we feel like an utter failure—like there is no way to repair our relationship with our child. We've made so many mistakes. We've said hurtful words that we can't take back. We've seen the damage reflected in that child's eyes, and it hurts so much.

Every parent faces moments like these. Sometimes it is more than a moment and seems to go on for days or weeks. We despair. We ache inside and out. The desire to reach out and heal the hurt is there, but we aren't able to do anything. As a parent, we want to fix what we've broken, but sometimes that isn't possible for us to do.

In the midst of the worst suffering any person could face, Job shows us what is important. The one truth that we can cling to when we hurt so much is that Jesus, our Redeemer, lives. He loves us. He is waiting for us. He hurts when we hurt, and He knows our every need. We can trust and rest in the hope we have in Him.

Jesus, You are my Redeemer and my Hope. Help me to be comforted in that and to truly know Your love. Amen.

What Possesses Us

Day 241

Then he said to them, "Watch out! Be on your guard against all kinds of greed; a man's life does not consist in the abundance of his possessions."
LUKE 12:15 NIV

It's easy to dwell on the "unfairness" of steplife. Someone always feels slighted, left out, taken advantage of, or overlooked. Someone always has more, and we can often grasp at possessions or covet what others have because of the seeming inequality of it all. And while we all need what we need, any undue attention to possessions simply masks something more important—what possesses *us*.

Is it greed? Is that what truly motivates us and steers our minds and hearts through the day? Or is it fear? Are we afraid someone else will have more and we'll be somehow less because of it? If greed or fear is possessing us, we can escape. We can change, overcome, and give ourselves to something better: generosity.

Being possessed by generosity—among other good things, such as understanding and mercy and grace—allows us to live Jesus' point. We focus on something more important, even in the grips of a steplife trauma or assault, because Jesus' point underscores God's forever premise: that we receive more only when we give away what we've been given. Let's start in our heart.

Father, I pray that You will possess me above all else. Please help me to reflect You to my family in every way, with generosity, grace, love, and compassion. Amen.

Day 242

Nothing Is Too Hard for God

Behold, I am the Lord, the God of all flesh: is there anything too hard for me?
Jeremiah 32:27 KJV

It's tough making one family from two families, isn't it? Don't give up. God wanted you to put your families together, and He will make sure your children and your husband's children bond as siblings. One day your kids will be good to one another and will love one another. One day you will be a strong family.

Even if your stepchildren spit venom at you today, they will appreciate you as a mother someday. Even if they blame you for mothering them in place of their biological mother today, one day they will remember that you were there for them when they needed you.

Sometimes it's comforting to remember that God is the only One who can change hearts. Only the Holy Spirit can get inside someone and turn hatred into love. Pray for your children and stepchildren every day. Ask God to help them love you, your husband, and each other. Pray that God will soften everyone's hearts and mold you into the family He wants you to be.

Remember—God is in the miracle business. Nothing is too hard for God!

Thank You, dear God, for changing hearts in my family so that we can love one another. I love You. In Jesus' name, amen.

Perfect Peace

You will keep in perfect peace all who trust in you, all whose thoughts are fixed on you!
Isaiah 26:3 NLT

While you're driving, do you constantly contemplate your car's inner workings? At home, do you stare at the lights and continually ponder the marvels of electricity? Do you clutch your bank card while meditating on the integrity of the banking system? Probably not. You just trust your car to get you where you need to go; you know that when you flip the switch the lights will come on; and you trust the bank to cover your checks and give you your money when you make a withdrawal. You just trust these things to happen without giving much thought to them.

However, when it comes to God, you not only need to trust Him, you also need to fix your thoughts on Him. Think about Him so much that He becomes the foundation of every thought, the basis for every word you speak, and the premise for every action. Make God's presence in your mind as sure as His presence in your heart. Let Him occupy your every thought, and trust Him with that difficult decision, touchy situation, or strained relationship. In return, He promises to keep you "in perfect peace." Not a bad trade.

Dear Lord, I'm trading in my worries and frustrations for Your peace. Please transform my mind so that my thoughts are fixed on You. Amen.

Day 244

Desires and Secret Petitions

Delight yourself also in the Lord, and He will give you the desires and secret petitions of your heart.
PSALM 37:4 AMP

God's promise in this verse is universal for His children. Delight in Him, and He will give us the desires of our hearts. What are your desires for your husband, your children, your stepchildren? What are your desires for yourself? Maybe you've never expressed your most secret desires aloud. But you can know that if your desires are in line with God's Word, our loving heavenly Father placed them there.

God delights in us, and He desires that we would delight in Him. But many times, the pressures of life, of expectations (whether our own or placed on us by someone else), of hopes and dreams steal away our quiet times with our Savior. When this happens, try getting up a little earlier—or stay up a little later if you're a night owl—and focus on Jesus. Remember how He has led you in the past. Claim His promises that He will never leave you nor forsake you. Revel in His love for you. Delight in Him. Delight in the small pleasures He sends each day. Make it a practice to look for Him everywhere. And rejoice when He gives you your desires and answers the secret petitions you've never shared with anyone else.

God is good, and He delights in blessing His children with good things. Trust Him with your deepest desires today.

Lord, please remind me that You want what's best for me. Help me to keep my focus always on You. Amen.

Think about These Things

Day 245

Finally, brothers, whatever is true, whatever is noble, whatever is right, whatever is pure, whatever is lovely, whatever is admirable—if anything is excellent or praiseworthy—think about such things.
Philippians 4:8 NIV

This family is too hard! I can't get through to the kids, and I'm exhausted from trying. No one cares how I feel. Even money is running low. Why should I bother? Tomorrow will just bring more of the same.

Have negative thoughts like these ever plagued you? If not, they undoubtedly will. Life has a way of overwhelming us from time to time—especially when problems in several arenas pile up at once.

Satan lies in wait for such moments. Sensing weakness, he launches a barrage of lies like flaming arrows aimed for our hearts and minds. He longs to derail our faith. We can and must fight back! Recognizing the battle is the first step. When fear-filled thoughts assail you, raise your shield. Reject the negatives that cross your mind, and replace them with affirmations of *anything* excellent or praiseworthy.

Look around—God is near! Praise Him for every need He's met, large and small. Has He sent a friend your way? Do you have food to eat? Are you able to walk, talk, think, or speak? These are excellent gifts from God. Allow nature to enchant you. Meditate on scripture and ponder the greatness of God. You'll find that Satan's lies cannot infiltrate a heart filled with praise.

Father, help me refocus my attention on Your faithfulness during this trial. You are worthy of all my praise! Amen.

Day 246

God Knows Best

"I know that You can do all things, and that no purpose of Yours can be thwarted."
JOB 42:2 NASB

Emma got laid off, and as she scoured the classifieds, she prayed that God would lead her to a new job. Soon she read about a job opportunity. The schedule would prevent her from picking up the kids after school, but she knew something would work out. After a promising interview and lots of prayers, Emma found out she didn't get the job. She was crushed, and she couldn't understand why God had disappointed her.

A few days later, the phone rang. The caller explained that she had spoken to an associate who mentioned Emma. The caller thought Emma sounded like a perfect fit for her company. Emma listened, dumbstruck, as the woman described the job as one that perfectly combined her experience and interests, was mornings only, and provided a better income than her previous job! Two weeks later Emma was employed again and still able to pick up her kids. As Emma reflected on all that had happened, she praised God. The first job would have been fine, but the second was perfect.

Sometimes we forget that God has a plan for us that He alone can see. While we may think we know what's best, we should remember that God has the big picture in mind. He can do anything, and His purpose for our lives cannot be thwarted.

Dear Lord, You can do all things. Please help me to trust that You see the big picture and that You have plans for me that I cannot envision. Amen.

God—Our Knight in Shining Armor

"Be strong and courageous! Don't be afraid or discouraged because of the. . .mighty army, for there is a power far greater on our side! . . .We have the LORD our God to help us and to fight our battles for us!"
2 CHRONICLES 32:7–8 NLT

There are times in our lives when we feel alone, as if we are going through what no one has ever gone through before. We hesitate to reach out, not wanting to bring anyone else down with our sorrows; or perhaps we are embarrassed to share about our situation. We then find ourselves closing up into a protective shell with an all-consuming despair not far behind.

Don't allow the army of despair and its soldiers—depression and discouragement—to defeat you. Seek help in the "big three." Start with prayer to the Man of Sorrows. He understands pain and rejection. Let Him know what you're feeling. Then seek consolation in the Bible, especially the Psalms, where you'll find amazing words of comfort. And, finally, look to fellow believers—a friend, pastor, older woman, someone you trust. Bare your soul, allowing the pain to come to the surface, the tears to flow.

By reaching out to God, His Word, and fellow believers, we find hope, love, and comfort. Once unburdened, we can put things in perspective. Most importantly, we can leave everything in God's hands, remembering He has promised to fight the battle for us.

Abba, You know what I'm up against. Don't allow me to be defeated by despair. Come to my aid by Your presence, through Your Word, and via a fellow believer. Make me strong and courageous! Amen.

Day 248

Mission Possible

"The kingdom of David is like a fallen tent, but in that day I will set it up again and mend its broken places. I will rebuild its ruins as it was before."

AMOS 9:11 NCV

Suzanne grew up in a Christian home and attended a Christian college. She met a wonderful guy named Matt who wanted to be a pastor. Suzanne dreamed of working in Christian education. When they became engaged, everybody celebrated! Suzanne anticipated a happy-ever-after life with a successful ministry and a Christian home.

But fifteen years later, Suzanne—weary from their demanding lifestyle and parenting four children—met a married Christian man who made her feel special. She walked away from Matt and her family and married Adam. Only over time did the two realize how much they hurt their ex-spouses and, especially, their children. The little ones clung to them, crying. The older kids wanted nothing to do with them.

"Oh, God, can You ever forgive us?"

Distraught, Suzanne and Adam sought biblical counseling. Confessing their sin, they subjected themselves to church discipline and slowly, with God's help, began to rebuild their lives and those of their children.

Some days Suzanne despaired of recovery. They and their families would bear scars until heaven healed them. But Jesus, who died so the broken could be repaired, would hold them together.

Holy Lord, how sin devastates a family! But if we repent, You can do the impossible. Thank You for Your sweet, powerful grace. Amen.

Just for Today

Therefore do not worry about tomorrow, for tomorrow will worry about its own things. Sufficient for the day is its own trouble.

MATTHEW 6:34 NKJV

Author Max Lucado says, "Worry is to joy what a vacuum cleaner is to dirt; you might as well attach your heart to a happiness-sucker and flip the switch." What a word picture. In the Sermon on the Mount, Jesus warned the people to drop their anxiety concerning their future and focus on the present.

What a difficult concept in today's world. With Day-Timers, BlackBerries, cell phones, and the Internet, we're in constant contact with others, yet are we focused on the here and now? How often we overlook the small pleasures God has put before us. The old adage "Take time to smell the roses" can become difficult in our hurry-scurry lives. Yet joy can be found when we stop and see a baby's smile, wildflowers, dirty dishes indicating a completed meal, or a pile of laundry showing our closets are full.

Jesus taught us to pray, "Give us this day our daily bread." We won't get the wisdom or resources to handle tomorrow's problems until we need them. God is faithful; He will provide. So relax and trust. Flip off the fretting switch and experience some joy.

Dear Lord, thank You for Your daily provisions. I bless Your name. Amen.

Unlocking the Heart

Let the words of my mouth and the meditation of my heart be acceptable in Your sight, O Lord, my strength and my Redeemer.

Psalm 19:14 NKJV

The desire for relationship is in your DNA. We all long for the mental, emotional, and physical benefits of relationship—especially when it comes to your new family dynamic. You want everyone to get along, but the natural tendency is to bicker, fight, and divide. This has been human nature since the devil targeted relationships in the Garden of Eden when Adam and Eve were separated from God by their sin.

God's heart is for reconciliation—to Himself and to one another. Relationships die over the stupidest things. Is proving who's right or wrong really worth the conflict and division? That's what the enemy is after—division. He wants to isolate each family member so he can conquer you and your family.

It's time to stop keeping score—instead, go to one another in love and be reconciled. Conflicts arise less frequently when we stay in the flow of God's presence. And a willingness to forgive can open the heart and allow God's love to flow and build a new relationship.

Dear God, help me not to be overly sensitive to the things that are said. Help me to understand my new family members and see them the way You do, and to speak to them with love and understanding. Amen.

All Sales Final

And the mother of the child said, As the LORD liveth, and as thy soul liveth, I will not leave thee.
2 KINGS 4:30 KJV

The popular saying is that children don't come with an instruction manual. But as a stepmom, you also know that they don't come with a gift receipt. Unlike sheet sets and toasters, your stepchildren can't be returned for a full refund or exchanged for a different product. They can't be discarded or donated to charity if they don't work out, and there is no 100 percent satisfaction guarantee.

This truth should be a matter of fact; but the sad reality is that too many parents have tried to get rid of their kids, and the results have been disastrous. Foster systems are full of unwanted children who often grow up to be insecure, embittered adults. Such tragedy is the result of selfishness and plays no role in the Christian family.

Your vow to remain faithful to the man you married applies to his children as well. Your stepkids have learned through experience that nothing endures forever and may wonder just how long *you* will last. Strive to convince them that, for better or worse, your commitment to them and their father is authentic. Show them that your choice to be their stepmother is one you take seriously, and your word is a warranty that will never expire.

Dear God, in this world of broken promises, help me to be a covenant keeper. Give me the grace to fulfill my vows as a wife and stepmother. Amen.

Regrets

Then said Jesus, Father, forgive them; for they know not what they do.
Luke 23:34 KJV

Regrets: the one thing we all possess but wish we didn't. Ignorance is responsible for many of our regrets. At the time we might be oblivious to the hurt caused by our actions or words. Perhaps years later we realize the pain that was levied by our own hands. Second chances are rare. Mistakes have consequences. Going back is not an option. So where should we go?

Forgiveness is the first step. As Jesus was being nailed to the cross, He extended forgiveness. He knew the men seeking His death were spiritually blind. They were unable to see that He was the promised Messiah who was willing to die so they might have eternal life. If Jesus forgave them, He will forgive you. There is no sin so big that Jesus' blood cannot cover it.

After receiving His forgiveness, forgive yourself. Let go of the pain, regret, or shame. Commit to going forward, not looking back. Ask the Lord to give you wisdom so that you won't live in ignorance. Think before speaking. Pray before taking action. Be guided and directed by the Lord. Then regrets will become fewer and fewer. The future will look bright and the past not so dark. Go forward in His love and forgiveness to embrace the life He has for you.

Dear Lord, forgive me for my past failings. Help me forgive myself so I don't live life with regret. Amen.

Excuse Me, Excuse Me, and Excuse Me!

I give eternal life to them. . .and no one will snatch them out of My hand.
John 10:28 NASB

"Excuse me, please!" It's hard to keep from bumping into others in crowded malls or busy airports, but the toughest challenge may come when you're in tight situations with your stepchildren's other family. *Should I step this way? On second thought, I'll take this side. Or should I make a run for it?* So, is there any spot to simply *be*?

Jesus has just the place for you: in His hand. This safe place isn't awkward or crowded, nor do you constantly have to wonder if you're in the way. He knows where you really belong, and that's in Him. In that security, Jesus also helps you find your way through the helter-skelter of life. With His ease and confidence directing your steps, you can get to where you need to go without taking anyone down in the process.

Poised with grace, you'll know when to stand in support of your husband, when to step aside out of respect for others, or when to step up in a responsible way for the children. You don't need to feel in the way; the Lord will give you a way to bless others.

You may find yourself saying, "Excuse me," less and less.

O, Lord, please help me move gracefully among others, knowing that I have a secure place in You. Amen.

Day 254

Squeaky Clean

"We will never find any basis for charges against this man Daniel unless it has something to do with the law of his God."

Daniel 6:5 NIV

Daniel had a stellar political career during his lifelong tenure in Babylon. The Bible tells us the faultfinders "could find no corruption in him, because he was trustworthy and neither corrupt nor negligent" (Daniel 6:4 NIV). If they wanted to feed Daniel to the lions (which they did), they would only be able to do so with regard to "the law of his God."

If we become victims of those who want to find fault with us, can we be like Daniel of old? Can we be faultless only in the exercise of our devotion to God? Can our conduct and conversation be "squeaky clean"? When others level criticism of how we measure up as stepmoms, can their only hope of making a charge stick be relegated to our integrity—our trustworthiness?

That won't come easily or naturally but will only occur supernaturally as we, like Daniel, devote ourselves to God. The Word says that three times a day Daniel prayed and asked God for help (see Daniel 6:10–11). There are no guarantees. Daniel did end up in the lions' den. But God called Daniel "highly esteemed" (Daniel 9:23 NIV)—in Hebrew, he was "counted precious."

When we're above reproach in the little and big things of our lives, God counts us as precious, too.

Father, let my life bring praise, honor, and glory to You. Help me to live with true integrity no matter what. Amen.

Playing Favorites

Jacob lay with Rachel also, and he loved Rachel more than Leah. And he worked for Laban another seven years. When the LORD saw that Leah was not loved, he opened her womb, but Rachel was barren.

GENESIS 29:30–31 NIV

Jacob was a man who played favorites. He had two wives and loved one more than the other. He had twelve sons and loved one best. While some might say it was only natural for him to love the wife he wanted to marry more than the wife he was tricked into marrying, his favoritism was still clearly wrong in God's eyes. It caused many problems in his family. His favoritism among his sons was even more troublesome: It caused such hatred between the brothers that Joseph was nearly murdered before being sold into slavery.

But God brought good out of the mess Jacob made of his family. Though initially a slave, Joseph rose to prominence in Egypt and eventually saved the lives of his entire family. God can turn any mess into a miracle. But just think of the joy we could have—and the heartache we could avoid—if He didn't have to!

In stepfamilies, it's easy to think in terms of "*my* child" or "*your* child" when we should be thinking "*our* child"—or, even more accurately, "*God's* child." We are all adopted into God's family by unmerited favor. We are all unworthy of Jesus' love, but He gives it to us all—freely and equally.

Dear heavenly Father, thank You for loving me so much.
Help me to love others as You love me. Amen.

Day 256

Worth It!

The sacrifices of God are a broken spirit, a broken and a contrite heart—these, O God, You will not despise.

Psalm 51:17 NKJV

On Sunday mornings, Phillipa scrambled to get her stepson, Lukas, ready for church. Lukas's dad didn't attend church, but he didn't mind if she took his son. This morning was particularly difficult, and Phillipa wondered again if it was worth the stress as she slid in the church doors—late. The only open seats were in the middle. She gave a sigh and made her way to the vacant spots. Once they were seated, Lukas started to cry. She tried to quiet him, but nothing worked. Phillipa felt humiliated and angry; here she was taking her stepson to church, and the Lord couldn't even keep him quiet! Why did she bother to come at all?

During prayer, Phillipa was brought to tears as the Lord gracefully showed her that "the sacrifice acceptable to God is a broken spirit." He never promised to make her life easier just because she attended church. She came with her stepson to worship God and teach Lukas the importance of making time for the Lord. She shouldn't expect to be *rewarded*. Bringing Lukas to church was important, but more important was her heart's attitude before the God of the universe.

Dear heavenly Father, help me to be willing to serve and worship You no matter the trials. I want a humble spirit so nothing shakes my faith. Amen.

Fairy Tales and Stepmothers

Day 257

Live happily with the woman you love. . . .
The wife God gives you is your reward.
Ecclesiastes 9:9 NLT

Stepmothers in fairy tales of old rightfully get a bad rap. Cinderella's stepmother abused her, eventually locking her up to keep her from marrying the prince. Snow White's stepmother was so jealous of the young girl's beauty that she solicited a man to murder her. Although these stories make for good reading, something went horribly wrong.

These stepmothers evidently did not understand their roles. First, the bond with their husband was not a healthy one. Whether the husband elevated the daughter above his new wife or she was threatened by their father-daughter bond, the marriage couldn't have been a deep, strong one.

Second, the stepmothers did not pursue a relationship with the girls. The interaction was ineffective, at best.

The good news is that you are starring in your own fairy tale and can have a much different outcome. You and your husband are a team. Your children need to know that you are each other's number-one priority (after God, of course!) and that you will back each other up. But they also need to know that they hold the number-two priority slot, and that you both love them and will always support them.

Be encouraged! You, your husband, and your children can truly live—happily ever after.

Father, I thank You for my role of stepmom. I pray that by Your strength I will fulfill my responsibility to our children and that we will be a "happily ever after" kind of family. Amen.

Day 258

Chosen Instruments

Before I formed you in the womb I knew [and] approved of you [as My chosen instrument], and before you were born I separated and set you apart, consecrating you.

Jeremiah 1:5 amp

The Bible tells us that long before the foundation of the world, He chose us to "be holy and blameless before Him" (Ephesians 1:4 NASB). "We are His workmanship, created in Christ Jesus for good works" (Ephesians 2:10 NASB). Our lives were important to Him then; they are important to Him now. Before we were born, He set us apart, separating us from the world, dedicating us to do His work.

Our influence may not go any further than the walls of our home. But the responsibility we as moms and stepmoms have within our families is just as divinely ordained as God's self-imposed responsibility for His children. He's put within us all we need to face the challenges and joys of raising children for His glory. He tells us that His plans for us are for good and not for evil, just like the dreams and wishes we have for our children. Those plans have a way of reminding us that He has placed us in the family He specially designed and formed for us.

How wonderful to know that He has placed His desires for our children and stepchildren within us! Holy plans. Plans to prosper us, to mold us into the image of His Son, to equip us to be the mothers and stepmothers He designed us to be.

Lord, thank You for providing me with the tools I need to mother my children. May I always rely on You for strength and encouragement when I need it most. Amen.

Making God Smile

Day 259

The LORD detests the sacrifice of the wicked, but the prayer of the upright pleases him.
PROVERBS 15:8 NIV

In Old Testament times, sacrifices were offered to the Lord in order to please Him. Yet the Lord has always been more concerned with who we are than with what we offer to Him. He doesn't *need* anything we may choose to offer as a sacrifice. He *wants* our hearts. If our hearts are wicked, depraved, and full of sin, then He will be disgusted by our sacrifice. We can offer money, time, or talent, and He will not be impressed.

A prayer, on the other hand, is more of a conversation than an offering. A prayer is often a request, a cry for help. But if the prayer is offered from a pure, righteous heart, then God is pleased! He would rather *give something* to an upright person than *get something* from a wicked person, for He has already received from the righteous person exactly what He wants—her heart!

This verse challenges us to examine our hearts and see what God sees. It challenges us to get on our knees before God and make the only sacrifice that will please Him: the sacrifice of a heart poured out for Him, the sacrifice of a righteous life lived to please Him. When we do that, we will bring a smile to His holy face. And a life that pleases God is a blessed life, indeed!

Dear Father, I want to please You. Help me to give You the one thing You long for: my heart. Amen.

Day 260 Strong, Firm, and Steadfast

And the God of all grace, who called you to his eternal glory in Christ, after you have suffered a little while, will himself restore you and make you strong, firm and steadfast.

1 Peter 5:10 NIV

Has your family been going through a difficult time lately? God has not forgotten you! The Bible tells us that God Himself will restore you after a time of suffering. God wants to make your family strong, firm, and steadfast. He wants you and your family to come to Him for wisdom. So gather your family and pray. There are several things that you can pray specifically during a time of suffering:

1. Pray that God's power will rest on each of you and make you strong. Ask that the Lord be close to you and your family during this trying time.

2. Pray that you will be able to stand firm on God's promises. Get into His word and allow God to speak to you. Read God's Word together as a family each day and discuss what you have read.

3. Pray that God will make you steadfast. Ask that the Lord give you the desire and the passion to remain faithful to Him and steadfast through all of life's challenges.

Dear heavenly Father, make me strong, firm, and steadfast. Soften my heart and speak to me through Your Word. Amen.

Day 261

So Much More Than a Nickname

He determines the number of the stars and calls them each by name.
Psalm 147:4 NIV

All that we know of the first time Jesus laid eyes on Simon was that He simply looked at him. Then Jesus changed Simon's name to Cephas, or Peter (John 1:40–42). What did Jesus mean? Why Cephas? It was more of an adjective, "the Rock," than a real name. Jesus recognized tremendous potential in Simon. He was calling an ordinary man to an extraordinary future.

What a wonderful example to us of how we should view our children. Filled with potential! Known by a special name to God.

But it was a long time before Simon became the Rock. In fact, Jesus never called Simon by that new name. Only later, in Acts, will Simon's name give way to Peter, in the same way "Christ" is a title that later became a part of Jesus' name. Despite many ups and many more downs, Jesus never gave up on Simon. Eventually, that potential was realized. Peter became a source of strength to the young church.

That, too, is a good reminder. Our children need time to be all that they can be. We should never give up on our children. With God's grace, they will be all they were meant to be.

Lord of names, thank You for seeing Simon's potential. Help me to believe in the potential of each one of my kids and to see them as You do—as extraordinary. Amen.

Day 262

The Choice Is Ours

You, Lord, are all I want! You are my choice, and you keep me safe.
You make my life pleasant, and my future is bright.
I praise you, Lord, for being my guide.
Psalm 16:5–7 CEV

Each morning, we can choose the attitude we will take as we face our day. Will we expect good things—or bad? See the best in people—or the worst? Speak evil—or good? See the light—or the darkness?

One way to stay on the bright/right/light side of life is to begin the day with God's Word and prayer. Find a Bible verse full of joy, like, "This is the day the Lord has made; we will rejoice and be glad in it" (Psalm 118:24 NKJV). Make it a point to find a scripture of joy every day. Then seek God's face in prayer, asking Him to watch over each step you make; to guide you in your words, thoughts, and deeds; to help you to brighten the world.

If and when you come up against someone or something negative, look for the good in the person or the situation. Don't allow the moods of others to affect you. If you need to, walk away physically or disengage mentally. Better yet—make it a point to do something nice for someone who has offended you.

There are a million ways to make this day a good and pleasant one. Find them and watch the Lord brighten your life—and, through you, the world!

Hallelujah, Lord! I have a whole day before me. With You as my guide, I now make the choice of looking for Your good everywhere. Thank You, God, for loving me, leading me, lightening me! Amen.

R.E.S.P.E.C.T.

Let the wife see that she respects her husband.
Ephesians 5:33 NKJV

We all want respect, especially from our children. Yet we often don't consider the type of example we are setting for them. If we are critical of our family's lifestyle choices, friends, and decisions without the balance of loving acceptance, our children will struggle with seeing the good in us. Their outlook toward us will become as negative as ours is toward them.

As mothers we are in a role that is under constant observation. How do we treat others: husband, pastor, friends, and neighbors? The driver who cuts us off? The store worker who is rude for no apparent reason? How do we react? We have to remember that our children might not say much, but they are very observant, even when they don't appear to be.

Respect always begins with our outlook to God. Are we thankful for His answer to our prayers, even when that answer is silence or not what we expected? When we can thank God for His guidance of our footsteps, we can become thankful of others around us. We begin to see others through God's eyes. This new light helps us to place them above ourselves.

We must try to thank God for our children, for everything about them. When they see that, they will return our respect.

Thank You, Lord, for those You have brought into my life. Help me see them through Your eyes and with Your love. Amen.

Day 264

A Ministry

For we must all appear before the judgment seat of Christ; that every one may receive the things done in his body, according to that he hath done, whether it be good or bad.
2 Corinthians 5:10 KJV

Everyone who has trusted Christ has been entrusted by Him with some sort of ministry for which she'll be held accountable. The work of being a stepmother has not been given to everyone. How do you respond to this unique opportunity? The age of your stepfamily isn't the main consideration; although that does, in large part, determine the role that you play in their lives.

Are you available for them? Will you be their mentor, their friend, their confidant? Will you be their mother if the situation warrants that? Do you realize that, just as in any other relationship, the most valuable part of your ministry to your stepchildren is prayer?

Depending on all that has transpired previously, they might reject you or welcome you into their lives with open arms, but your praying for them is something over which they have no control. That is between you and God. What have you done with the ministry God has bestowed upon you? Are you pleasing Him? In what areas could you improve?

Someday you will stand before our great heavenly Father. On that day will you hear Him say, "Well done"?

Give me the heart of a servant, O God. Let my family see You in me. Amen.

Saint Stepmom Need Not Apply

We have different gifts, according to the grace given us.
ROMANS 12:6 NIV

We all know those generously gifted stepmoms who seem to sail through their role with the humility of Mary, the wisdom of Solomon, and the patience of Job. Their names are probably already inscribed on the rolls of the saints.

But what if you've looked for your gifts and haven't found them? What if you can't cook your stepkids' favorite foods or play the games they like or meet their difficult personalities with understanding and grace? What if you don't have a calm voice and words of encouragement, mercy for their mistakes, and tolerance for their tantrums?

Of course, we each have some gifts, at least one or two where our stepkids are concerned, and we're grateful. But we still want to be like Saint Stepmom. We want those special gifts even if we weren't given them, but wait—maybe we were.

Maybe we have those gifts of humility, wisdom, and patience buried deep somewhere; but because God made us all different, our grace for them isn't as great as someone else's. That's okay, because we can still develop them to the highest point God has chosen. We can use up every ounce of grace He poured on us in those areas we feel lacking.

Saint Stepmom? Probably not, but the gifted stepmom our families need? You bet.

Father, please help me to appreciate the gifts You've given me and to use them all the best I can for my family. There's nothing we can't do together. Amen.

Day 266 The Power of Almighty God

"Have you visited the storehouses of the snow or seen the storehouses of hail?"
Job 38:22 NLT

Job is really challenged when God allows Satan to test his faith. Satan destroys Job's wealth, health, and family; but Job continues to trust in God. However, toward the end of the story, Job cries out, asserting his innocence in front of God. God's answer to Job is terrifying in its power. God asks Job a number of questions, including the one written above. As God continues to question him, Job realizes that God has ultimate control and that God's infinite power and wisdom should not be questioned by mere humans.

From time to time, we find ourselves in situations we don't understand. When we are tempted to question God, however, we should remember Job's questions and God's response. Our God is more powerful than we could ever imagine or dream. He built the treasuries of snow and the storehouses of hail. He filled them and pours them out on earth when He chooses! God has a plan for our lives that we cannot begin to understand. We simply must put our trust in God—a God who is not only all-powerful but who loves each one of us more than we could ever conceive.

Dear Lord, Your power is infinite, yet You love me more than I can even imagine. Please help me to trust You in everything. Amen.

Envy, Be Gone!

For where envy and self-seeking exist, confusion and every evil thing are there.
James 3:16 NKJV

Though she hated to admit it, the new bride struggled with feelings of envy. Whenever her husband's two boys came to visit, she sensed the bond between father and sons but felt completely left out of the loop. Instead of sharing her feelings or trying to join in, she found herself retreating to a private, quiet place whenever the kids were around. This just seemed easier. Unfortunately, over time more distance grew between them; and before long, she felt completely left out.

Maybe you understand this woman's dilemma. Perhaps you're the sort to slip away instead of joining in, especially if you feel out of place. One of the hardest things about being a stepmom is the feeling that you're a "fifth wheel," especially when you're around people who have a strong history together. They share common memories and relationships, and you wonder if you'll ever be a part of that.

So, what can you do? First, deal with your feelings of envy. Acknowledge them before your heavenly Father. He knows all about them anyway, but it will make you feel better to get them off your chest. Then, join in the fun. Come up with a plan of action and implement it whenever the whole family is together. That way you will create new memories that you can all look back on.

Father, today I ask You to take away my envy. Replace it with a renewed sense of purpose within my family. Amen.

Day 268

The Lord Has Made a Way

O Lord, You are my God; I will exalt You, I will give thanks to Your name; for You have worked wonders, plans formed long ago, with perfect faithfulness.

Isaiah 25:1 NASB

He was diagnosed with lung cancer at almost seventy-eight years old. His wife of nearly forty-eight years and their six children cared for him throughout his nineteen-month illness until he passed away. The woman who loved this man more than life itself resolutely faced the rest of her life alone. However, God had plans for her, and those plans included an old family friend whose wife died in a car accident two years later.

The two "seventy-somethings" began spending time together, no doubt sharing their grief, but also awakening to the possibility that they could love again. Almost two years after finding each other, they married. God even gave them a song for their wedding entitled "The Lord Has Made a Way," based on Isaiah 25:1. The new bride was amazed at how the lyrics so accurately described her feelings.

In His infinite wisdom, the Lord knew they would need each other. In "perfect faithfulness," He blessed them with new love and a new start. He took their sadness, heartache, and loss and showered them with happiness, healing, and restoration. He transformed their grief and sorrow into acceptance and joy. He gave them a second chance at love. Hasn't He done the same for you and your husband?

Precious Lord, thank You so much for this second chance for my husband, our children, and me. You are so good to us. Amen.

Portraits

Who hath saved us, and called us with an holy calling.
2 TIMOTHY 1:9 KJV

Claudia frowned in the mirror at the gray hairs that seemed to have sprouted overnight. How different she looked from the starry-eyed bride in the framed wedding portrait propped on her dresser. She was so lovely then!

And so naive, she thought, as she looked at the photo sitting next to it—a group shot of her and her husband with the children from his first marriage. The hesitant, half smiles spoke volumes about their early days as a family. It had been anything but functional, and Claudia remembered how close she'd come to walking out.

But I couldn't, she thought. *God wouldn't let me.*

Claudia hadn't planned or even wanted to be a stepmother, but she knew in her heart that it was the work God had called her to do. His grace and strength had sustained her in her lowest times, making the scene in the final framed photograph possible. Her stepchildren and the children she had conceived with her husband, clustered tightly around their parents. The bright, happy faces smiling boldly into the camera were a testament to their success as a blended family.

Maybe it's not what I planned to do with my life, Claudia thought, as she considered the years of toil and love that had earned her every one of those gray hairs, *but I'd do it all over again.*

Lord, strengthen me for the work You have called me to do, so that I may look back on my years as a stepmother and smile. Amen.

Fruit of the Vine

"Abide in Me, and I in you. As the branch cannot bear fruit of itself unless it abides in the vine, so neither can you unless you abide in Me."

John 15:4 NASB

A visit to a vineyard deeply impressed a young stepmom. She knelt to look at the knotty limbs and the way they spread from the main trunk. Hanging from the branches were bunches of juicy grapes, bursting with sweetness. "They don't struggle to produce fruit," she said to herself. "It's a natural process of being part of the vine."

That revelation changed her life. Until then, she had suffered endless frustrations trying to mother another woman's children. Anger, bitterness, and exhaustion had been her constant companions. Drawing on the knowledge that she was part of God's vine, she amended her ways. Instead of moaning, she would pick up the Bible and read God's Word. Instead of flopping on her bed, she would kneel and pray. As she discovered the secrets of abiding in the Vine, her life began to change. The fruit of the Spirit began to appear in her life, and the children were easier to love as they responded to the new gentleness in her.

God's desire is that each of us abide in the Vine. The sap that sustains us is the life-giving power of God's Word. As we soak up words of healing and salvation from the Bible, we too can bear abundant fruit.

Dear Lord, help me to abide in You and produce much fruit. Give me a fresh desire for Your Word. Amen.

Think! Before You Think

Day 271

Do not be shaped by this world; instead be changed within by a new way of thinking.
ROMANS 12:2 NCV

When traveling to a drastically different time zone, you have to rethink when to do the daily things of life, like getting up, eating meals, or going to bed. Your host may say, "That's how we do things here." Similarly, followers of Christ must have a new frame of mind when entering His kingdom. Former selfish thought patterns simply won't work, just as Hannah discovered in her journey with God.

Selfish thoughts no doubt flooded Hannah's mind in her own world. Her husband's other wife constantly poked fun at Hannah's barren womb. Year after year, Peninnah "kept provoking her in order to irritate her" (1 Samuel 1:6 NIV). One day Hannah decided to look at things differently. Instead of taking her gripe to the other wife, she took her grief to the Lord. In the process of pouring her heart out to the Lord, Hannah left the temple in a new frame of mind. So powerfully was her mind set on the Lord that it renewed her appetite and revived her countenance!

As a stepmom, are you adjusting your thoughts to God's way of doing things? Instead of going toe to toe with the Peninnah in your stepmom world, why not go heart to heart with God? He says, "That's the way we do things around here!"

Lord, please forgive me when I conduct myself like I did before coming to You. Help me to think Your way. Amen.

Day 272

Don't Quit

Go to work in the morning and stick to it until evening without watching the clock. You never know from moment to moment how your work will turn out in the end.

Ecclesiastes 11:6 msg

Sometimes it feels as if life is meaningless. We face the same boring routines day in and day out—like the hamster running endlessly, uselessly, on its wheel. We don't seem to get anywhere. Nothing seems to work. We're not even sure what the goal is anymore.

Maybe the people in our lives are the ones who never change, no matter how much prayer and effort we put into them. Our husbands, our children and stepchildren, our extended family members, coworkers, and friends—believers or unbelievers—don't seem to care about our concerns for them.

Yet the Lord encourages us to continue working diligently, trying new methods, new ways to accomplish the goal. Paul tells us in Galatians 6:9 (nasb) to "not lose heart in doing good, for in due time we will reap if we do not grow weary." We don't know how our efforts will turn out; but as we continue to seek God's plan and purpose for our loved ones and ourselves, God promises that we will reap the rewards if we don't give up too soon.

So be diligent. Continue to seek the Lord's guidance for new methods, new ways, new desires, and new plans in order to accomplish His purposes. You will not be disappointed.

Lord, thank You for giving me the strength to keep on going—even when life isn't going as I'd planned. Amen.

Mistaken Identity

Day 273

Immediately Jesus spoke to them, saying, "Be of good cheer! It is I; do not be afraid."
Matthew 14:27 NKJV

First, unforeseen circumstances blew their getaway dreams to bits. Then a storm threatened the boat ride that was supposed to relax them.

A page out of your vacation history? Actually, a biblical one with which we all identify. The disciples, worn out by ministry demands and saddened by the murder of John the Baptist, had looked forward to quiet time with Jesus. But thousands of sick people followed Him to the "solitary place," begging Him to heal them. Jesus canceled their vacation plans, ministering to the crowd and feeding five thousand men, plus women and children, with miracle food.

When Jesus finally sent the disciples across the lake, they hoped to enjoy a little R & R. As a storm blasted Galilee, however, they found themselves rowing for their lives. The men probably prayed fervently for God's help. But they didn't expect Jesus to walk on water!

How often in the midst of trouble we plead for God's presence; yet, like the disciples, we panic when He shows up. Full of fear, they deduced He was a ghost. Ravaged by doubt, we, too, may see His help as a threat. Yet Jesus soothes us like little children and reassures us, "It is I."

That's all we need to know.

Lord Jesus, You stop at nothing to rescue me. When You walk my way, please help me recognize Your love. Amen.

Day 274

No Matter What

I trust in your unfailing love; my heart rejoices in your salvation. I will sing to the LORD, for he has been good to me.

PSALM 13:5–6 NIV

In this world, so many things are uncertain. But there is one thing of which we can be eternally secure. And it's one of the most amazing things about God: His unconditional love.

Knowing God loves us—no matter what, just as we are—we have the confidence to get through anything, the faith to endure any hardship. Now wouldn't it be great to let our stepchildren know we feel the same way toward them? That no matter what, we will love them?

Let's face it. We all make mistakes. And there are times when we fall short of God's goal for our lives or disappoint Him in some way. But God loves us so much, He forgives us. Are we that forgiving to the children He puts in our care?

Let's love and forgive our stepchildren unconditionally. Let's raise secure adults for our Lord and Master.

Make it a point each day—by word or deed—to assure your stepchildren of your love. Let them know that although they may have made a mistake, you forgive them. That even though they may have disappointed you, nothing can take your love away.

Be like Jesus. Love your children unconditionally. And watch their light shine.

God, I thank You for Your unfailing love. Help me be a better parent by showing this same love to my own children. And may my doing so shine a light on their path to Your door. Amen.

First-Rate Speech

Be pleasant and hold their interest when you speak the message. Choose your words carefully.
Colossians 4:6 CEV

Some days it's easy for a mom to "tune out." After all, there is so much to remember! Recital dates, sports activities, bill paying, not to mention keeping the house stocked with groceries.

But how easy is it—especially when we're having a bad day, are tired, or are mentally overwhelmed—to snap at our kids, spouting off words before they are filtered through our brain.

The Bible equates our tongue with the rudder of a boat. It is the rudder's job to get the vessel to its destination. What a huge responsibility for a small controller! But just think of the power it holds.

Moms are vital examples of pure, godly speech for their children. The Bible instructs us to "be pleasant" as we speak and to "choose [our] words carefully." Because those words can never be snatched back, it is crucial that we think before releasing our words. Not only in the everyday routine, but also during times of godly teaching, select words that will build up your kids. This practice is for their encouragement, but it also trains them in how God desires that they speak to others. If they seek to imitate your speech, how will they be doing in communicating with you?

Lord Jesus, I give You control of my tongue today. May my words please You and build others up. Amen.

Day 276

The One Opinion That Counts

The fear of human opinion disables; trusting in God protects you from that.
PROVERBS 29:25 MSG

It's amazing how much the voice of a child can alter our opinion. "Please, can I stay up a few minutes more?" Or the voice of a friend can change our way of thinking. "Maybe you shouldn't be so hard on your kids. Another mother I know lets her kids do that."

Everyone has an opinion about how you should mother or how to keep your marriage strong, but only one opinion really matters. What direction from God's Word has the Lord given you for your life? When you've heard from the Lord, that opinion should be the one you cling to above all others.

Opinions, thoughts, and distractions will always come your way in an attempt to distract you from following God. "Dad may like you, but I never will." "His kids won't love you like a real mom." "Why are you marrying such a complicated family?" Pray about it, and trust God to lead you down the right path. Once you have His direction, cling firmly to your path as you walk out the plan He has for you. Never let human opinions get you off track from the one opinion that matters the most—God's.

Lord, help me to trust Your opinion above all others. Let nothing pull me aside from my goal of following You. In Jesus' name, amen.

Blender Families

Day 277

When Rachel saw that she bore Jacob no children, she envied her sister. . . .
So she gave him her servant Bilhah as a wife, and Jacob went in to her.
Genesis 30:1, 4 ESV

In the days of the patriarch Jacob, men of different religions, including Judaism, had multiple wives. Although "everybody's doing it" may have been the cultural norm, problems were commonplace—and of no small consequence. That's clear as the story of Jacob's family unfolds with infighting and worse. Even at the time of Jesus' ministry on earth, Jewish men married the widow of their deceased brother to continue the late brother's name in the family line. Children growing up in these homes—like Jacob's where two of his wives were sisters—had cousins who were also their stepsiblings. "Blended families"? How about "blender families"?

We may feel we're living in a blender family. Everyone is getting stirred up, mashed up, and beaten up in our frenetic pace. Sometimes we have to roll with it. Sometimes we can laugh at it. Sometimes we can only throw up our hands and beg, "Mercy, Lord!"

God heard the prayers of Rachel. He heard the prayers of her sister and co-wife, Leah. He heard and answered their prayers and the prayers of their husband and children. Thankfully, God is always in the mix with us. Let's not hesitate to enlist His help today.

Father, You call all kinds of people to Yourself and call them "family." Help our family to blend together in all the right ways. Amen.

Day 278

Heart Probe

I am asking you to respond as if you were my own children. Open your hearts to us!
2 Corinthians 6:13 NLT

Questions and statements take up a lot of everyday conversation with kids: *When will you be home? You forgot to take out the garbage. Your socks don't match! Why didn't you come straight home from school?* How about taking a break and craft a plea to your stepchildren? The apostle Paul surely wouldn't mind if you model yours after the one he wrote to his "stepchildren" at Corinth.

First, state clearly what it is you want or are asking for. Paul didn't make them guess what he wanted them to do to build their relationship: open their hearts! It's a simple, straightforward plea but not a cerebral request. It originates in the heart. Second, use an inviting "voice" over a commanding or corrective tone. Paul desired to connect with people, not drive them away. Third, Paul practiced what he was pleading—he took the initiative by opening his heart to the Corinthians.

A plea even with practice doesn't guarantee a positive response from the other party, but it is a beautiful way to communicate that you're ready to go further than the daily exchange of information. You can begin today to get to the heart of the matter.

Dear God, help me get beyond the information stage, willing to move into the connection stage of my relationship to my stepchildren. Amen.

Who Holds the Future?

Day 279

But one thing I do: Forgetting what is behind and straining toward what is ahead, I press on toward the goal to win the prize for which God has called me heavenward in Christ Jesus.

PHILIPPIANS 3:13–14 NIV

Being a stepmom presupposes a hard truth: We were not the first. Our husbands had other wives before us and other children. There are a lot of *firsts* that we will never share with them and many memories we don't hold in common. We have to share their past with others; often, with joint custody and other relatives still in the picture, we have to share their present also. It is hard to share the ones we love, and we may wonder why God allowed this.

But this is no longer Eden, where Adam and Eve came to each other as new creations with no history before God breathed life into their nostrils. We all have things in our past that make living with another person more difficult. Our great God, however, is a God of new beginnings and second chances. Lot's wife looked behind her and was turned into a pillar of salt. The Israelites looked behind to the things they left behind in Egypt and were unable to appreciate the miracles that God was doing for them *right then* in the desert.

The real question is not "Why, Lord?" but "Who holds my future in the palm of His hand?"

Dear God, You are too awesome for words. I bow before You in thanksgiving and acknowledge that You alone are the Lord of my life. Amen.

Day 280

A Bleeding Ear

Then Simon Peter, who had a sword, drew it and struck the high priest's servant, cutting off his right ear. . . . Jesus commanded Peter, "Put your sword away! Shall I not drink the cup the Father has given me?"

John 18:10–11 NIV

In a fit of rage, combined with fear and exhaustion, Simon Peter rushed forward, pulled his short sword from under his cloak, and aimed for the closest guard.

Simon, Simon, Simon.

Not a smart move. Simon's weapon was illegal. Luke, with his love for medical details, tells us that Jesus quietly healed the guard's bleeding ear. Had He not, Simon would have been arrested. More importantly, this was not his battle. Jesus had already told him that (many, many times). This battle belonged to Jesus alone.

But don't we all relate to Simon's impulsive response to protect a loved one? It's a natural instinct of parents. We let protective emotions get the better of us. We overhelp and step in where we don't belong. We use our own means to solve a problem—a problem that isn't ours to begin with.

We need to let our kids work out their own solutions to their problems, even if it means they make mistakes. They're practicing skills they will need as adults. And how else will they learn to depend on God if we are always rushing forward, brandishing our own sword of overprotection?

Lord, this is a hard lesson to learn. Teach me to look to You for direction of when to step in and when to step back. Amen.

Stand Your Ground

Day 281

Many seek the ruler's favor, but justice for man comes from the Lord.
Proverbs 29:26 NASB

You probably came into your new marriage as a stepmom with high expectations—we all do. Then life begins to happen, the perfect dream fades, and we have to take each challenge as it comes. The ups and downs of blending a family can take a toll on all of you. And then you wonder, *What have I gotten myself into? Was that Your plan, God? Did I miss it? Hello? Are You still there?*

Don't let the hope you had before you became an instant family escape you. Anything worth having is worth working for. Hold tightly to the things you held in your heart when you first said, "I do." When you're tempted to give up—or throw your hands up in defeat—don't let go!

The enemy of your family wants you to turn tail and run! Don't give him the pleasure; stand strong and hold your ground. Be bold! Be courageous. Take God at His word and believe the unbelievable. You can beat the odds. God is a God of second (and third and fourth) chances. With God on your side, you can succeed and make your dreams of a second-chance family a reality.

Heavenly Father, You gave me a dream, and with Your help I know it can become a reality. I'm in this for the long haul. I refuse to give up. Give me wisdom to unite this family and bring us all closer to You. Amen.

Day 282

Staying in Touch

"Call to me and I will answer you and tell you great and unsearchable things you do not know."
Jeremiah 33:3 niv

The mother glanced again at her watch. She should have heard from her daughter an hour ago, but the girl hadn't checked in. She wasn't answering her cell, either. The mother's emotions had gone from anger to concern to fear. For now she could only pray that her child would come home safe.

Often, our children don't see the need to let us know they are okay. They don't understand why we want them to check in—that this is for their safety, not to restrict their fun. They get busy and lose track of time, unwilling to concede to the importance of letting their mother know they are all right. As parents, we want our child to call; and we will answer.

We often do the same with God. His desire is to hear from us often, but not so He can keep track of every move we're making; He can do that already. God wants us to keep Him at the forefront of our thoughts for our protection. He doesn't want us to contact Him only if we need help in some way. He wants to be our intimate friend, to tell us and show us those things we need to know for life.

Lord, I want to put You first. Thank You for being there to answer when I call. Amen.

Trusting Pursuit

Let us go right into the presence of God with sincere hearts fully trusting him.
HEBREWS 10:22 NLT

Phoebe is a long-haired black cat with an unusual habit: she's a chaser and a flopper. When her master leaves the room, Phoebe pursues him; and when he stops, she flops down, belly-up, at his feet. Rolling from side to side, warbling, and stretching toward his toes, Phoebe begs for her master's attention. And she will get it. Her master simply cannot resist!

There's no fluff in Phoebe's conduct. She acts out of pure desire and absolute trust. Her constant, eager pursuit is always followed by belly-up vulnerability. It's clear Phoebe knows she won't be stepped on, mistreated, or ignored. Her master loves her and has earned her trust. No wonder she pursues him with abandon!

We can learn from Phoebe. We, too, have a Master who is faithful and true. He is worthy of our pursuit. Our God not only created the universe, but sent His beloved Son to die for our sins—that's how valuable we are to Him. Despite His greatness, He desires intimate fellowship with us. He calls us by name and numbers the hairs on our heads. And even though He knows our depravity, God chooses to lavish His love upon us and cover us with mercy and grace.

We are forever safe in the presence of the Lord. Shouldn't we pursue Him with abandon, trusting Him to give us the loving attention we need?

Father, remind me to chase after You and hold nothing back. You are my God in whom I trust! Amen.

Day 284

Helping Hands

For I the Lord thy God will hold thy right hand, saying unto thee, Fear not; I will help thee.

Isaiah 41:13 KJV

Were you ever frightened as a little girl? Maybe you were lost or had to go somewhere you had never been before. Remember how much better you felt when a trusted adult held your hand? Strong, capable fingers gripping your own trembling ones gave you courage, confidence, and the promise of help.

You're not a child anymore, but the fears you confront today are just as real. As a stepmom, you're forced to make decisions that affect the lives and futures of the people you love most. With such high stakes, you can't afford to fail; and the dread of doing just that can be paralyzing at times.

God did not call you to stepmotherhood only to abandon you there. He understands your great responsibilities and knows that you are incapable of fulfilling them on your own. He has promised never to leave or forsake His children, and He stands ready to help as soon as you call. Like that trusted adult who held your hand when you were a frightened child, God reaches out to your trembling spirit and offers limitless strength and wisdom. He knows that you want to be a good stepmother, and as the Supreme Father, He has all of the tools available to make you just that.

Dear Lord, teach me to cast all of my fears upon You, and remind me that with Your help, failure is a foe that I need never face. Amen.

Guard the Treasure

You have been trusted with a wonderful treasure.
Guard it with the help of the Holy Spirit, who lives within you.
2 Timothy 1:14 CEV

As a stepparent, you have been entrusted with the most precious of treasures: your husband's children. If you have children of your own, you know how much these stepchildren mean to their father. Whether the children live with you or only visit occasionally, you have the great responsibility of nurturing them and giving them love when they are with you.

When children are young, they are easy to mold and shape with love and consistent guidance. As they become teenagers, human nature sometimes takes over and tries to undermine what you have worked to accomplish. Guard the treasure given you. Remember to encourage them daily, and show the love of Christ through your actions and words.

Prayer will guide you through the rough years of acceptance and approval. The Holy Spirit, through prayer and scripture reading, will give you the answers you seek. Nothing you do for your stepchildren in the name of the Lord will be in vain. Although they may not always appreciate your guidance and your rules when they are young, they will have respect for you and will thank you later. God's promises never fail, and He will guide you as you live each day and guide your children in the ways of the Lord.

Heavenly Father, help us to guard the treasure You have given to us.
May our words and actions always be filled with love. Amen.

Day 286

Supernatural Love

Beloved, let us love one another, for love is of God; and everyone who loves is born of God and knows God. He who does not love does not know God, for God is love.

1 John 4:7–8 NKJV

Did you ever picture yourself as a superhero? You are. Taking on the job of stepmom is a job worthy of a superhero.

Just think about it. Stepmoms need a lot of courage. We need insight into the feelings of our stepchildren and into the feelings of the biological mother and father. We need to be able to create our own space within a new family. We need to remember to be slow to criticize and quick to praise our stepchildren. Sounds like a job for a superhero to me!

Maybe we don't have superhuman strength, but we do have supernatural strength. God gives us the ability to love when we are hated, to forgive when we are spitefully used, and to believe that He can change our families, especially when things seem hopeless.

No one but God can give us that kind of strength. Ask God for courage today. Ask Him to help you see your stepchildren through His eyes. Ask Him to let you see your husband through His eyes. He'll help you.

God of love, please help me see my stepchildren and my husband through Your eyes. Please give me Your eyes of love today. In Jesus' name, Amen.

God's Love, Our Love

Day 287

Watch what God does, and then you do it, like children who learn proper behavior from their parents. Mostly what God does is love you. Keep company with him and learn a life of love. Observe how Christ loved us. His love was not cautious but extravagant. He didn't love in order to get something from us but to give everything of himself to us. Love like that.

Ephesians 5:1–2 MSG

Paul was writing to believers in Ephesus to encourage them to think with a new identity. What better time to do the same than when we become a stepmom? How can we put Paul's words into practice and "love like that"?

1. Keep company with God. We can imagine Him always at our side (as He is), during the delightful and the disastrous. We can receive His love and pass it on, picturing in our minds the actual transfer of a double handful from Him to us and then to those around us.

2. Be extravagant and giving. We can reach out with all we have, trusting that we're supported on God's grace, strength, and love. We can be unafraid to open our hearts to our stepkids and hug them to us in the spirit that God hugs us to Him—completely free to empty everything we have onto them, knowing God will resupply all we give away.

God's love has transformed us, and it's our privilege to follow His lead.

Father, thank You for Your example of how to love and grow and be like You. Please make me an example of You to my family. Amen.

Day 288

Sticks and Stones

The heart of the righteous ponders how to answer,
but the mouth of the wicked blurts out evil things.
PROVERBS 15:28 NASB

"*Sticks and stones may break my bones, but words will never hurt me.*" Whoever wrote that little rhyme was wrong. Words hurt a lot worse than sticks and stones. And the wounds they inflict take much longer to heal, too. Words are fierce weapons and must be handled with great care.

A wicked person doesn't really care whom she hurts. For the wicked, there is no need to think before speaking. After all, who cares if feelings get hurt or if a life gets destroyed? Unkind people just let words tumble out as soon as they enter their thoughts. Mean people aren't concerned about the damage their words may cause. They even delight in the broken hearts and shredded lives their words leave behind! Their speech brings destruction.

The righteous person, on the other hand, knows to handle words with sensitivity and care. Though he or she does not cower from speaking what is right, this person knows to precede any speech with great thought and prayer. Because of this, the words of the righteous person bring peace, joy, and healing. The words of the upright are a fountain of life.

Dear Father, please help me to think before I speak. Let my words always bring healing and not destruction. Amen.

Passing Through

"When you pass through the waters, I will be with you; and when you pass through the rivers, they will not sweep over you. When you walk through the fire, you will not be burned; the flames will not set you ablaze."

Isaiah 43:2 NIV

Israel was God's chosen people: the redeemed. They were called by His name and created for His glory. They were His. The Lord made many promises to Israel. In Isaiah 43:2, God reassured them that although they would experience trials and difficulties, they would endure because of His love and presence. The word *through* in this verse indicates that they would eventually reach the other side, that hardship would be behind them, that they would taste victory.

Have you ever felt as though you were about to be engulfed by a raging river or a consuming fire? If you are a child of God, you, too, have been redeemed. Never forget that the Lord is with you! Although trials and difficulties will come, God's love and presence will enable you to *pass through* to the other side. The Lord will give you the strength to persevere, to endure, to be victorious.

Trust the Lord in your current situation. Do not fear. Claim His promise to be with you. Remember His unconditional love for you. Believe that He will indeed help you pass through to the other side.

Dear Lord, thank You for enabling me to pass through difficulties. May the hope of reaching the other side encourage me to persevere. Amen.

Spring Rains

Brothers and sisters, be patient until the Lord comes again. A farmer patiently waits for his valuable crop to grow from the earth and for it to receive the autumn and spring rains.

James 5:7 NCV

Marrying into a ready-made family can be a challenge, particularly if the children are older and set in their ways. Remember the old adage: Rome wasn't built in a day. Neither were families, especially merging families. It takes time for relationships to build and for trust to be established. Sure, you want to see it happen overnight. You want your love for your stepchildren—and their love for you—to be as natural as your love for your spouse. Be patient! It will happen. . .in time.

So what do you do in the meantime? As the scripture indicates, you wait patiently. That means you don't let your anxieties get the best of you. You don't fret. You don't speak negative words over your situation. You believe in your heart of hearts that when the next season comes, the crop will grow. And it will!

Take your cues from the farmer in today's scripture. Be on the lookout for spring rains. They're an indicator that seasons are changing. Prepare your heart for new things. Likely, they're just around the bend.

Lord, sometimes I feel so impatient. I want things to happen—now! I'm so impatient! Help me control my urge to fix things on my own, and give me patience when I need it most. Amen.

The Next Generation

Day 291

"David. . .served the purpose of God in his own generation."
Acts 13:36 NASB

When God designed David, He had a definite game plan. This shepherd boy, the son of Jesse, was known as "a skillful musician, a mighty man of valor, a warrior, one prudent in speech, and a handsome man" (1 Samuel 16:18 NASB). God knew David's potential, and He used it to work His will.

God looked at the shepherd boy David and saw a king. He looked at Moses, a murderer with a speech impediment, and saw a performer of miracles and a leader of His chosen people. He looked at the murderous Paul and saw an evangelist. He looked at the promiscuous Samaritan woman at the well and saw a true worshipper who brought others to the knowledge of Him.

God sees the potential in all His children, including our stepchildren. Do we? Are we looking to see where their talents lie, where they can best serve the Lord? Are we encouraging them in their endeavors? Are we raising up children that will serve the purpose of God in their own generation?

Look at your children. How do you see God using them? For what have they been designed? Take a good look at this next generation; then encourage and strengthen them to serve God's purpose.

God, You know the plans You have for my children. Show me the ways in which they can best serve You. Help me to steer them in the right direction. And if neither they nor I are sure of their path, help me to encourage them to pray, "Lord, what do You want me to do?" (Acts 9:6 NKJV). Amen.

Day 292

Can You Hear Me?

Listen to good advice if you want to live well.
PROVERBS 15:31 MSG

Have you ever felt as if you're talking but no one is listening? Does that ever happen in your home? As a loving, intuitive mom, sometimes you may just want to crawl up onto the roof and yell your words of wisdom at the top of your lungs; but other than the neighbors thinking you're quirky, nothing would really come of that.

Getting a young person's attention can potentially be even more difficult in a stepparent situation. The parties involved can be more defensive, which results in a dividing wall. The wall, if left alone, tends to extend higher, totally ruining the possibility of any effective communication.

What is the "wall level" like in your house? Why not take some time with each of the kids and have a heart-to-heart chat? There can be positive results from this interaction: You can learn more about each other, deepen respect for one another, and even have a few lighthearted, fun moments along the way.

Talk with your kids today. Start the dialogue flowing. But the sofa or the kitchen table will work fine—much better than the roof!

Dear God, help me to be a better communicator with my children. Please grant them the ability to listen and to see my genuine love and concern for them. Amen.

Mother Knows Best

Day 293

"Age should speak; advanced years should teach wisdom."
JOB 32:7 NIV

"I'm beginning to think I've made a mistake," Libby said. "I never should have married a man with kids."

"What makes you think that?" her mother asked. Libby sighed and named off a laundry list of personal failures and shortcomings.

"I don't know what I'm doing," she admitted. "I'm just flying by the seat of my pants and hoping that everything will turn out all right!"

Her mother chuckled knowingly.

"Mom, it's not funny!" Libby cried.

"Oh, but it is, dear. Maybe not right now, but trust me when I say that it will be."

Libby raised a doubtful eyebrow.

"Honey," her mother said. "Of course you're flying by the seat of your pants. All parents do, step or otherwise. So, you've made some mistakes. What matters is that you're learning from them." She gazed directly into her daughter's eyes. "Becoming a mother to those kids wasn't a mistake. It was a good, noble, and loving decision. You stick with it and see how much easier it gets."

Libby sighed. "Of course I'll stick with it. I love my stepkids. But how long does it take to feel like you know what you're doing?"

Libby's mother smiled and draped an arm around her daughter's shoulders.

"If I only knew," she said.

Lord, I don't have all the answers. Lead me to those who have sound advice to give, and help me to take it. Amen.

Day 294

Turn to Jesus

The tongue that brings healing is a tree of life,
but a deceitful tongue crushes the spirit.
Proverbs 15:4 NIV

"You can't tell me what to do! You're not my mom!"

"I hate it here! I want to go to my *real* mom's house!"

If you're a stepmom, and you've heard these or similar words, you know how much they hurt. Sometimes an actual stone, sharp edges and all, would be preferable to this sort of verbal missile. A bruise heals quickly, but the ache from words spoken in anger may take months to fade—if it fades at all.

But the thought to cling to when harsh words are flung is that even though they cause hurt, the hurt from which they arise is much greater. It may be hard for us to comprehend the anger and grief and guilt that stepchildren feel—and can continue to feel for years—if we have never gone through a similar situation.

Instead of matching them rock for rock, we can return blessings for cursings; we can give love when all that is given us is anger and disdain. We can love without counting the cost or the bruises. This may be our greatest chance to show Jesus to our stepchildren.

Turn away from anger, from wrath and harsh words. Turn to Jesus instead.

Dear Lord, I am so easily tripped up by angry words. Please guard my tongue, Lord, and help me speak only words of peace. Amen.

Focus

Day 295

For he who sows to his flesh will of the flesh reap corruption, but he who sows to the Spirit will of the Spirit reap everlasting life.
Galatians 6:8 NKJV

Two women discussed the idea of starting an organization to help people cope with life. But they differed on how to implement the idea, so they parted ways. The first woman became a life coach. She charged people for classes that taught them how to get a GED, do a job interview, keep house, parent, and budget. Her idea caught on. She went on TV talk shows and became nationally known. She held seminars teaching others to become life coaches. She won awards and became wealthy.

The second woman held all the same classes as the first woman, but she didn't charge people for her help. She taught people how to help themselves and how to help others. Only those she helped knew her name, and they rose up and called her blessed. They also volunteered with her to help their community.

What made the difference? The first woman taught people how to live in this world. She got her reward in this world. The second woman taught people how to prepare to live in the next world. She set her mind on what is above and not on the things of this earth. We, too, have the choice of where our focus lies: here or there.

Father, please help me to remember that whatever I am doing for You, I need to do it now because I will never pass this way again. Amen.

Day 296

Unwelcome Guests

He said to the woman, Thy faith hath saved thee; go in peace.
Luke 7:50 KJV

Somehow she found her way into the house. Perhaps she worked as a cook or server, because Simon the Pharisee would never invite even a righteous woman to dine, as men and women in his culture ate separately. Certainly, Simon never would have welcomed a woman of her reputation to join him and his guests. The fact Simon permitted her presence makes us question whether he intended to show disrespect for Jesus in the same way he neglected common courtesies of that day: providing water to wash His feet, oil for His head, and a welcome kiss. If Simon hoped to embarrass Jesus, his scheme backfired. He and his Pharisee friends had to watch the woman rub Jesus' feet with oil, dry them with her hair, and cover them with kisses—intimate actions that shocked them down to their self-righteous toes and fueled endless gossip in the town.

While society viewed her as a brazen hussy, Jesus understood the devotion behind her "inappropriate" behavior and loved her for it. How He must have welcomed her authenticity in a house of hypocrisy! He forgave the woman's many sins. She left with His blessing still ringing in her ears: "Your faith has saved you. Go in peace."

Lord Jesus, even when religious people don't understand my love for You, You receive it and forgive my sins. Help me do the same for even the Simons in my world. Amen.

Day 297

Rejoice!

Do not be surprised at the painful trial you are suffering, as though something strange were happening to you. But rejoice that you participate in the sufferings of Christ, so that you may be overjoyed when his glory is revealed.

1 Peter 4:12–13 NIV

Are you sick of all the problems that seem to be lurking around every corner? You solve one problem just to start over with a new one the very next day, or so it seems. The Bible says for us not to be surprised at the trials that we face. In fact, the Bible warns us that we will have trouble (John 16:33). Problems make us wiser, and we have fellowship with Christ through sufferings. Problems bring us into a deeper relationship with the Lord. God's Word tells us to "rejoice" that we are participating in the sufferings of Christ. Now, this doesn't mean that we should go looking for trouble and be happy that we've found it! It means that we can be encouraged when we do face hard times; the Lord is with us, and He longs to draw us closer to Himself through our trials. To rejoice means to take delight in knowing that God is in control. He knows what you are going through, and He will be with you every step of the way.

Dear Father, help me to rejoice in knowing that You are always in control. Draw me closer to You through the issues I face each day. Amen.

Day 298

Accepted and Accessible

[God] hath made us accepted in the beloved.
Ephesians 1:6 KJV

Not until after she was a teenager did she learn the truth. Her parents were not her birth parents. In her twenties, she learned she had never even been legally adopted. That made her mom her foster mother. After she was reunited with her biological father, she learned that her birth mother had died within a year of her birth. She not only had older brothers and sisters (and stepsiblings) to meet for the first time, but she had a stepmother with whom to get acquainted, too.

Her "new" stepmom welcomed her into the family. Not long after that, however, her birth father died. When a rift ensued between her stepmom's children and her biological siblings, she found herself caught in the middle. Yet she and her stepmom maintained their new bond. They accepted one another because of the beloved one they shared: her stepmom's husband and her dad.

What a blessing to be accepted simply because of a love connection between others. There's no expected standard to measure up to or tests to pass. For most of those in blended families, this doesn't happen automatically. But if we as mature women can give our stepchildren that edge—that acceptance—it may smooth the rough spots that are sure to give us all bumps and bruises along the way.

Lord God, You have accepted me out of love for Your Son. Empower me to accept my stepchildren out of love for my husband. Amen.

Wonderful Counselor

Day 299

I will praise the Lord, who counsels me; even at night my heart instructs me. I have set the Lord always before me. Because he is at my right hand, I will not be shaken.

Psalm 16:7–8 NIV

Are you in the middle of a particularly difficult situation right now? Are you puzzled as to what course of action you should take? Whether you have your own biological children or are "just" trying to be a mother to your husband's children, you are striving to do a good job of raising them. That is not an easy task for a nonblended family, yet you deal with the dubious honor of having that big *S* stamped on your forehead. (Unfortunately, that *S* stands for Stepmom, not Supermom.) You struggle with the regular "mom stuff" (guilt, fatigue, doubt, inadequacy), and then pile on top of that all the "stepmom stuff" (guilt, fatigue, doubt, inadequacy), and *squash*! You're buried under a double helping of confusion and discouragement. Your sticky situation is stickier because of the complexities inherent in a blended family, and you just don't know what to do. Good news! The Lord is in the counseling business—*and* He doesn't charge by the hour. The verses say that not only will He counsel you, but your heart will teach you, even while you sleep. So focus on the Lord, seek His counsel, and you will find the answers you need.

Father, I praise You because You give me wise counsel. I trust that You are right beside me holding me steady. Amen.

Day 300

Riding High or Low?

Fitting every loose thought and emotion and impulse into the structure of life shaped by Christ.
2 Corinthians 10:5 msg

Living according to our fickle feelings is like riding a roller coaster: one day up, one day down. It's easy to fall into the trap of believing our thoughts more than what God says in His Word. Don't let every emotion that surfaces dictate the direction of the day. Capture loose thoughts with a Christ-centered net.

To begin this process, we need to latch on to God's promises and steady our course. We need to line up our feelings with what we know the Bible says. The apostle Paul said, "We walk by faith, not by sight" (2 Corinthians 5:7 nasb). Sometimes we won't sense God's presence, but because He has promised He'll never leave us, we must believe He's there. Jesus said, "Peace I leave with you; My peace I give to you" (John 14:27 nasb). Accept that peace. Let it rule in your heart. Concerned about having enough? "My God will supply all your needs" (Philippians 4:19 nasb). These are proven promises to stand on, promises we can live by.

God is a God of faith, and He works in ways that faith, not feelings, can discern. Trust Him. We must—even when we don't feel like it.

Dear heavenly Father, as a child of the King, I choose to accept Your promises. Thank You for all You've done for me. Amen.

A Glimpse Inside

He left the meeting place and went to Simon's house. Simon's mother-in-law was running a high fever and they asked him to do something for her. He stood over her, told the fever to leave—and it left. Before they knew it, she was up getting dinner for them.

Luke 4:38–39 MSG

In the first century, a high fever meant death was near.

Simon had just accepted the call to follow Jesus. Right on the heels of his decision, his plans were jeopardized. If his mother-in-law died, could that derail Simon's plan to be a disciple to Jesus? Could he leave his wife and family alone?

Have you ever been in a similar situation? Efforts to follow Christ in a deeper way get interrupted with a left curve that involves pressing family needs. Could that left curve be from the enemy in an attempt to derail you?

After Jesus miraculously healed Simon's mother-in-law, she was instantly back on the job, serving the Lord. Her response gives us a glimpse inside of Simon's household, of how loved and needed this woman was. We get a glimpse of what Jesus already knew.

This story reminds us that we will be facing tests and trials as we grow deeper in our faith. Jesus did not disappoint Simon's family. We can trust Him to care for our family's needs, even when we feel pressed from all sides. He won't disappoint us.

Lord, as I seek to follow You, let me trust You to straighten out the left curves. Amen.

Day 302

Follow the Leader

"I will lead the blind by ways they have not known, along unfamiliar paths I will guide them; I will turn the darkness into light before them and make the rough places smooth."

Isaiah 42:16 NIV

Do you ever feel like you are groping in the darkness? Sometimes life has a way of overwhelming us. We have no idea what is coming or how to deal with what has already come. We feel like we are stumbling around, with no clue where to step next.

But rather than stumbling, we can just stand still! God wants us to calm down, take a deep breath, and reach for His hand. He can see even in the dark. He knows all the bumps, all the curves, all the twists and turns that our lives will bring. And He will guide us.

In addition to guiding us, He will provide light for our journeys. He is light, and His wisdom will serve to illuminate our choices. He will also smooth out our paths, for His way is always the best way. By seeking Him in prayer, and by reading His Word, we will find that our darkness fades, our stumbling ceases, and our fears diminish.

Dear Father, thank You for guiding me. Help me to seek You in all my decisions, for I know You will never lead me in the wrong direction. Amen.

God's People

At one time you were not a people, but now you are God's people. In the past you had never received mercy, but now you have received God's mercy.

1 Peter 2:10 NCV

If you've served the Lord for a long period of time, it might be difficult to remember what your life was like before you entered into that life-changing relationship with Him. There was a time—for all of us—when we were alienated from God. But when we put our trust in Christ, we were swept into His family. We became "His" people. Isn't it a wonderful feeling to belong?

Maybe you're in the process of merging families and understand all too well the difference between "real" belonging and "forced." Maybe you don't think you'll ever all feel like one cohesive unit. Take heart! If God is truly your Father, then you will all learn to walk together in peace. Remember, you are all His children. Sure, there's bound to be some squabbling, but your Dad will get it all worked out—in time.

God mercifully, lovingly swept you under His wing; and He longs for you to have that same heart toward your children. They need to feel a part of something. They have to know that they belong.

Dear Lord, I want to extend the same nurturing love to my children that You offer to me. Help me create the right family environment—one where everyone feels safe and loved. Amen.

Day 304

Wise Planning

The plans of the mind and orderly thinking belong to man,
but from the Lord comes the [wise] answer of the tongue.
PROVERBS 16:1 AMP

It has been said that a woman's work is never done. To keep on top of caring for children, keeping the house clean, and managing a career takes careful planning. Some women are more successful at this than others and order their lives around schedules, lists, and planners.

There is no harm in doing this, but sometimes routine can get in the way of true mothering. It may be a choice between a clean bathroom or a story and cuddle with a child; or maybe a roast dinner needs to be sacrificed for an expedition to catch tadpoles. Stepmoms often feel this pressure more intensely, as they feel the other mother may be judging her home and assessing the way she handles the children.

The important thing is to remember to listen to God's voice. If we ask Him to speak to us and give us wisdom, we will know when it is right to abandon our plans and take time to do something with our families. The end results often speak for themselves: increased energy levels, joy, and stronger relationships. Plans and orderly thinking are needed to run a household, but don't forget to listen to God's voice. Sometimes He has a better plan for a situation.

Dear God, may I always be aware that Your wisdom can override my plans. Help me to listen for Your voice in every situation. Amen.

Day 305

God's Glory

The heavens declare the glory of God; the skies proclaim the work of his hands. Day after day they pour forth speech; night after night they display knowledge.

Psalm 19:1–2 NIV

God is speaking! Are we listening? It's easy to ignore or overlook the obvious. Each morning, God creates a unique sunrise that ushers in a brand-new day. Every evening, a sunset graces our landscape with colors that the most gifted artist can't accurately capture on canvas. As we hurry about our day, many times we are oblivious to God's creation—our backs turned, our ears closed.

Creation shouts God's glory! Majestic oak trees draw eyes heavenward while providing a home for birds and shade for animals. Water in rivers and lakes quietly sustains life. Seeds germinate and reproduce themselves, thus providing nourishment. The sun, moon, and stars are held in their exact place by His power. Even the tides can be accurately calculated because of God's sovereignty and faithfulness. Can you see it? Are you listening?

As Jesus entered Jerusalem on a donkey prior to His crucifixion, the people threw their cloaks on the road and shouted, "Hosanna!" When some of the Pharisees asked Jesus to rebuke His disciples, Jesus responded by telling them that even if they kept quiet, the stones would cry out! Do not miss it! Do not ignore God's creation. Listen to what God is revealing through His creation—the speech and knowledge that declare His glory!

Dear Lord, thank You for the beauty of Your creation. May I listen and learn so that I can give You glory! Amen.

Day 306

Such a Time

"Yet who knows whether you have come to the kingdom for such a time as this?"
Esther 4:14 NKJV

Being a stepmom is tough. We don't have the nine months of preparation and planning of a mother giving birth. There are often resentments, awkwardness, and other strong emotions with which to contend. To top it off, we're dealing with children who often don't understand how to cope with the change in their life. They can lash out from uncertainty and fear, not because they wish us ill will.

No woman wants to be thought of as the wicked stepmother portrayed so often in stories. We want to be loved by our new children. Our desire is to be a family unit that gets along well. Sometimes we may be tempted not to take a strong stand on issues in order to promote harmony or peace. However, we must always take a firm stance on important matters.

Take heart. Realize that God allowed you to be where you are for a purpose. Through the tough times, love with God's unconditional love, which may mean doing hard things. That's okay, because God's purpose will be fulfilled. He will bring beauty out of any situation, no matter how hopeless the outlook. We can trust our new family, with all its complexities, to God, knowing He has only our best interests in mind.

Thank You, Jesus, for the example You set—of love being a difficult walk that ended in beauty. Amen.

Day 307

Faithful to the End

Being confident of this very thing, that he which hath begun a good work in you will perform it until the day of Jesus Christ.
Philippians 1:6 KJV

Karlena stared at the stacks of wood surrounding her in the cabinetmaker's shop. It was a little overwhelming, but she was determined to choose just the right grain for her new kitchen. Suddenly, her eyes came to rest on a smaller pile. It was the most unique wood she'd ever seen.

"What is this?" she asked.

"Oh, that's wormy maple," said the cabinetmaker. "A nasty little worm gets in and crawls all through leaving a path in the wood. Bummer for the tree, but it sure makes a unique and pretty wood."

Karlena nodded slowly. "Yes," she said quietly. "That's what I want." It was such a reflection of her own life. She'd had quite a few rough times lately. She knew she wasn't always the stepmom she should be. She made a lot of mistakes and became easily frustrated; but just like the worm in the maple tree, she knew all of her weakness could be used for God's glory—to make an even more beautiful product in the end. He wasn't finished with her yet, but He wouldn't stop until He'd completed it.

Karlena smiled as she signed her contract. Her new cabinets would be a daily reminder of this truth.

You aren't finished with me yet, Lord. What a joy to know You're always at work in my life! Amen.

Day 308 Security in the Simplicity

Make it your ambition to lead a quiet life, to mind your own business and to work with your hands, just as we told you.

1 Thessalonians 4:11 NIV

Sometimes steplife seems to circle round us like a tornado, spinning and spinning faster and faster, spitting out debris with neither thought nor care. And when it gets so chaotic, a grasp of the basics is a source of peace. Grounded by simplicity, we can stand solid in the turmoil.

It helps us to focus on the simple and practical when the emotions and the understanding and all the intricacies of steplife are hard to grasp. Paul's principles are applicable to us, too, because the practical, the tactile, and the simplicity of obedience can offer quiet, comfort, and purpose in troubling times.

We can "lead a quiet life" by cleaning out the clutter in our minds and hearts, by spending some time alone, by refusing to be pulled into a fight or to overextend ourselves at others' requests.

We can "mind our own business" by accepting responsibility for ourselves and allowing others to do the same, by focusing on the choices we make and responding well to the choices of others.

We can "work with our hands" by focusing on the tasks before us, by not neglecting or procrastinating on the jobs we need to do, by helping those around us with a tangible example of our care and concern.

Father, help me to find great peace in my simple, everyday choices that bring You into everything I do, so that I may share You with others. Amen.

Joy Is a Command

For the kingdom of God is not eating and drinking, but righteousness and peace and joy in the Holy Spirit. For he who in this way serves Christ is acceptable to God and approved by men.

Romans 14:17–18 NASB

The Bible is full of hard teachings: to love when you don't feel like it, to sacrifice your most prized possessions if God asks it of you, to pour yourself out for others, to keep praying when you get no answers, to trust God in the midst of suffering. These things don't come naturally to us, while selfishness, greed, revenge, anger, and doubt seem a lot easier!

As Christians, we often define ourselves negatively: We *don't* do this; we *can't* do that; we *won't* do such and such. We put on glum faces and, Pharisee-like, glory in our self-deprivation. But in this passage, Paul tells us that we can serve Christ best by putting on joy. For some people this may be hard. But this and other passages make it clear that God expects us to be joyful, that it is a natural outpouring of our thankfulness for what Jesus has done for us.

We can win people to Jesus with our joy! This includes friends, children, stepchildren, husbands, relatives, and mere acquaintances. So put away those frowns, glares, and gloomy looks, and put on joy.

Dear Father, I praise You that You are a God of joy. I pray that those around me might be drawn closer to You through the joy I show. Amen.

Be Generous

Be generous, and someday you will be rewarded.
Ecclesiastes 11:1 CEV

The old adage that you can't out-give God is very true. When Ecclesiastes 11:1 speaks of giving, it isn't only in terms of possessions or money, but also time. In order for stepchildren, or even your own children, to love and respect you, they must have quality time with you.

The more we give of our time and efforts to our children, the more they will learn to trust and respect us. Children hunger for guidance and regulations in their lives even though they may rebel and complain about them. They prefer structure to chaos and limits rather than unrestrained freedom.

So many times parents make the mistake of giving their children "things" to replace the time spent away from them. As much as the children love and enjoy the toys and possessions, they much prefer that parents spend time with them.

When children are young, the opportunities for time together abound. Trips to the museum, library, zoo, park, or other places of interest in your town will create wonderful memories that will be returned with love years later.

When they are teens, we can give the gift of trust and some independence in their decision making. We may not always reap the harvest at the time we think it should come, but the generous giving of time and effort will make a difference in our lives as well as the lives of our precious children.

Precious Lord, help me today to give of myself generously to the lives of my children. Amen.

Difficult People

Recompense to no man evil for evil. Provide things honest in the sight of all men. If it be possible, as much as lieth in you, live peaceably with all men.

Romans 12:17–18 KJV

Cheri gritted her teeth as she hung up the phone, trying not to slam it down. Her father, usually drunk, only called to harangue her with tirades at the government and hassle her for money. After supper her stepdaughter Rachel called with similar demands. Even eight-year-old Andy, sensing her weakness, manipulated her about bedtime. Cheri held her head in her hands. Why did God surround her with people who kept her insides churning? And why couldn't her husband, Lee, understand her exhaustion? Somehow, she always ended up answering the phone.

Sensing she needed a break, Cheri visited her sister for a weekend. Refreshed, she returned home determined to deal with her relatives God's way. When she stopped berating herself for their struggles, Cheri felt less temptation to get revenge for their selfishness. She prayed for them daily and tried to help when possible. But when Dad or Rachel became abusive, Cheri turned on the answering machine and clicked off her cell. She shared Rachel's problems and Andy's stubbornness with Lee, refusing to play family martyr. Andy, sensing her resolve, argued less.

And their home, while not perfect, became a place where she, Lee, Rachel, and Andy all found peace.

Lord Jesus, please show me the best way to care for difficult people, and remind me to pray faithfully for them. Amen.

Day 312

Stepmothering for Dummies

Teach me thy way, O Lord, and lead me in a plain path.
Psalm 27:11 KJV

If only there were a comprehensive guide to stepparenting. A handy, do-it-yourself instruction manual guaranteed to equip you for stepmothering success. How to handle ex-wives? See page 124. Dealing with angry adolescents? Check out page 207. For tips on solving your toughest dilemmas, consult the Frequently Asked Questions in the back of the book. Then sit back and enjoy the bliss of stress-free stepparenting.

Such a book might sell millions of copies and secure a comfortable retirement for the author, but it could not teach you what practical experience can. Your family and the circumstances that brought you together are hardly textbook material, and nothing can better instruct you on what works and what doesn't than good old-fashioned trial and error.

There is no such thing as a perfect parent. You may be expected to know it all, but the truth is that you don't. Despite your best efforts, you will make mistakes. The key to overcoming them is to keep a "teach me" attitude toward God. Let Him turn your bloopers and blunders into on-the-job training. The knowledge you gain won't make you a perfect stepmother, but it will make you a successful one.

Dear heavenly Father, as discouraging as my failures are, remind me that they are also my best teachers. Help me to learn from my mistakes so that I don't have to repeat them. Amen.

Damage Control

They pay me back misery for mercy, leaving my soul empty.
Psalm 35:12 msg

Of all the books written on stepmothering, few deal with the other side of the blended families: sending our biological children to be with their father and stepmom. If, like our husbands, we came into a second marriage with our own children, we may not be the only stepmom in the mix. We have to share our children with their stepmom. Our children return from their time—and different house rules—with their dads and stepmoms. We dread our kids' times away and our mutual readjustment period upon their return.

There's not much we can do to control many of the circumstances in our lives, let alone those of our children. We do our best to be good stepmoms, but we suspect the stepmother of our children doesn't reciprocate. We refuse to badmouth our ex's wife. We try to help our children be more charitable to their stepmom (for their dad's sake, if no one else). But it's tough—or seemingly impossible.

We can learn from real people in the Bible who had overwhelming challenges totally out of their control, too. Or we can find a trusted friend to whom we can vent. We can pour out our sickness at heart to God. That may be all we can do for now, while we pray for a better day tomorrow.

God, I get so frustrated! Too often I have no control over the pain that comes into my kids' lives. Give me wisdom, Father. Protect my children from hurt. Amen.

Day 314

Finding Friendship

A man who has friends must himself be friendly, but there is a friend who sticks closer than a brother.

PROVERBS 18:24 NKJV

Stepmoms need friends. Can I get an "amen"? We need our friends' encouragement, friendship, and prayers. We need to have people we can call and vent to for ten minutes.

One stepmom, Jodie, purposely looked for successful stepmoms and talked to them. Talking through her problems helped her feel like she wasn't alone.

Sometimes we can see the root of our problems more clearly after we've talked with a friend. We need encouragement as stepmoms, but we also need empathy and wisdom. A true friend can give you all three.

Do you have any friends who are stepmoms? Why not ask God to send some empathizers into your life? Ask Him to lead you to other stepmoms who can listen, encourage, and cry with you. God loves meeting our needs.

But do you know who is your very best friend? Jesus. Jesus is the very best friend we could ever ask for. Proverbs 17:17 (NKJV) says, "A friend loves at all times." Jesus died so we could be with Him in heaven. Now that's a true friend. Aren't you glad Jesus is your friend, too?

Lord Jesus, thank You for being the best friend of all. Please help me through this day. I love You. In Your name, amen.

Memory Stones

Having predestined us to adoption as sons by Jesus Christ to Himself, according to the good pleasure of his will.
Ephesians 1:5 KJV

Anna felt lost. She had hoped this trip to the mountains of Colorado would produce a wonderful new memory for her blended family, but four days had produced nothing but hurt feelings and a lot of nasty bug bites on everyone.

She drifted around the campsite, lost in her thoughts. Most of the family had reluctantly gone with her husband, Dean, to gather firewood. Her eyes fell on Michael, her five-year-old stepson, who had stayed behind to finish constructing his pile of stones. Quietly, she watched him as he examined each stone carefully before setting it into its own place in his pile.

"What are you doing?" she asked softly.

"I'm remembering," Michael told her.

Anna couldn't resist. "Remembering what?" He turned and faced her, stone in hand. "This rock made me remember my tree house. And this one remembers the hospital where I got my tonsils out and Mommy and Daddy were *both* there.

"And this rock remembers our new house when you said you would love me. . . ." His voice trailed off, but Anna's tearful eyes urged him on. "It remembers that you love me—not instead of my mommy—but on top of all my mommy's love."

Take a moment to examine the memory stones in your life today.

Dear God, I remember the times and places You were there for me. Help me to cherish each one in my heart and never forget that Your promises always overcome anything I'm facing today. Amen.

Day 316 Prepare to Be Amazed!

With God's power working in us, God can do much, much more than anything we can ask or imagine. To him be glory.

EPHESIANS 3:20–21 NCV

Some situations in life seem so impossible. In our minds, we cannot image how God will work things out. Or how He can possibly use us to improve such sorry circumstances. But the Word tells us that we have an amazing strength within us. It's the power of God! With Him as our source, He can do anything—more than we can possibly ask or imagine—through us!

So the next time you have to go to court to face a custody battle, are dealing with stepkids that resent your presence in their lives, have to confront an unreasonable ex-spouse, or can't find a schedule that works for you *and* two other sets of parents, remember that with God's power within us, He can do anything!

Nothing is impossible when we are walking in God's way, allowing His Spirit free rein within us, and letting the love of Christ flow freely through us. All we need to do is give way to His will and then prepare to be amazed!

Father, I am amazed at how You work Your will in this world. You know the situations I face. You know the present circumstances in my life. I have run out of ideas for how to solve the problems. But You see all, know all, and are in all. You know how all this will turn out. Help me to rest in that knowledge and allow Your power to work through me. To You be all the glory! Amen.

Be Thankful

Day 317

So then, just as you received Christ Jesus as Lord, continue to live in him, rooted and built up in him, strengthened in the faith as you were taught, and overflowing with thankfulness.

Colossians 2:6–7 NIV

Are you known for being a thankful family? Or do you have some family members who struggle with grumbling and complaining? Do you look around at all that God has blessed you with and thank Him abundantly? Or do you look around and see clutter and chaos? Gather your family, and hold a group discussion. Even if the grumblers protest, let them know how important this is to you. Get out of your comfort zone, and be transparent with each other. Read this passage aloud, and discuss what it means. Commit together as a family that you will continue to live in Christ. Count your blessings as a family and pray. Thank God for all that He is and for all that He has done. Make this a regular event in your home. Try going around the dinner table several times a week and have everyone tell what he or she is specifically thankful for that day. You will be amazed at how an "attitude of gratitude" can change the atmosphere in your home. Be thankful!

Dear Father, thank You for all that You have blessed me with. Change my attitude to reflect my thankfulness. Amen.

Day 318

Trained to Listen

The LORD came and stood there, calling as at other times, "Samuel! Samuel!" Then Samuel said, "Speak, for your servant is listening."

1 SAMUEL 3:10 NIV

How many times do we have to repeat ourselves because our child is distracted: watching television, playing a game, reading a book, or any of a multitude of other things. The end result is that our request is ignored because he or she would rather continue doing something else. In our frustration, we often react with anger, causing more of a problem, instead of using wisdom to get the obedience we need.

If we are honest, we can admit to being distracted when our children want our attention. Of course, we always have an excuse because we are busy with something important. How funny! If questioned, our children would feel the same about their lack of consideration to us.

Learning to listen takes discipline. We must realize the importance of answering our children's questions, and we need to impress upon them the significance of listening to us. When we consider the number of times God has tried to "talk" with us, only to have us disregard Him for various reasons, we can begin to understand the necessity of teaching ourselves and our children to truly hear. When we begin to take the time to hear God, we will also hear our children, and by example they will be training to listen to us and to God.

Thank You for Your patience, Lord, as You show me how to listen. Amen.

Healing Hearts by Hand

And let us consider and give attentive, continuous care to watching over one another, studying how we may stir up (stimulate and incite) to love and helpful deeds and noble activities.

HEBREWS 10:24 AMP

Stepfamily holidays are tough. Time, money, gifts, traditions, expectations—it can be too much for a family struggling with painful wounds and emotions. But sometimes we can help.

The stepmom was hurting deeply herself, and she had neither the insight nor the experience to know how her stepkids were feeling. But she was willing to take a risk.

She helped her young stepdaughters with paint and glue and mismatched finds to create something only a mother could love. There was no grand pronouncement, no great plot, just a sunny afternoon at the kitchen table as they made a present for the woman she'd never met: their mom. They stuffed the creations into their backpacks and promised to hide them safely until Mother's Day.

Her stepkids were too young to understand the significance of the act, to know the hours she spent wondering if it was the right thing to do. But it was a start. It was a stitch over the cuts for her and, hopefully, a spot of salve for her stepdaughters, as together they would find their way to healing.

All we can do is leave the past behind and focus on now. May our efforts reach our own wounds and touch those around us as well.

Father, stir me up with Your grace so that my behavior matches the healing You bring. And help me pass that on. Amen.

Day 320

Children of God

What marvelous love the Father has extended to us! Just look at it—we're called children of God! That's who we really are.

1 John 3:1 MSG

Our wonderful, loving God never thinks twice about it. We're His kids, plain and simple. We've been adopted into His family, and we're grafted in. . .forever. And the love of God is beyond comprehension! What heights! What lengths! It meets us coming and going, no matter what we've done. And He love us, even when we feel completely unlovable. Talk about unconditional love!

Since you're a child of the King, you already know what it feels like to be a recipient of that amazing love. But what does it feel like to extend it to others, even those hardest to love? Sometimes loving the unlovable brings the most satisfaction of all. But can we really love like that? Is it possible to look at absolutely everyone with the same condition-free love and affection? If we ask the Lord for His thoughts on the matter, yes!

Today, make a special effort to experience and show "marvelous" love. It works like a healing balm, mending broken relationships. You will be amazed at its miraculous effect—on both you and the one you're loving.

Heavenly Father, thank You so much for extending such marvelous love. I can't understand it, Lord, but I want to share it with others. Show me how to do that, especially when it's hard. Amen.

I Know I Can

I can do all things through Christ which strengtheneth me.
Philippians 4:13 KJV

The Little Engine That Could by Watty Piper is a classic that has charmed children for decades. It tells the simple story of a plucky little engine who pulled a train of cars over the mountain when no other was willing to try. Her ability stemmed, not from might or size, but from her eager, optimistic belief that "I think I can."

The duties of stepmotherhood can be a burdensome, gravity-defying climb that leaves you breathless from the exertion. At times you may feel like the tired, old engine who puffed, "I cannot. . .I cannot. . . ," as it sadly retreated to the roundhouse. But with God as your engineer, no mountain is too high, no burden too heavy. His grace is sufficient at all times; His strength is made perfect in moments of your weakness.

No matter what kind of difficulty you are facing as a stepmother, you can overcome. Not by your own physical power or intellectual strength, but by the omnipotence of your heavenly Father. Trust in Him, and you'll be able to say with confidence, "I know I can!"

Dear heavenly Father, be my strength when I am weak. Give me courage when I am afraid. Refresh me when I am weary, and bless me with the kind of optimism that makes me eager to climb mountains for the view that awaits me at the top. Amen.

Day 322

Step Up to the Plate

When Jesus saw his mother and the disciple whom he loved standing nearby, he said to his mother, "Woman, behold, your son!" Then he said to the disciple, "Behold, your mother!" And from that hour the disciple took her to his own home.

John 19:26–27 ESV

In our culture we've borrowed all kinds of expressions from sports.

"Keep your stick on the ice."

"When in doubt, punt."

"Step up to the plate."

All take on additional meanings outside the arena or ball field.

As Christ hung on the cross, He shared a final poignant moment with His mother and dearest friend. Even though He had brothers and sisters in His birth family (Matthew 13:55–56), He relinquished the care of His mother to the apostle John. For reasons we don't know, the Lord knew that John would be the one to "step up to the plate" and care for His mother.

As stepmoms, we have also been called upon to "step up to the plate." No matter what the relationship is between our stepchildren and their birth mothers, we have a role to fill that belongs to us alone. No pinch hitter sits in the dugout. The ball has been thrown to us. We have the responsibility to do the best we can for our team—our family. Sometimes we may strike out. Sometimes we'll sacrifice for someone else and bunt.

But once in while we might just hit a home run!

Thank you, Father, for the unique position You've given me as a stepmom. Help me to do my part well and to finish strong. Amen.

Those Who Trust Him

Day 323

The LORD *is good, a refuge in times of trouble.*
He cares for those who trust in him.
NAHUM 1:7 NIV

These days, it's hard to trust anyone. We see horrible stories on the news, and we convince ourselves that there is no refuge in this world. We lock our dead bolts and carry our tiny bottles of mace, and we hope the boogeymen will stay away.

But there is a refuge, and His name is Jehovah! Our God is good. He is a strong protector, and His arms are a safe place. When we trust in Him, we have nothing to fear.

The problem comes when we forget to trust Him. All too often we take our eyes off of God and focus on the terrible things going on around us. Like Peter walking on the water (Matthew 14), we place our attention on the crashing waves instead of looking at the One who will keep us safe.

God wants us to look at Him. He longs for us to trust Him and Him alone. He loves us more than anything and wants to protect us. But He won't force Himself on anyone. We have to make the decision to run to Him, to stay close to Him, and to trust Him. When we do, He will care for us, and we can find rest and peace in His perfect refuge.

Dear Father, please help me to keep my eyes on You. I trust You.
Thank You for caring for me in times of trouble. Amen.

Day 324

Winning through Kindness

Therefore if thine enemy hunger, feed him; if he thirst, give him drink: for in so doing thou shalt heap coals of fire on his head. Be not overcome of evil, but overcome evil with good.
ROMANS 12:20–21 KJV

Candace connected well with her stepsons, Jace and Jack. She and their mother cooperated in arranging the twins' activities.

But the moment Candace met Brent's elderly mother, Adele, she realized her mother-in-law might never accept her. Adele never displayed family pictures that included Candace. She tried to engineer family get-togethers without Candace's input, generating quarrels between Candace and Brent.

One Christmas Adele caught a cold and remained home, refusing offers of help. Candace hadn't enjoyed the holidays so much in years. She was tempted to let Adele suffer the isolation she demanded. But Candace prayed for her and encouraged her husband to call and visit for a while when he and the boys shoveled her snow. Candace brought Adele's favorite comfort food: roast, potatoes, and carrots. From then on, Candace took this dinner to her mother-in-law whenever she was ill—and occasionally, just because.

Adele didn't change much. But she couldn't hide her delight when Candace brought the steaming dish. Adele once mentioned that her mother cooked this favorite when she was ill, and Candace finally glimpsed the person hiding inside the armor of stubbornness. Shortly before Adele died, Candace received a thank-you note signed, "Love, Adele."

Lord, I don't know what flame You'll light inside others through my actions. But I pray the kindness You strengthen me to give will do Your work. Amen.

Look at Me, Look at You

Day 325

When they measure themselves with themselves and compare themselves with one another, they are without understanding and behave unwisely.
2 Corinthians 10:12 AMP

In a world of trying to "measure up," just imagine a square boasting to a triangle about having more sides. Or an inch straining to be a yard. A dozen striving to redefine the number twelve. Such endeavors are exercises in futility, to be sure; but God also cautions people against thinking themselves superior or inferior to another. Like the stepmom situation down the street. You'd feel better, look better, or do stepmothering better in her shoes. Or, *I'm glad I'm not her*. So, how does God want to help you let her be her and let you be you?

God jumps at the opportunity to say that each one is made in His image (Genesis 1:26). Also, He personally crafted you and her differently (Psalm 139:13–16). You are the only one to fill your spot and she, hers. On top of that, God has good work for each one in Christ to do (Ephesians 2:10). Now this, God says, is an exercise in "fruit-ility."

Taking the opportunity to get to know her or to learn from her will bring out Christ's best in you. With that perspective, why would anyone want to fall back into the slush of comparison?

Dear Lord, please help me to bear fruit through who I am in You instead of thinking I could do it better if I was like. . . Amen.

Day 326

Worry Free!

The Lord is good to those who wait hopefully and expectantly for Him, to those who seek Him [inquire of and for Him and require Him by right of necessity and on the authority of God's word]. It is good that one should hope in and wait quietly for the salvation (the safety and ease) of the Lord.

LAMENTATIONS 3:25–26 AMP

In this society of instant gratification, we can easily become impatient when problems are not immediately resolved or circumstances remain unchanged for the better. Instead of praying and placing the problem at God's feet, we wring our hands. In lieu of hope, we are filled with despair. Instead of seeking God's power and will, we try to resolve problems under our own power and with our own agenda in mind.

Jeremiah tells us that the Lord is good to those of us who wait for Him with hope and expectancy, to those who ask Him to work in the situation, relying on the promises found in His Word.

Want to reduce stress? Write Lamentations 3:25–26 on an index card and make this promise your morning and evening mantra. Believe it. Claim it. Make it a part of your life. When you do, your worries will ease away, as will the wrinkles they are bound to bring.

I wait for You, Lord, with hope and expectations of good things to come. Today I seek Your face, relying on Your promises and the authority of Your Word. I fold my hands, resting secure in the knowledge that You will bring good things to pass in Your time—not mine. And in doing so, I am at peace. Praise be to Your wonderful name! Amen.

Things Above

If ye then be risen with Christ, seek those things which are above, where Christ sitteth on the right hand of God. Set your affection on things above, not on things on the earth.

Colossians 3:1–2 KJV

There are two ways we can choose to live. We can spend time and energy seeking earthly treasures or heavenly ones. The choices are diametrically opposed to one another and have eternal consequences. The battle is a daily one.

When earthly affections govern our hearts, our lives reflect temporary treasures. We may spend our lives seeking beautiful homes, fulfilling careers, or satisfying hobbies. Fashion may drive our spending. Food may rule our appetites. Someday, however, homes, careers, hobbies, clothes, and food will all be gone. What will be left?

When we choose to set our affections on things above, we are choosing to love God and love people. At the conclusion of our earthly lives, eternal rewards will remain. Loving God means investing time and energy in our personal relationship with Him by reading His Word and communicating through prayer. Our hearts are changed as we grow in His image. Loving people means pouring our lives into them—encouraging them on their spiritual journey.

Homes, careers, and hobbies are fine. But there is so much more to life. Don't miss it! Keep your eyes where Jesus is. Set your affection on things above.

Dear Lord, help me set my affection on You and eternal priorities. Amen.

Day 328

Feeling the Forecast

Be humble and gentle. Be patient. . .
making allowance for each other's faults.
Ephesians 4:2 NLT

Folks who deal with certain health issues can sense imminent weather changes. They say their discomfort increases even before the low-pressure system arrives. On the other hand, in response to a sunny and dry forecast the same people say, "Bring it on!" By the way, what do your loved ones sense or feel ahead of your expected arrival?

When Paul asked his friends from Ephesus to meet him in Miletus (Acts 20:17), what did they sense as he approached? No doubt they sensed refreshing breezes of encouragement and warmth because they were actually sad to the point of tears when Paul departed.

What do your stepchildren feel before you come through the door? Instead of sensing more pressure, do they relax at the thought of a gentle and humble spirit? Can they anticipate a glad-to-see-you smile? Can they count on a hug? If a delicate issue is on their minds, can they expect a listening ear? Now that's a forecast that everyone anticipates.

Dear Lord, please forgive me for fulfilling a gloomy forecast. Instead of more aches and pains, may I brighten my stepchildren's day! Amen.

Day 329

Hold His Hand

Trust in the Lord *with all thine heart; and lean not unto thine own understanding. In all thy ways acknowledge him, and he shall direct thy paths.*

Proverbs 3:5–6 KJV

Life's journey will take us over many peaks and through many valleys. At the top of a mountain, we know we can trust God's plan. But down in the dark shadows, we're not so sure. Is He really there? Does He really care? His Word says He does.

The psalmist David was faced with many trials. He was on the run for his life, hiding in caves, clamoring for God's help. Did God relieve him of all his trials? No. Yet David penned songs full of praise for a magnificent Creator. Paul sat chained in a prison and wrote of a faithful Lord who would never let him down. Hebrews 11 records name after name of people who trusted in their heavenly Father despite their circumstances.

Trust. We're often leery of releasing what's in our hands and trusting God. Yet scripture directs us to do that very thing. Not to try to understand, but to follow Him. God rules both the mountaintops and the valleys with love and wisdom. Corrie ten Boom said, "Never be afraid to trust an unknown future to a known God." Let go. He'll be there.

Father, thank You for Your promises. I trust in You. Amen.

Day 330

True Need

For everyone who asks receives, and he who seeks finds, and to him who knocks it will be opened.
Luke 11:10 NKJV

The age of the child doesn't matter much when we go to the grocery store. They all want something that isn't on the shopping list—something they can't do without for another minute. They ask. They cajole. They beg. Sometimes there are tears or tantrums.

This behavior is annoying because, as mothers, we know they don't truly need the item they are wanting. It is a desire or want that usually comes from their peers or a commercial on television, not from any actual hunger or deprivation. When money is tight, we have the responsibility to teach our children the difference between wants and needs and not give in to every whim they have, because this only promotes selfishness.

How many times do we ask God for something that is a selfish desire couched in a feeling of desperate need? Our emotions have taken over and we feel we have to have our prayer answered in a certain way. We may be disappointed when God's answer isn't what we expected.

We can teach our children much by setting the example of begging God for the things that matter most: His will for our lives and His divine guidance. When we are walking close to Him, all worldly fears and concerns take a backseat. We can know we have received exactly what we need.

Thank You, Lord, for providing all I need. Amen.

Day 331

Habit of Grace

Therefore, rid yourselves of all malice and all deceit, hypocrisy, envy, and slander of every kind.
1 Peter 2:1 NIV

Malice, deceit, hypocrisy, envy, slander—not flattering character traits. Yet stepmothering tends to bring out the worst in us sometimes, turning even the most generous and even-tempered soul into a crazy person. But we can fight it when we learn to make the opposite a habit. We need something to put in the place of all those undesirable emotions, and *grace* fits the bill.

Sure, we can respond with grace during the easy times; and it's even fun to be generous and kind and compassionate when that's what we're getting in return. But what about the hard times, when our first and natural response is something far less than graciousness? That's when our habit will help.

We can learn to be aware of our grace and generosity and kindness and compassion when we practice it, notice what it feels like, and consciously make the choice to ingrain the behavior within so that we can repeat it. Then, when a steplife ripple or tidal wave hits, we can grab onto our habit, review our practices, and act with grace despite the pull to behave otherwise.

When we have something in our arsenal with which to battle the malice, deceit, hypocrisy, envy, and slander, fighting is easier. And our habit of grace will serve us well as the battle rages.

Father, thank You for Your grace that lives in me and enables me to rise above damaging choices. Please help me practice this habit of grace every day. Amen.

Day 332

God's Purposes

Though I walk in the midst of trouble, you preserve my life; you stretch out your hand against the wrath of my enemies, and your right hand delivers me. The Lord will fulfill his purpose for me; your steadfast love, O Lord, endures forever. Do not forsake the work of your hands.

Psalm 138:7–8 ESV

Do you ever feel that God has abandoned you? Left you to face your difficulties alone? Perhaps you've even said to Him what the psalmist said in Psalm 138: "Do not forsake the work of your hands." He created us; He put us into the families we're in, whether by birth or by marriage.

Yet too many times our circumstances don't meet our expectations. Whatever happened to "happily ever after"? Those children who aren't yours by birth, but are yours by choice, turn into little monsters, resisting your attempts to love them unconditionally. Outside influences, things, or people you thought were supporting you, turn away and become obstacles to realizing your dreams.

Yet through all of it, God is working out His purposes, using the good and the bad. He has a plan, a purpose for each one of us, and He delights in using blessing and trouble to bring it about. He loves us too much to forsake us and leave us helpless and hurting. It probably won't happen overnight, but we can know that God is working, fulfilling His purpose of conforming us to the image of His Son, using the bad, as well as the good (see Romans 8:28–29).

Father, on difficult days, please remind me of Your amazing plan for my life. Amen.

Cling-Free Motives

We didn't have any hidden motives when we won you over,
and we didn't try to fool or trick anyone.
1 THESSALONIANS 2:3 CEV

Even more tenaciously than lint adheres to a black sweater, subtle, impure motives cling to the things we do for others, no matter how hard we try to shake them off. Like this: A stepmom runs out to buy her stepdaughter a new outfit—she felt guilty for making up an excuse why she couldn't sit down to play her favorite game. Another stepmom dishes out compliments to her stepson, only to get him to watch his younger siblings Saturday night. Can your actions be free of clingy selfish and impure motives?

Writing as a sort of stepparent to the Thessalonians, Paul made it clear that no under-the-table-motives clung to his message of Christ or to his ministry among them. He could have preached about Christ just to meet his weekly evangelism quota. He could shorten his visit on the pretense that he had a busy week or pretend to care about them, only to impress them with his charisma. Instead, he presented himself free of "lint" so it didn't detract from the beauty of Christ and His gift of salvation.

The next time you wear a black outfit, may it remind you to check your motives for "clingies." Like Paul, it'll be your joy to communicate a cling-free message.

O, Lord, I confess that linty motives have clung to my actions.
Please help me not detract others from Your beauty. Amen.

Day 334

Ambassador for Christ

And he took a child, and set him in the midst of them: and when he had taken him in his arms, he said unto them, Whosoever shall receive one of such children in my name, receiveth me.

Mark 9:36–37 KJV

Our Savior had a special place in His heart for children. It was a distinguishing quality that set Him apart from the male-dominated society in which He lived. He urged His followers to embrace the innocent qualities of little ones and pronounced judgment on those who offended them. Jesus was an ambassador for children, and now He has passed that torch on to you.

You didn't bring your stepkids into the world. They automatically joined your life when you married their father. As "just" their stepmother, you might feel like the low gal on the totem pole, but the truth is that you have answered a high calling.

Jesus went out of His way to address the children in His midst. He took time out of His busy ministry to hold, bless, feed, and heal them. As you set aside some of your own plans and dreams to make room for your stepchildren, know that you are not only receiving *them*, you are receiving Christ as well.

Dear Father, help me treat my stepchildren as You would, and remind me that my acts of kindness and love are done not just to them, but to You as well. Amen.

Before and After Eden

Day 335

So the L*ORD* *God sent them out of the Garden of Eden, where they would have to work the ground from which the man had been made.*
GENESIS 3:23 CEV

We have no idea how long Adam and Eve lived in the Garden of Eden before the tempter settled in. Nor do we know how much time elapsed before Adam and Eve succumbed to the temptation. By the third chapter of Genesis, everything in Eden was upside down. What had been a blissful home was now a place of insecurity, fears, and doubts.

How quickly things can change! Love that had been effortless and innocent now required commitment and forgiveness. And a lot of hard work. But Adam and Eve endured. They shared love first in a perfect Eden and afterward in a thorny exile. Yes, God had banished them from the Garden because of their sinful choices. Yes, their life was filled with bitter trials. But they were never *abandoned* by God. He stuck with them, even in exile.

It doesn't take long before our own Eden seems to turn upside down. Reality settles in quickly. Like Adam and Eve, our marriage can't escape the consequences of our own sinfulness. But we are not in this marriage alone. God is with us and can help us find our way back to Eden.

Thank You, Lord, for glimpses of Eden in our romance. During those times, when we are communicating well, appreciating each other, and aware of how richly You have blessed us, we get a taste of perfect love. It gives us a longing to get back to Eden. Amen.

Above All

Above all, love each other deeply, because love covers over a multitude of sins.
1 Peter 4:8 NIV

Every family goes through its share of rough patches. You might not be facing a major crisis, but it's the little annoying things that have got you down lately: You come home to find the house a mess after spending all day cleaning it; you made a batch of cookies for a special party, and you find that the kids have gotten into them; your youngest child has made a juice trail all over the new carpet—the list goes on. Things just never seem to get any easier. And that's the truth we all must face. Life isn't easy, and it never will be easy. We must come to grips with that fact. Accept the truth with grace and a sense of humor. Love is the tie that binds us all together. Laugh a bunch and love a lot! Love covers over a multitude of messes! Life might actually start to *seem* a little less difficult with a different perspective. Ask the Lord to give you a new perspective today. Invite Him to fill your heart to overflowing with love for Him and for your family.

Dear Father, I confess that I have been more
focused on all of life's little problems than on You.
Please change my heart and fill me up with Your love. Amen.

Pray Without Ceasing

Day 337

The earnest (heartfelt, continued) prayer of a righteous man makes tremendous power available.

James 5:16 AMP

Stepchildren often lead a fractured existence: shuffled from one house to another at arbitrary intervals, continually packing and unpacking, switching from one set of schedules, rules, and expectations to another. And for stepmoms, it can be equally difficult to be constantly adjusting roles and responsibilities. At one moment we are deep in the challenges of loving, disciplining, training, and teaching our children; the next moment we have to stop all that and let them go to someone else. In a joint custody situation, they can be out of our control and influence more than they are with us.

In this situation, there is nothing we can do but recognize that, ultimately, these are God's children and lift them up to Him in prayer. Prayer is a great gift. It allows us to partner with God in the work He is doing in other people's lives and hearts. This includes our stepchildren, whether we are together or apart.

While we are sleeping, God is watching over and loving them. While we are watching television, God is watching over and loving them. While we are in line at the supermarket, God is watching over and loving them. He can take care of them far better than we can!

Dear Father, thank You for how much You love me and my children. Please help me remember to lift them up to You in prayer hour by hour. Amen.

Day 338

Motivated by Love

Although in Christ I could be bold and order you to do what you ought to do, yet I appeal to you on the basis of love.
Philemon 8–9 NIV

Living in twenty-first-century America, we cannot comprehend Paul's dilemma in writing this letter. First, he wrote from prison on behalf of his dear friend Onesimus, a slave who had run away from Philemon. In the ancient Roman world, recaptured slaves could expect crucifixion or equally horrible fates. Paul's letter could have sealed Onesimus's death. Paul also admitted he had harbored the escaped slave. This not only might have destroyed his close relationship with Philemon, but put him in great personal danger, as Romans regarded sheltering a runaway slave as theft.

But Paul did not shrink from the complicated situation. With holy boldness, he lovingly but firmly asked Philemon, in the name of love, to forgive Onesimus and welcome him back not as a slave, but as a brother in Christ. Paul, a prisoner with little money, even offered to reimburse Philemon for any financial losses he suffered.

We may find ourselves dealing with difficulties involving new and ex-spouses, stepchildren, and multiple in-laws. Our culture may demand one action when we believe God's Word directs us to do the opposite. If we, like Paul, act with Christ's authority and—above all—love, we open the door for relationship miracles.

Loving, merciful God, thank You for liberating me when I was a spiritual slave. Help me to be bold and generous in setting others free. Amen.

Prayer Replaces Worry

Day 339

Don't worry about anything; instead, pray about everything. Tell God what you need, and thank him for all he has done.

PHILIPPIANS 4:6 NLT

How easy it is to tell someone not to worry, but how difficult it is in practice. All mothers tend to worry about their children. Stepmoms seem to have even more worries. They may fret about whether their stepchildren will accept them and love them. Stepmoms also stew over the same things as the birth mother—things such as illnesses, poor attitudes, disobedience, and rebellion. These things will come whether the child is by birth or by marriage.

This scripture reminds us to pray about everything. This includes any and all problems that arise during stepparenting. God knows our needs before we ask Him for help; but just like any parent, He desires our asking Him to help. We see the needs of our children before they do many times; but when we are patient and let them come to us for help, they are usually more open to the advice we have for them.

The other part of this verse is just as important. When God intervenes and works a miracle or when He answers a simple prayer, He deserves our prayer of thanksgiving and our praise. Then the peace that passes all understanding will come to us and sustain us, because that is His promise.

Precious Lord, help us today to remember You are concerned about every part of our lives, and we can come to You in prayer, thanking You for Your promises and love. Amen.

Day 340

Courage in the Face of Opposition

They were all trying to frighten us, thinking, "Their hands will get too weak for the work, and it will not be completed."

NEHEMIAH 6:9 NIV

Nehemiah was an amazing man. He heard that the walls of Jerusalem had been torn down; and immediately he requested permission from the king of Persia to return to Jerusalem and rebuild the walls of the city. While he and his fellow Jews were rebuilding the walls, troublemakers tried to halt the work. They made fun of and even threatened the Jews in the hopes that they would abandon their project. In each case, Nehemiah encouraged the workers and prayed to the Lord for strength. The Jews didn't give up, and eventually the walls of Jerusalem were rebuilt.

Do you ever feel that fear is hindering your calling from God? Are you confronted by people who do not believe in you or by those who want your mission to fail? Do you feel Satan dragging you down and discouraging you as you try to complete the work God has called you to? Take heart! Your task may be daunting, but the Lord is with you. Be inspired by Nehemiah's courage in the face of hostility. Follow his example by praying to the Lord for strength. Despite any opposition, trust in the Lord, and He will see you through.

Dear Lord, although I am afraid, I put my trust in You. Strengthen my hands for Your work. Give me the courage to prevail. Amen.

Look at Me, Child

Day 341

Keep your eyes on Jesus, who both began and finished this race we're in.
HEBREWS 12:2 MSG

A mom tried to get her three-year-old son to look at the photographer because he kept gawking at everything *but* the camera. Getting him to focus was no small task. So what causes grown-ups to sometimes get their eyes on everything *but* Jesus?

Well, many disciples turned away from Jesus when His teaching became too difficult to accept (John 6:60). Peter took his eyes off Jesus to gawk at his circumstances (Matt. 14:29–30).

As a stepmom, what catches your eye, causing you to look away from Christ? Perhaps anger grabs your attention when the "mom" makes more demands about what her children can and can't do at your house. Maybe insecurity stares you in the face when your stepson defies you—again. Perhaps an "if only I'd gotten off to a better start" clamors for you to look in its direction.

Like the little boy, no matter what is going on around you, Jesus wants your eyes fixed on Him. Some issues may require some time to work through them, but Christ can keep them from having the power to gain your full attention. Only Christ is worthy of that! He loves to have you look at Him, refusing to let other things distract you. Now that's a picture!

Lord, please forgive me for letting so many things get my attention. Help me to keep my eyes upon You. Amen.

Day 342

On Prayer

Continue in prayer, and watch in the same with thanksgiving.
Colossians 4:2 KJV

True prayer is a powerful tool. It's how we communicate with our heavenly Father. But that's just the point. We must actively communicate with Him.

The first word in this verse is *continue*. It is a significant word in that it indicates a need for consistency. How faithful are you in your prayer life? There needs to be more thoughtful discipline in most of our prayer lives. We shouldn't be throwing a bunch of mismatched thoughts together and calling them prayer. It's true that sometimes our hearts will be so heavy that all we can muster are groanings and broken thoughts. The Holy Spirit intervenes at those times (Romans 8:26). However, we must be sure that we truly are concentrating and putting effort into our prayers—not just spouting words to soothe our consciences.

Consider also the word *watch*. In other words, pay attention. Concentrate. Make time to pray free of distraction. When you go to God, go with a purpose and watch for results.

Prayer is a powerful tool and a wonderful gift. Use it. Get involved with it. Let God bless you and your family through it. Realize that it's worth the effort you put into it.

Thank You, God, that I may come to You with my joys and burdens. Let me be a blessing to others through my prayer life. Amen.

Day 343

Well Placed

I shall place you in your own land: then shall ye know that I the Lord have spoken it, and performed it.
Ezekiel 37:14 KJV

Have you ever felt as if you don't belong? I think we all have at one time or another. When we walk into a room full of strangers, when we step out to do something for the Lord that we've never done before, or when we look at the children we are responsible for raising and wonder why we were given this work.

Children can also feel alienated from those around them. Anytime they are in a new situation, such as at church, school, or sporting events, they can easily believe they don't fit in. Even a confident child can use bravado to cover insecurity. We need to be encouraging and understanding of what they are experiencing, because we have felt that before, too.

One of the truths we can share with our children is that they are in this situation because God has placed them there for a purpose. We can trust God in that. We can also impart that being uncomfortable is okay and will only last for a time. Making new friends, or learning something that will last a lifetime, can come from these uncomfortable situations. God knows why He performs certain things in our lives. We only have to trust.

Lord, help me to know my place is with You, wherever You would have me to be. Amen.

Day 344

It's All in the Seeking

"God will stick with you as long as you stick with him. If you look for him he will let himself be found; but if you leave him he'll leave you."
2 Chronicles 15:2 msg

Have you ever played hide-and-seek with a small child? If you are the one hiding, you might hide behind a door or under the kitchen table, letting your feet "accidentally" show. You certainly wouldn't hide in the attic or in a dark closet full of coats. Why? Because the child would never be able to find you. She would give up because finding you is too difficult, or she would cry because she lost you.

When we lose sight of God, He will never be far away. Just as in a game of hide-and-seek with a child, God allows Himself to be found when we're ready to search for Him. He desires that we make an effort in seeking Him—through prayer, reading our Bibles, and communing with other Christians—but He will never be impossible to find as long as we are searching. However, if we give up looking for God, we will never find Him. Our communion with God must be intentional. He desires to walk with us; and He will always be there, waiting for us to find Him and celebrating when we do.

Dear Lord, thank You for sticking with me. When I lose You, help me to find You again. I never want to leave You. Amen.

Dealing with the Fear Factor

There is no fear in love. But perfect love drives out fear, because fear has to do with punishment. The one who fears is not made perfect in love.
1 John 4:18 niv

A stepmother worked for years to develop a better relationship with her husband's teenage sons. They plowed over her, emotionally, verbally, and sometimes physically. As a result, fear set in. She wondered if things would ever change, if the situation could possibly improve. Worse still, she wondered if she had the gumption to keep trying.

Fear can be a real showstopper. It can freeze us in our tracks, keep us from moving forward. That's why it's such a relief to realize that perfect love casts out fear. When we trust God enough to hand our fears over to Him, He bathes us in His love. We can't drive away fears, try as we may. But He can.

Today, allow God's perfect, holy love to drive away any fears you've been struggling with. Don't allow them to serve as speed bumps to your faith. Acknowledge them, and give them to the One who is capable of handling your fears. Then watch as He showers you with His perfect love.

Lord, I'll admit I've been afraid at times. . .afraid of rejection from others in my family. . .afraid of making mistakes. Today I give my fears to You. Remind me daily that there is no fear in love. And may I never forget that You are love. Amen.

Day 346

The Trust of the Powerless

"O Lord, no one but you can help the powerless against the mighty! Help us, O Lord our God, for we trust in you alone."

2 Chronicles 14:11 NLT

Asa was the third king of Judah, and he did what was right in the eyes of the Lord. He tore down idols and removed pagan altars, looking to God for wisdom and strength. During this time, God gave the people of Judah rest from their enemies until the Cushites attacked them. King Asa easily could have listened to the advice of his palace advisers or his military men as Judah prepared to go into battle. However, Asa, king of Judah, called on the name of the Lord. He affirmed Judah's trust in God and sought to do the Lord's will. Indeed, God crushed the Cushite army and gave Judah a great victory because Asa relied on God and not on his own power.

Sometimes we feel powerless against the mighty stresses that we feel in our lives. Between our husbands, children, work, church, and all of the other things we manage to squeeze into each of our days, we are overburdened, overworked, and overwhelmed. King Asa offers a model for us to live by. We must acknowledge that we are weak and that we need God's help; and then we must trust, not in ourselves, but in God. God will see us through.

Dear Lord, I am powerless without You. I offer You my life right now. Take control and help me, Lord, as I put all my trust in You. Amen.

My Little Darling

Now Israel loved Joseph more than all his children.
Genesis 37:3 KJV

Israel (Jacob) was a blessed man. His quiver was filled to the brim with twelve strapping boys and his daughter, Dinah. But there was one child, the son of his beloved Rachel, who held the key to his heart—Joseph. A smart boy, well behaved and obedient. A dreamer with ambition and wisdom beyond his years. Joseph, the joy of his father's old age, the promise of Israel's future, was despised by his brothers.

The animosity between Joseph and his ten brothers stemmed from their father's unbridled favoritism. Israel's preference was well known among the tents of his people, and the result was disastrous. Twelve young men who should have been devoted to one another as brothers were divided into two groups: Rachel's children and not Rachel's children.

Do you have a child who holds a special place in your heart? Maybe it is the babe of your own womb, adored long before your stepchildren came along. Perhaps it is the best behaved or most loving child in your family. Regardless, your responsibility to your children is to love them equally. Don't divide them into categories of "his" and "mine." Distribute your affection evenly, and work to enforce their unity as siblings. Children have antennae tuned to detect partiality. You aren't doing your little darling any favors by setting him or her apart from the others.

Dear Lord, help me learn Israel's lesson. Bless my heart with the ability to love all of my children equally, and may my actions never foster jealousy and hatred among them. Amen.

Day 348

Claiming the Promises of God

"And now, O Lord, I am your servant; do as you have promised concerning me and my family. May it be a promise that will last forever."
1 Chronicles 17:23 NLT

David had been given an extraordinary promise from the Lord—that one of his sons would build a temple for the Lord. In addition, God promised to establish the throne of David, through his son, forever. David celebrated this promise in wonder. He was amazed that God had taken him from a lowly shepherd boy to the king of Israel and that He promised to extend his family line forever. In this verse, David claimed the Lord's promises as he rejoiced.

As we read about God's promises to David, we should feel cause for celebration as well. We know the rest of the story. Through David's line came Jesus Christ who will rule as king in heaven for all eternity. This story should also help to increase our faith. We may not have received the same promises that David did, but as believers, we have certainly received promises from God. God loves each of us and cares about our lives. He assures us that He will take care of our families; and as we read here about David, we also know that we can trust God. Like David, we must simply believe God and claim the promises He has given to us.

Dear Lord, You have richly blessed me and my family. Reveal Your promises to me, teaching me to trust You enough to claim those promises in Your name. Amen.

Day 349

Hospitality Revisited

Offer hospitality to one another without grumbling.
1 Peter 4:9 NIV

Hospitality is far more than inviting friends for dinner. It's a practice we can adopt as part of our daily lives, and we'll come to see the benefits right away.

Hospitality promotes community and connection. We may think it sounds funny to practice hospitality with our family in our homes, but that's the perfect place to start—and often the hardest. Practicing hospitality means focusing on the other person, overlooking her flaws or looking past her own inhospitable behavior to seek what would make her feel welcome, safe, wanted, and nourished.

We can *welcome* our stepkids with love and respect. Sometimes, the same isn't returned, but we can keep practicing our hospitality as an example for them.

We can create a *safe* environment where no one is belittled, judged, or treated unfairly because of a difference in genealogy. Practicing our hospitality here means looking out for those who can't look out for themselves.

We can *want* the family we have. Everyone may not always get along; members may argue or jockey for position; but despite the struggles, we can practice our hospitality by cherishing our family and working hard to help everyone succeed.

We can *nourish* those around us with good words and good times that make good memories. Dinner may be nice, and special occasions may mean lavish spreads, but the goodness of our hearts will fill our loved ones even more.

Father, please guide me to practice Your kind of hospitality every day to help me create an environment of Your kind of love and joy. Amen.

Day 350

Not Alone

For I am convinced that neither death nor life, neither angels nor demons, neither the present nor the future, nor any powers, neither height nor depth, nor anything else in all creation, will be able to separate us from the love of God that is in Christ Jesus our Lord.

Romans 8:38–39 niv

Cell phones. Internet. Text messages. Today it is easier than ever for people to stay connected to one another. It's almost as simple to keep in touch with someone living across the ocean as with someone living across town. Yet statistics show that people are lonelier than ever.

We sit at desks and stare at screens, and we feel isolated and alone. More than anything, we long to feel a connection with someone. But no matter how lonely or secluded we may feel, God is right there! He loves us more than anything, and nothing can ever separate us from that love.

God loved you and me before time began. He calls each of us by name. He created us, He knows our thoughts, and He sees our hearts. And the love He has for us is more powerful than anything we can imagine. He has always loved us, and He will never stop loving us. We are not alone.

Dear Father, thank You for Your love, which transcends time and space and is bigger and more powerful than any barrier. Amen.

Build on Solid Rock

Day 351

Anyone who hears and obeys these teaching of mine is like a wise person who built a house on solid rock. Rain poured down, rivers flooded, and winds beat aganist that house. But it did not fall, because it was built on solid rock.

Matthew 7:24–25 CEV

The day started like any other. Meg ate breakfast, read the paper, and spent some time alone in prayer. Then she left the house for her yearly mammogram appointment. She was not prepared for what happened next—or was she? Over the following week, Meg was diagnosed with breast cancer. Discussions of treatment seemed unreal. Her world had been turned upside down. Meg would never be the same.

None of us can accurately predict what tomorrow may bring. Yet we can best prepare by building on the solid foundation of Jesus Christ, the Rock, today. When our life is built on His truth, we will never be destroyed. Paul describes Christian hardship in 2 Corinthians 4:8–9 (NIV): "We are hard pressed on every side, but not crushed; perplexed, but not in despair; persecuted, but not abandoned; struck down, but not destroyed."

Although battling cancer was not easy, Meg endured. Her chemo treatments became opportunities to tell others about the love of Jesus. Hope and peace defined her. Meg had built her life on solid rock. What about you? Are you preparing for tomorrow by building on Jesus Christ today?

Dear Lord, help me follow You today so that I am prepared for whatever I may face tomorrow. Amen.

Day 352

Do Not Be Afraid

An angel of the Lord appeared to them, and the glory of the Lord shone around them, and they were terrified. But the angel said to them, "Do not be afraid. I bring you good news of great joy that will be for all the people."

Luke 2:9–10 NIV

"Do not be afraid."

Those comforting words were the first words on the lips of angels when delivering a message from heaven to mere mortals. Jesus used that phrase many times with His disciples after a miracle or unexpected turn of events. As He approached the disciples' boat, walking on the water, He calmly called out, "It is I; don't be afraid." Later, when He was raised from the dead, He said to the women at the tomb, "Don't be afraid."

It is interesting that when we have a brush with the power and glory of God, our first response is fear. It's that same kind of fear as if we were in the midst of an earthquake. Or the fear that grips us as we watch our teenager drive away in our beloved minivan for the first time, alone and unsupervised. We suddenly feel small and impotent, realizing what little control we truly wield.

But even more interesting is how quickly God seeks to reassure us that we have nothing to fear. With a loving God at work on our behalf, what do we have to fear?

Holy Father, how wonderful it is to know that You don't want us to be afraid of You. Replace my fear with awe at Your power and majesty and love. Amen.

Not By My Might

"Peace and prosperity be with you, and success to all who help you, for your God is the one who helps you."
1 Chronicles 12:18 NLT

After King Saul banished David from his presence, David went into hiding. A great number of seasoned and daring warriors came and devoted themselves to David. In 1 Chronicles we read that some of these men could shoot their bows and arrows right- or left-handed. Others were adept at using spears and shields. They had fierce faces and were fleet of foot. They fearlessly crossed swollen rivers, and they put to flight all armies that opposed them. The weakest man, we are told, could have defeated one hundred men; the strongest man could have defeated one thousand. These mighty men committed themselves to David with the assurance that he would succeed in returning to Israel as king. However, their confidence came from knowing that it was God who helped David. Despite their remarkable strength and extraordinary military prowess, these men humbly devoted themselves to God.

Sometimes we think that we can make our own peace and prosperity. We think that we will succeed—through our own power alone. When we slip into this attitude, we must remind ourselves that our success comes only from God, no matter how capable we believe we are. God is the One who helps us. Let us put our trust in Him today.

Dear Lord, You are my help in all things. Forgive me for trying to do everything myself. Teach me to trust in Your power and look to You for peace. Amen.

Day 354

A Sweet Role, Anyone?

The more you grow like this, the more productive and useful you will be in your knowledge of our Lord Jesus Christ.

2 Peter 1:8 NLT

You expect more than floury, sticky dough when you buy fresh cinnamon rolls. The baker's off to a good start, but she has to keep adding ingredients to eventually give you a mouth-watering roll. The stepmom role also starts with the basics—but, oh, to enhance it! So, how does a stepmom turn sticky dough into a "sweet role"?

Check out this recipe: "So don't lose a minute in building on what you've been given, complementing your basic faith with good character, spiritual understanding, alert discipline, passionate patience, reverent wonder, warm friendliness, and generous love" (2 Peter 1:5–7 MSG).

In other words, add a splash of friendliness to your hello when your stepchildren come through the front door. To a tense conversation, add a generous handful of understanding. And when you check a kid's version of a clean room, pour in a generous amount of passionate patience. Oh, and to a toddler's fall, add lots of lovin'.

Does the sticky dough in your hands need the additional ingredients in God's recipe? As you stir in these essentials, you'll be amazed at how much they enhance the role you're in the process of developing.

O, Lord, help me to daily add Your ingredients—it will make all the difference in the role I serve up. Amen.

The Power of the Almighty

Day 355

Then Moses raised his hand over the sea, and the LORD opened up a path through the water with a strong east wind. The wind blew all that night, turning the seabed into dry land. So the people of Israel walked through the middle of the sea on dry ground, with walls of water on each side!

EXODUS 14:21–22 NLT

Imagine being a slave in Egypt your entire life. One day two fellows named Moses and Aaron demand that Pharaoh let your entire nation leave Egypt. Crazy things begin to happen: All the water in Egypt turns to blood; frogs, gnats, flies, locusts, and hail cover the land; the livestock dies; the Egyptians develop horrible boils; the land turns completely dark; the firstborn children of the unbelieving Egyptians are killed. Suddenly, you're marching freely out of Egypt because of the miraculous wonders of God.

But God isn't finished. The Egyptians change their minds and are now in pursuit. You are trapped between the Red Sea and their enormous army. And then, through His amazing power, God parts the Red Sea, and you escape to the other side on dry land! Saved! You are saved by the Lord God Almighty!

The awesome power of God still exists today. God cares about us and wants what is best for us. We just have to believe that He will provide. Revel in God's power today! Delight in His love! Our God still saves! Bless His name!

Dear Lord, Your power is awesome, and Your love is amazing. Thank You for loving me so much. Open my eyes to Your miraculous power and love each day. Amen.

One Step at a Time

Behold, how good and how pleasant it is. . .to dwell together in unity!
Psalm 133:1 nasb

Ah, transitions. They can be good, and they can be. . .well. . .

You've heard the saying, "The only thing that stays the same is change." You have already experienced many changes in the merging of your two families and acquiring the title *stepmom*. For some families, the transition seems rather smooth while others take the patience of Job—and then some!

Some members of the family may have moved to a new town—or at least to a new house. There may be a change in workplaces or schools. And now this group of people is living together under the same roof.

In the midst of change, it may be of benefit to take some "baby steps" toward a family routine. Begin a tradition unique to your family: Make pizza together on Saturday nights, have a game night on Friday nights, or take a walk together on Sunday afternoons. This time together can help build stronger relationships and family cohesion as you learn more about each other and play together.

Change is inevitable, but routine can help make the adjustment a little easier for everyone involved.

Dear Jesus, thank You for each member of our family. Help us to develop some routines so that we can become closer to one another as we have fun together. Amen.

Tried and True Instructions

"Son of man, take into your heart all My words which I will speak to you and listen closely."
EZEKIEL 3:10 NASB

In the verse above, God is calling Ezekiel to be his prophet. Ezekiel has seen some pretty crazy visions, including two wheels in the sky, and he has just been commanded by God to eat a scroll that tastes as sweet as honey. Now God tells Ezekiel that He is sending him to the Israelites to preach to them and to warn them about their rebellion against God. God tells Ezekiel that though the Israelites are stubborn and will not listen, Ezekiel should go and preach to them anyway. But first, Ezekiel must soak up all the words God speaks, listening closely so that he may tell others what he has heard.

Like Ezekiel, we have been called to tell others about God. Amazingly, God's instructions to one of Israel's most powerful prophets are the same for us today. Absorb God's words into your heart, and listen to Him closely. Spending time in God's Word is the best way to get to know Him and to hear His voice. By impressing His words upon our hearts, we will be prepared to share the Good News of Jesus Christ with those who have not yet heard it.

Dear Lord, please open my heart to Your Word so that I may know You. Open my ears so that I might hear You speak. Amen.

Day 358

Be Prepared

But in your hearts set apart Christ as Lord. Always be prepared to give an answer to everyone who asks you to give the reason for the hope that you have. But do this with gentleness and respect.

1 Peter 3:15 NIV

Living in a blended family isn't always easy. It takes a lot of patience and prayer. When it comes to your husband's children, it's always better to win them over with gentleness and respect. If you are putting Christ first in your life, He will help you to accomplish this goal. It's not a good idea to "preach" to your blended family about how things should be. It's much better to show them by how you live—and by how you love. God's Word tells us it is much more important to love with actions than with words (1 John 3:18). But be ready with answers and understanding when the day arrives when one of your stepchildren comes and initiates a conversation. Then you have gained an open door in which to share your heart. Always be prepared to share the hope of Christ's love with your blended family, because you never know when the opportunity might present itself.

Dear Father, help me to set apart Christ as Lord. Grant me wisdom that I might love my blended family gently and respectfully. Amen.

Getting Serious about Repentance

"Who knows? God may yet relent and with compassion turn from his fierce anger so that we will not perish."
Jonah 3:9 NIV

Nineveh was full of wicked people who hated the Israelites—it was not exactly the kind of place a prophet like Jonah would choose to vacation. However, when Jonah eventually arrived in Nineveh, something miraculous happened. Even though his preaching was halfhearted (he didn't want God to relent), the moment the Ninevites heard God's Word, they believed God.

The king commanded that everyone—even the animals!—fast and dress in sackcloth. Then he spoke the line written above. Even though the people knew little about the God of Israel, they put their hope in Him. They trusted in God's compassion and relied on Him to relent from the destruction He promised to pour out on them. The people of Nineveh were serious about repentance.

Unfortunately, when we compare our response to God's Word with Nineveh's, we find ourselves coming up short. The Ninevites repented wholeheartedly, even though they were not at all certain God would relent. We have the assurance of God's love and compassion, but we often repent halfheartedly. Today let's look to their example and repent with all our hearts. We have the promise of new life through Jesus Christ. Let's listen to God's Word and obey today.

Dear Lord, thank You for Your love and compassion. Please teach me to repent unconditionally. Let me listen and obey Your Word with an open heart and with eagerness. Amen.

Day 360

The Pickle Blessing

So then, as occasion and opportunity open to us, let us do good. . . . Be mindful to be a blessing.
GALATIANS 6:10 AMP

Kerrin was having one of those days. She was out of coffee. Her last pair of pantyhose tore. Her car had a flat tire; and by the time she got it fixed, she was late for work. In a really bad mood, Kerrin rushed into her office mumbling harsh words under her breath. At her cubicle she stopped short. There, sitting in the middle of her desk, was a jar of her favorite bread-and-butter pickles. The sight of those pickles immediately changed Kerrin's mood from bad to glad.

As Kerrin picked up the jar of pickles, one of her coworkers said, "I was at the store on my way in, and I saw those and thought of you."

"I'm so glad you did," Kerrin replied. She told her coworker all that had gone wrong that morning. "But this," Kerrin said, indicating the pickles, "has made this day all better. Thank you."

We have no idea what those around us may be going through. So we are wise to listen to the still, small voice of God when He prompts us to do something for someone. God can use even a jar of pickles to bless someone if we let Him.

Father, today please help me not just to count all the blessings You have given me but to share them. Let me reflect Your blessing to others. Amen.

Choosing Love, Waiting for More

We love each other because he loved us first.
1 John 4:19 NLT

In the verse preceding today's scripture, the apostle John says that God is love and there's no fear in that kind of love. That's a good point to keep in mind in our steplife.

Sometimes we expect to love our stepkids deeply, like their dad. Sometimes we believe it will be easy; and then when it's not, we wonder how we'll make this life work. Trying to love where loving is hard seems quite fearful indeed. But we can still trust John's point.

We discover that we don't have to understand, like, enjoy, or feel particular affection for our stepkids; but we can love them without fear, and in that choice, we can carry on. We can *choose* to love them because their dad loved them first. We can *choose* to love them because our God has taught us how to love. We can *choose* to love them because we want to, and we'll love them from afar if we have to.

This approach allows us to fearlessly care for them even if they don't want us to. It allows us to fearlessly put their welfare first without asking for anything in return. It allows us to fearlessly love them now while we wait faithfully for more.

Father, thank You for loving me when I didn't know how to love You. Please help me to practice that kind of love with my stepkids and trust in Your control of everything else. Amen.

Day 362

Let's Stick Together

A friend loves at all times.
PROVERBS 17:17 NIV

The dictionary defines the word *friend* as "a person who is attached to another by feelings of affection or personal regard." This is an accurate definition, but friendship means so much more. A true friend is trustworthy, loyal, helpful, kind, encouraging, understanding, forgiving. Genuine friendship should be treasured and nourished.

In 1 Samuel we read of David and Jonathan's friendship. Jonathan's father, King Saul, was hunting David to kill him. David enlisted his friend's help to discern which way he should flee. Once Jonathan realized his father's treacherous plan, he told David to leave. He said, "You will be missed, because your seat will be empty." He could no longer be in David's presence for fear of David's safety, and he realized what a loss that would be.

Friendship involves treasured times with those we love and who love us. We form wonderful friendships with hours spent together and listening ears to hear what the other has to say. So it is when we form a friendship with Jesus. He is there to support us, uphold us, and encourage us. He's a true friend. Joni Eareckson Tada has said, "In friendship, God opens your eyes to the glories of Himself." We can be assured of His love when we have a relationship with the Son—our true friend.

Dear Lord, thank You for sending Your Son to become my friend. Amen.

My Father's Eyes

Day 363

For those whom he foreknew he also predestined to be conformed to the image of his Son, in order that he might be the firstborn among many brothers.
Romans 8:29 ESV

Although biological children may inherit physical attributes and personality traits from their natural parents, adopted and stepchildren display mannerisms and characteristics of the parents who raise them. Children are greatly influenced by their environment. Adults are no different.

Friends and family affect us. Books, magazines, and television impact us. We are most influenced by our greatest priority. King David was called a man after God's own heart. He sought God first and meditated on His Word continually. He spent large amounts of time alone with God. Because of that, God dramatically influenced David's heart.

As Christians, it is God's will that we be conformed to the image of His Son. In order for that to happen, Christ should be the most influential person in our lives—the One we spend time with, the One we listen to, the One we worship. With each passing day, do you look more and more like Christ? Are you taking on His characteristics and priorities? The fruit of the Spirit is a good litmus test. Love, joy, peace, patience, kindness, goodness, faithfulness, gentleness, and self-control should be displayed more and more as we spend time with Jesus. May it be so!

Dear Lord, may I be conformed to the image of Jesus by spending time with You. Amen.

Day 364

Face-to-Face

I have much more to say to you, but I don't want to write it with pen and ink. For I hope to see you soon, and then we will talk face to face.

3 John 13–14 NLT

There's nothing like a face-to-face chat to get to the bottom of things—good or bad. When you're looking someone in the eye, your words take on added power.

How do you feel about that? Are you the sort of person who is comfortable settling issues face-to-face, or are you afraid of confrontation? Good or bad, it's better to deal with it eyeball to eyeball. Why? For one thing, Jesus always confronted head-on. He didn't deal with people behind their backs. He cut to the chase. Talk about leading by example. Also, it's great to chat face-to-face, because the countenance of a person's face speaks volumes.

Today, whether you have something difficult to share or something encouraging, don't be afraid to open up. Skip the e-mail. Don't mess with the phone call. Share your heart—face-to-face. Looking that person in the eye will give you the calm assurance you need to speak the truth in love.

Dear Lord, please bring to mind anyone You would have me meet with face-to-face. If You're calling me to encourage that person, then give me the words to share. If I need to confront in love, then show me Your heart for that person before I do. Amen.

Wish List

Day 365

*And this is the confidence that we have toward him,
that if we ask anything according to his will he hears us.
And if we know that he hears us in whatever we ask,
we know that we have the requests that we have asked of him.*
1 John 5:14–15 ESV

Wow! This passage sounds as if God is issuing a blank check, doesn't it? Just think of all the great stuff we can have. Many of us reading this have already started on our lists! But we must go back and read a little more closely. John isn't saying that God is like Santa Claus, standing by to fill our never-ending wish lists. He says if we ask anything "*according to his will he hears us.*" That changes things a little, doesn't it?

When we seek to line up our lives with God's will, we have the assurance that *He hears us.* When we come to Him with outlandish requests that have nothing to do with His will for our lives, He may or may not listen. But when we seek His will and ask accordingly, He will always listen! And He will always give us the things that He desires for us to have. We can rest in knowing that He loves us more than we can imagine, and His gifts for us are always good.

Dear Father, thank You for Your good gifts. Please help me to desire only those things that You desire for me. Amen.

Contributors

Brumbaugh, Renae Days 6, 27, 45, 72, 92, 100, 124, 146, 165, 180, 197, 211, 226, 233, 259, 288, 302, 323, 350, 365
Renae Brumbaugh lives in Copperas Cove, Texas, with her pastor-husband and two children. You can read more of her devotionals at www.RenaeBrumbaugh.com.

Cecil, Cheryl Days 26, 36, 60, 77, 114, 139, 144, 161, 172, 181, 213, 229, 253, 271, 278, 325, 328, 333, 341, 354
Cheryl Cecil resides in northeast Indiana. Her writings appear in various publications. She enjoys coffee dates with her hubby, time with family, and teaching Bible studies.

Douglas, Katherine Days 11, 53, 89, 106, 130, 155, 175, 192, 209, 230, 254, 277, 298, 313, 322
Katherine Douglas says stepmothering continues to bring lifelong blessings. She is now the proud (step)grandma of triplets Adam, Daniel, and Christian.

Downs, Emily Days 4, 76, 118, 169, 256
Emily Downs is a freelance writer living near Lake Michigan; her work has appeared in magazines, books, newspapers, and on the radio.

Farrier, Nancy Days 16, 34, 51, 69, 85, 103, 119, 133, 149, 164, 182, 202, 217, 240, 263, 282, 306, 318, 330, 343
Nancy J. Farrier is the author of twelve books and numerous articles and short stories. She is married and has five children. Nancy lives with her family in Southern California.

Fisher, Suzanne Woods Days 2, 15, 35, 71, 98, 126, 150, 174, 193, 228, 261, 280, 301, 335, 352
Suzanne Woods Fisher is the author of *Amish Peace: Simple Wisdom for Complicated Lives* and many other books. Find Suzanne online at www.suzannewoodsfisher.com.

Freudig, Laura Days 13, 57, 73, 96, 120, 138, 160, 196, 216, 237, 255, 279, 294, 309, 337

Laura Freudig has lived most of her life on islands along the Maine coast. She enjoys reading, hiking, and singing with her husband and three (soon to be four) children.

Goodman, Karon Days 14, 31, 52, 66, 80, 95, 113, 132, 157, 179, 199, 222, 241, 265, 287, 308, 319, 331, 349, 361

Karon Goodman is a Christian writer and speaker from Alabama. She has one son and has been a stepmom to two sons since 1996. Find Karon online at www.karongoodman.com.

Gregor, Shanna Days 3, 48, 99, 134, 167, 191, 223, 250, 281, 315

As a freelance writer, editor, and product developer, **Shanna D. Gregor** has served various ministries and publishers since 1996. The mother of two young men, Shanna and her husband reside in Tucson, Arizona. Find her at www.gregorswrite.com.

Hahn, Jennifer Days 24, 44, 67, 82, 115, 127, 153, 188, 205, 219, 232, 257, 275, 292, 356

Jennifer Hahn is a freelance writer, compiler, and proofreader who lives in Pennsylvania's Amish country. She and her husband, Mark, have two daughters and a son.

Hanna, Janice Days 1, 18, 39, 58, 70, 91, 105, 123, 143, 168, 186, 194, 212, 234, 267, 290, 303, 320, 345, 364

Janice Hanna hails from south Texas. She is a Christian author and mother of four grown daughters. Janice has written over forty books, most under the name Janice Thompson.

Hyatt, Gale Days 22, 37, 64, 83, 109, 136, 148, 170, 184, 207, 227, 236, 251, 269, 284, 293, 312, 321, 334, 347

Gale Hyatt has been writing since the third grade. She and her husband live in Valrico, Florida, with their two handsome sons and one precious princess.

Key, Eileen Days 7, 49, 90, 131, 176, 218, 249, 300, 329, 362

Eileen Key resides in Texas. She has published numerous articles and devotionals. Her first mystery novel, *Dog Gone*, is from Barbour Publishing.

Lindsay, Christy Days 17, 54, 87, 122, 156, 190, 215, 242, 286, 314

Christy Lindsay has been published in *Guideposts*, *Christian Communicator*, and ChristianBibleStudies.com. She also writes a column for her hometown weekly newspaper.

Maltese, Donna Days 25, 30, 56, 78, 102, 112, 137, 142, 163, 178, 208, 214, 221, 235, 247, 262, 274, 291, 316, 326

Donna Maltese is a freelance writer, editor, and proofreader; publicist for a local Mennonite project; and the assistant director of RevWriter Writers Conferences. Donna resides in Pennsylvania with her husband and two children.

Nydegger, Mandy Days 32, 41, 68, 81, 145, 246, 266, 340, 344, 346, 348, 353, 355, 357, 359

Mandy Nydegger lives with her husband, David, in Waco, Texas. She loves Christmas, snow, and the Indianapolis Colts.

Parrish, MariLee Days 23, 42, 61, 86, 108, 128, 159, 187, 210, 231, 260, 297, 317, 336, 358

MariLee Parrish lives in Colorado with her husband, Eric, and young son, Jake. She's a freelance musician and writer who desires to paint a picture of God with her life.

Patrick, Wanda Days 19, 38, 62, 84, 111, 140, 171, 206, 245, 283

Wanda Patrick, mother of five grown children and stepchildren, enjoys writing, leading Bible studies, and travel. She lives in Norcross, Georgia, with her husband, Dack.

Phillips, Rachael Days 21, 40, 65, 97, 121, 152, 183, 203, 225, 248, 273, 296, 311, 324, 338

Award-winning writer **Rachael Phillips** (www.rachaelwrites.com) has authored four Barbour biographies and four hundred articles, columns, and devotional pieces. Rachael and her husband, Steve, have three children and four grandchildren.

Powell, Janice Days 5, 47, 88, 125, 151, 185, 204, 243, 268, 299

Janice Powell graduated from college and married in 1985. She lives for her Savior, her husband and seven kids (and their laundry), homeschooling, music, writing, reading, and chocolate.

Quillin, Rachel Days 20, 59, 94, 117, 154, 189, 220, 264, 307, 342

Rachel Quillin is a freelance writer and homeschool mom. She and her husband, Eric, live in Stone Creek, Ohio, with their six children.

Rayburn, Julie Days 12, 43, 74, 101, 110, 129, 158, 195, 224, 252, 289, 305, 327, 351, 363

Julie Rayburn is a public speaker and an operating room nurse. She lives in Atlanta with her husband, Scott. They have two grown children and two grandchildren. Find her at www.julierayburn.com.

Rogers, Martha Days 9, 46, 75, 116, 166, 200, 238, 285, 310, 339

Martha Rogers has written many devotions, with a number of them appearing in published anthologies. She is a member of ACFW and lives in Houston with her husband.

Roome, Debbie Days 8, 50, 79, 104, 135, 173, 201, 239, 270, 304

Debbie Roome was raised in Africa and moved to New Zealand with her husband and five children in 2006. She works as a freelance writer.

Swofford, Conover Days 29, 93, 162, 295, 360

Conover Swofford resides in Columbus, Georgia. In addition to writing, she loves reading and singing in her church choir. Conover also loves her day job—a receiver at a Christian bookstore.

Vawter, Marjorie Days 28, 33, 63, 141, 147, 177, 244, 258, 272, 332

Margie Vawter is a freelance writer who loves to encourage others to Christlikeness. Married to Roger and mom to two adult children, she lives in Colorado.

Wegener, Laura Days 10, 55, 107, 198, 276

A musician, writer, and newlywed, **Laura Wegener** loves using her writing degree in a full-time capacity writing for various ministries.

Scripture Index

Old Testament